C000173585

NICHOLS

GUIDE TO THE WA...

birmingham &
the heart of england

Also available:

Nicholson Guide to the Waterways
1. Grand Union, Oxford & the South East
2. Severn, Avon & Birmingham
4. Four Counties & the Welsh Canals
5. North West & the Pennines
6. Nottingham, York & the North East
7. River Thames & the Southern Waterways
8. Scotland – the Highland and Lowland Waterways

Nicholson Inland Waterways Map of Great Britain

Published by Nicholson
An imprint of HarperCollins*Publishers*
77–85 Fulham Palace Road
Hammersmith, London W6 8JB

www.collins.co.uk
www.bartholomewmaps.com

First published by Nicholson and Ordnance Survey 1997
Reprinted 1998
New edition published by Nicholson 2000, 2003

Researched and written by David Perrott and Jonathan Mosse.
Designed by Bob Vickers.

The publishers gratefully acknowledge the assistance given by British Waterways and
their staff in the preparation of this guide.

Grateful thanks is also due to the Environment Agency and members of the
Inland Waterways Association, CAMRA representatives and branch members.

Photographs reproduced by kind permission of Derek Pratt Photography.

Printed in Hong Kong.

ISBN 0 00 713666 8
PJ11165 03/3/54

The publishers welcome comments from readers. Please address your letters to:
Nicholson Guides to the Waterways, HarperCollins Reference,
HarperCollins Publishers, Westerhill Road, Bishopbriggs, Glasgow, G64 2QT or
email nicholson@harpercollins.co.uk

Wending their quiet way through town and country, the inland navigations of Britain offer boaters, walkers and cyclists a unique insight into a fascinating, but once almost lost, world. When built this was the province of the boatmen and their families, who lived a mainly itinerant lifestyle: often colourful, to our eyes picturesque but, for them, remarkably harsh. Transporting the nation's goods during the late 1700s and early 1800s, negotiating locks, traversing aqueducts and passing through long narrow tunnels, canals were the arteries of trade during the initial part of the industrial revolution.

Then the railways came: the waterways were eclipsed in a remarkably short time by a faster and more flexible transport system, and a steady decline began. In a desperate fight for survival canal tolls were cut, crews toiled for longer hours and worked the boats with their whole family living aboard. Canal companies merged, totally uneconomic waterways were abandoned, some were modernised but it was all to no avail. Large scale commercial carrying on inland waterways had reached the finale of its short life.

At the end of World War II a few enthusiasts roamed this hidden world and harboured a vision of what it could become: a living transport museum which stretched the length and breadth of the country; a place where people could spend their leisure time and, on just a few of the wider waterways, a still modestly viable transport system.

The restoration struggle began and, from modest beginnings, Britain's inland waterways are now seen as an irreplaceable part of the fabric of the nation. Existing canals are expertly maintained while long abandoned waterways, once seen as an eyesore and a danger, are recognised for the valuable contribution they make to our quality of life, and restoration schemes are integrating them back into the network.

This series of guides offers the most comprehensive coverage of Britain's inland waterways, all clearly detailed on splendid Ordnance Survey® maps. Whether you are boating, walking, cycling or just visiting, these books will give you all the information you need.

▍CONTENTS

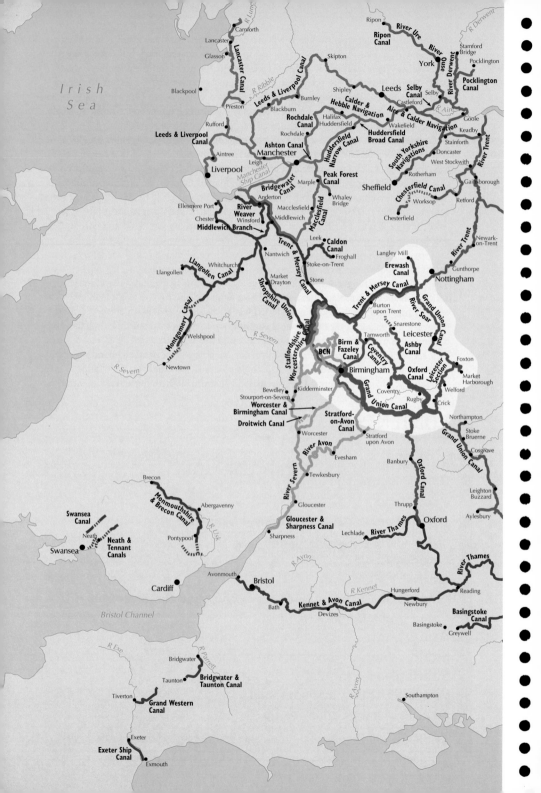

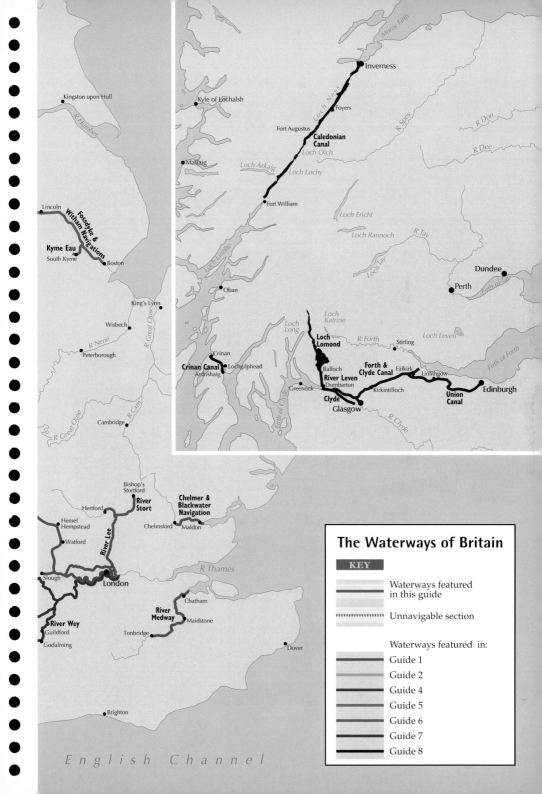

Kingston upon Hull

R Humber

Lincoln
**Fosdyke &
Witham Navigations**
Kyme Eau
South Kyme
Boston

King's Lynn
Wisbech

R Nene
Peterborough

R Great Ouse

Cambridge

R Cam

R Great Ouse

Kyle of Lochalsh

Mallaig

Loch Ness
Inverness
Foyers
Fort Augustus
**Caledonian
Canal**
Loch Oich
Loch Arkaig
Loch Lochy

Fort William

Loch Linnhe

Oban

Crinan
Crinan Canal Lochgilphead
Ardrishaig

Loch Long
Loch Katrine
**Loch
Lomond**
Balloch
River Leven
Dumbarton
Greenock
Clyde
Glasgow

Firth of Clyde

R Clyde

Moray Firth

R Spey
R Don

R Dee

Loch Ericht

Loch Rannoch
R Tay

Loch Tay

Dundee
Perth
Firth of Tay

R Forth
Stirling
Loch Leven

**Forth &
Clyde Canal** Falkirk
Linlithgow
Kirkintilloch
**Union
Canal**
Edinburgh

Firth of Forth

Bishop's
Stortford
Hertford
**River
Stort**
**Chelmer &
Blackwater
Navigation**
Chelmsford
Maldon
Hemel
Hempstead
Watford
River Lee
Slough
London
River Wey
Guildford
Godalming

R Thames

Chatham
**River
Medway**
Maidstone
Tonbridge

Dover

Brighton

E n g l i s h   C h a n n e l

The Waterways of Britain

KEY

━━━ Waterways featured
in this guide

┈┈┈┈┈ Unnavigable section

Waterways featured in:
━━━ Guide 1
━━━ Guide 2
━━━ Guide 4
━━━ Guide 5
━━━ Guide 6
━━━ Guide 7
━━━ Guide 8

Leaving Hatton Bottom Lock, Grand Union Canal (see page 107)

GENERAL INFORMATION FOR WATERWAYS USERS

The slogan 'Waterways For All' was coined to take account of the wide diversity of people using the inland waterways for recreation.

Today boaters, walkers, fishermen, cyclists and gongoozlers (on-lookers) throng our canals and rivers, to share in the enjoyment of a quite amazing waterway heritage. British Waterways (BW), along with other navigation authorities, is empowered to develop, maintain and control this resource in order to maximise its potential. It is to this end that a series of guides, codes, and regulations have come into existence over the years, evolving to match a burgeoning – and occasionally conflicting – demand. Set out below are key points as they relate to everyone wishing to enjoy the waterways. Please see the inside front cover for details on how to contact British Waterways.

LICENSING – BOATS

The majority of the navigations covered in this book are controlled by BW and are managed on a day-to-day basis by local Waterway Offices. Waterway Managers are detailed in the introduction to each waterway. All craft using BW waterways must be licenced and charges are based on the length of the craft. This licence covers all navigable waterways under BW's control and in a few cases includes reciprocal agreements with other waterway authorities (as indicated in the text). BW and the Environment Agency now offer an optional Gold Licence which covers unlimited navigation on the waterways of both authorities. Permits for permanent mooring on the canals are also issued by BW. For further information contact BW Customer Services. You can download licence fees and charges and an application form from the BW website.

BW and the Environment Agency operate the Boat Safety Scheme, setting technical requirements for good and safe boat-building practice. A Boat Safety Certificate or, for new boats, a Declaration of Conformity, is necessary to obtain a craft licence. For powered boats proof of insurance for Third Party Liability for a minimum of £1,000,000 is also required. Further details from BW Customer Services. Other navigational authorities relevant to this book are mentioned where appropriate.

LICENSING – CYCLISTS

Not all towpaths are open to cyclists. This is because many stretches are considered to be too rough or narrow, or because cyclists are considered to cause a risk to other users. Maps on the BW website show which stretches of towpath are open to cyclists, and local offices can supply more detailed information relevant to their area. A cycle permit is required (except on the Caledonian and Crinan Canals), and this is available free of charge (except for the Kennet & Avon Canal, where a charge is made) from BW Customer Services.

When using the towpath for cycling, you will encounter other towpath users, such as fishermen, walkers and boaters. The Waterways Code gives advice on taking care and staying safe, considering others and helping to look after the waterways.

TOWPATHS

Few, if any, artificial cuts or canals in this country are without an intact towpath accessible to the walker at least. However, on river navigations towpaths have on occasion fallen into disuse or, sometimes, been lost to erosion. Considerable efforts are being made to provide access to all towpaths, with some available to the disabled. Notes on individual waterways in this book detail the supposed status of the path, but the indication of a towpath does not necessarily imply a public right of way or mean that a right to cycle along it exists. Maps on the BW website show all towpaths on the BW network, and whether they are open to cyclists. Motorcycling and horse riding are forbidden on all towpaths.

INDIVIDUAL WATERWAY GUIDES

No national guide can cover the minutiae of individual waterways and some Waterway Managers produce guides to specific navigations under their charge. Copies of individual guides (where they are available) can be obtained from the Waterway Office detailed in the introduction. Please note that times – such as operating times of bridges and locks – do change year by year and from winter to summer.

STOPPAGES

BW works hard to programme its major engineering works into the winter period when demand for cruising is low. It publishes a *National Stoppage Programme* and *Winter Opening Hours* leaflet which is sent out to all licence holders, boatyards and hire companies. Inevitably, emergencies occur necessitating the unexpected closure of a waterway, perhaps during the peak season. You can check for stoppages on individual waterways between specific dates on the BW website. Details are also announced on lockside noticeboards and on Canalphone (*see* inside front cover).

STARTING OUT

Extensive information and advice on booking a boating holiday is available on the BW website. Please book a waterway holiday from a licenced operator – only in this way can you be sure that you have proper insurance cover, service and support during your holiday. It is illegal for private boat owners to hire out their craft. If in doubt, please contact BW Customer Services. If you are hiring a canal boat for the first time, the boatyard will brief you thoroughly. Take notes, follow their instructions and *don't be afraid to ask* if there is anything you do not understand. BW have produced a short video giving basic information on using a boat safely. Copies of the video, and the *Boater's Handbook*, are available free of charge from BW Customer Services. Sections of the *Boater's Safety Toolkit* can also be downloaded from the internet, *see* www.aina.org.uk.

GENERAL CRUISING NOTES

Most canals are saucer-shaped in section so are deepest at the middle. Few have more than 3–4ft of water and many have much less. Keep to the centre of the channel except on bends, where the deepest water is on the outside of the bend. When you meet another boat, keep to the right, slow down and aim to miss the approaching craft by a couple of yards: do not steer right over to the bank or you are likely to run aground. If you meet a loaded commercial boat keep right out of the way and be prepared to follow his instructions. Do not assume that you should pass on the right. If you meet a boat being towed from the bank, pass it on the outside. When overtaking, keep the other boat on your right side.

A large number of BW facilities – pump outs, showers, electrical hook-ups and so on – are operated by pre-paid cards, obtainable from BW regional offices; local waterways offices (*see* introductions to individual navigations); lock keepers and some boatyards within the region. Cards are available in £5, £6, £10 and £15 denominations. Please note that if you are a weekend visitor, you should purchase cards in advance.

Speed

There is a general speed limit of 4 mph on most BW canals. This is not just an arbitrary limit: there is no need to go any faster and in many cases it is impossible to cruise even at this speed: if the wash is breaking against the bank or causing large waves, slow down.

Slow down also when passing moored craft, engineering works and anglers; when there is a lot of floating rubbish on the water (and try to drift over obvious obstructions in neutral); when approaching blind corners, narrow bridges and junctions.

Mooring

Generally speaking you may moor where you wish on BW property, as long as there is sufficient depth of water, and you are *not causing an obstruction*. Your boat should carry metal mooring stakes, and these should be driven firmly into the ground with a mallet if there are no mooring rings. Do not stretch mooring lines across the towpath. Always consider the security of your boat when there is no one aboard. On tideways and commercial waterways it is advisable to moor only at recognised sites, and allow for any rise or fall of the tide.

Bridges

On narrow canals slow down and aim to miss one side (usually the towpath side) by about 9 inches. *Keep everyone inboard when passing under bridges,* and take special care with moveable structures – the crew member operating the bridge should be strong enough and heavy enough to hold it steady as the boat passes through.

Tunnels

Make sure the tunnel is clear before you enter, and use your headlight. Follow any instructions given on notice boards by the entrance.

Fuel

Hire craft usually carry fuel sufficient for the rental period.

Water

It is advisable to top up daily.

Lavatories

Hire craft usually have pump out toilets. Have these emptied *before* things become critical. Keep the receipt and your boatyard will usually reimburse you for this expense.

Boatyards

Hire fleets are usually turned around on a Saturday, making this a bad time to call in for services. Remember that moorings at popular destinations fill quickly during the summer months, so do not assume there will be room for your boat. Always ask.

LOCKS AND THEIR USE

A lock is a simple and ingenious device for transporting your craft from one water level to another. When both sets of gates are closed it may

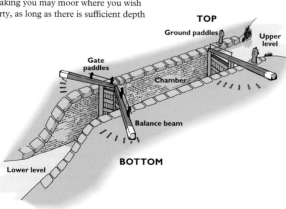

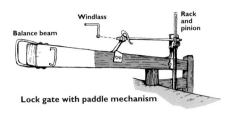

Lock gate with paddle mechanism

Labels on diagram: Windlass, Rack and pinion, Balance beam

be filled or emptied using gate or ground paddles at the top or bottom of the lock. These are operated with a windlass.

General tips
- Make safety your prime concern. *Keep a close eye on young children.*
- Always take your time, and do not leap about.
- Never open the paddles at one end without ensuring those at the other end are closed.
- Never drop the paddles – always wind them down.
- Keep to the landward side of the balance beam when opening and closing gates.
- *Never* leave your windlass slotted onto the paddle spindle – it will be dangerous should anything slip.
- Keep your boat away from the top and bottom gates to prevent it getting caught on the gate or the lock cill.
- Be wary of fierce *top gate* paddles, especially in wide locks. Operate them slowly, and close them if there is *any* adverse effect.
- Always follow the navigation authority's instructions, where these are given on notices or by their staff.

PLANNING A CRUISE

Many a canal holiday has been spoiled by trying to go too far too fast. Go slowly, don't be too ambitious, and enjoy the experience. Note that mileages indicated on the maps are for guidance only.

A *rough* calculation of time taken to cover the ground is the lock-miles system:

Add the number of *miles* to the number of *locks* on your proposed journey, and divide the resulting figure by three. This will give you a guide to the number of *hours* it will take. But don't forget your service stops (water, shopping, pump out), and allow plenty of time to visit that special pub!

TIDAL WATERWAYS

The typical steel narrow boat found on the inland waterways system has all the seagoing characteristics of a bathtub, which renders it totally unsuitable for all-weather cruising on tidal estuaries. However, the more adventurous will inevitably wish to add additional 'ring cruises' to the more predictable circuits within the calm havens of inland Britain. Passage is possible in most estuaries if careful consideration is given to the key factors of weather conditions, tides, crew experience, the condition of the boat and its equipment and, perhaps of over-riding importance, the need to take expert advice.

In many cases it will be prudent to employ the skilled services of a local pilot. Within the text, where inland navigations connect with a tidal waterway, details are given of sources of both advice and pilotage. It is also advisable to inform your insurance company of your intention to navigate on tidal waterways as they may very well have special requirements or wish to levy an additional premium. This guide is to the inland waterways of Britain and therefore recognizes that tideways – and especially estuaries – require a different approach and many additional skills. We therefore do not hesitate to draw the boater's attention to the appropriate source material.

GENERAL

Most inland navigations are managed by BW or the Environment Agency, but there are several other navigation authorities responsible for smaller stretches of canals and rivers. For details of these, contact the Association of Inland Navigation Authorities at www.aina.org.uk or BW Customer Services. The boater, conditioned perhaps by the uniformity of our national road network, should be sensitive to the need to observe different codes and operating practices. Similarly it is important to be aware that some waterways are only available for navigation today solely because of the care and dedication of a particular restoration body, often using volunteer labour and usually taking several decades to complete the project. This is the reason that, in cruising the national waterways network, additional licence charges are sometimes incurred. The introduction to each waterway gives its background history, details of recent restoration (where relevant) and also lists the operating authority.

BW is a public corporation, responsible to the Department of Environment, Food and Rural Affairs and, as subscribers to the Citizen's Charter, they are linked with an ombudsman. BW has a comprehensive complaints procedure and a free explanatory leaflet is available from Customer Services. Problems and complaints should be addressed to the local Waterway Manager in the first instance – the telephone number is listed in the introduction to individual waterways.

The Inland Waterways Association campaigns for the 'conservation, use, maintenance, restoration and development of the inland waterways', through branches all over the country. For more information contact them at PO Box 114, Rickmansworth, WD3 1ZY, telephone 01923 711114, fax 01923 897000, email iwa@waterways.org.uk or visit their website at www.waterways.org.uk.

BRITISH WATERWAYS EMERGENCY HELPLINE

Emergency help is available from BW outside normal office hours on weekdays and throughout weekends via British Waterways' Emergency Helpline (*see* inside front cover). You should give details of the problem and your location.

*Cruising Ashby Canal at Dadlington (*see *page 15)*

ASHBY CANAL

MAXIMUM DIMENSIONS
Length: 70'
Beam: 7'
Headroom: 6' 6"

MILEAGE
MARSTON JUNCTION (Coventry Canal) to:
Burton Hastings: 3 miles
Hinckley Wharf: 6 miles
Stoke Golding Wharf: 8³/4 miles
Dadlington: 10 miles
Shenton Aqueduct: 13 miles

Market Bosworth Wharf: 15 miles
Congerstone: 17¹/4 miles
Shackerstone: 18¹/4 miles
Snarestone Tunnel: 21 miles
CANAL TERMINUS: 22 miles

No locks

MANAGER
01283 790236
enquiries.fradley@britishwaterways.co.uk

Looking at this canal on a map it appears to be very much out on a limb. In fact the Ashby Canal was originally intended to be a through route from the River Trent at Burton to the Coventry Canal near Bedworth, but this plan was repeatedly shelved. In 1792, however, an Ashby Canal Company was formed and a Bill promoted, mostly by the owners of Leicestershire limeworks and the new coalfields near Ashby de la Zouch, who decided that an outlet southwards was required from their various works. The problem that soon arose was that, while the proposed canal could be built level for 30 miles (following the 300ft contour) from the junction with the Coventry Canal at Marston Jabbett, near Bedworth, to Moira, the section north of Moira would require expensive and complicated works, including locks, reservoirs, pumping engines and possibly a tunnel. Part of this cost was, in fact, avoided by building an extensive system of tramroads to and around the various coalmines and limeworks. However, while the canal was still being built (by a succession of engineers – Jessop, Outram, Whitworth senior and junior, and Thomas Newbold), the new coalmines near Ashby Wolds were found to be less productive than had been hoped. This, combined with the fact that the canal was never extended north to the Trent, was instrumental in preventing the Ashby Canal from making a profit for 20 years. However, a new coal mine sunk at Moira in 1804 eventually produced coal of such excellent quality that it became widely demanded in London and southern England. The canal flourished at last.

In 1845 the Midland Railway bought up the Ashby Canal – with the approval of all concerned except the Coventry and Oxford canal companies, who stood to lose a lot in tolls if the coal traffic from Moira switched to rail carriage. These two companies managed to hamstring the Midland Railway so effectively over its management of the canal that, instead of switching to carriage by rail, the coal traffic from Moira continued along the canal at a substantial level through to the turn of the century. It is therefore hard to see what real benefit the railway company gained from buying the canal. Subsidence from the coal mines near Measham (now stabilised with the completion of mining in the area) has caused great damage in this century to the canal that served them. This subsidence has brought about the abandonment of over 8 miles of the canal, so that the waterway now terminates just north of Snarestone, outside the coalfield. The last load to be carried along the canal was coal to Croxley (Herts), from Gopsall Wharf in 1970. Ambitious plans are in hand to re-open the waterway through to Moira, making use of the abandoned railway line in Measham. Already a new half-mile section, complete with a lock in water, has been constructed beside Moira Furnace.

Burton Hastings

At Marston Junction the Ashby Canal branches east off the Coventry Canal. Under the bridge there is a box containing guides to the waterway produced by the Ashby Canal Association. As soon as it leaves Marston, the canal changes completely and dramatically. The industry and housing estates that had accompanied the Coventry Canal through the Nuneaton–Bedworth conurbation suddenly vanish to be replaced by green fields, farms and trees. In this way the character of the Ashby Canal is established at once: also the first of the typical stone-arched bridges occurs which, together with the shallow and relatively clear water, suggests a rurality far from the industrial Midlands. Only the power lines that criss-cross this stretch are a memory of the other world to the west. A long wooded cutting leads the canal towards Burton Hastings, a typical farming village. Then the canal turns north, setting a course for Hinckley passing, to the east of bridge 13, Stretton Baskerville, a 'lost' village and scheduled ancient monument. The A5 (Watling Street) and the A47 cross near Hinckley. There is no navigation on the Hinckley Wharf Arm, which is used as a boat club mooring. However there are good moorings west of bridge 16 and to the north and south of the marina complex beyond bridge 17 (but ask at the marina first). Keeping west of the town, the canal continues through the fine rolling farmland that typifies the Ashby Canal.

Boatyards

Ⓑ **Trinity Marinas** Wharf Farm, Coventry Road, Hinkley (01455 896820; www.trinitymarinas.co.uk). 🚽 🛢 ⚓ D E Pump-out, gas, overnight and long-term mooring, slipway, wet dock, DIY facilities, chandlery, books, maps and gifts, telephone, toilets, showers, solid fuel, laundrette, café and restaurant. *Emergency call-out.*

WALKING & CYCLING
The condition of the towpath has been greatly improved of late and erosion in the bridgeholes has been made good. This is a very rural waterway, so few sections of the towpath have an all-weather surface, making progress for walker and cyclist difficult in some areas during the winter months. Hinkley and Bosworth Borough Council publish four guides which detail walks that include sections of the canal. These are available from local Tourist Information Centres.

NAVIGATIONAL NOTES
The canal is still shallow in places although a robust dredging programme has done a great deal to improve things. Headroom under bridge 17 is very limited. Random mooring may be awkward due to shallow sides, so use the wharfs and recognised moorings.

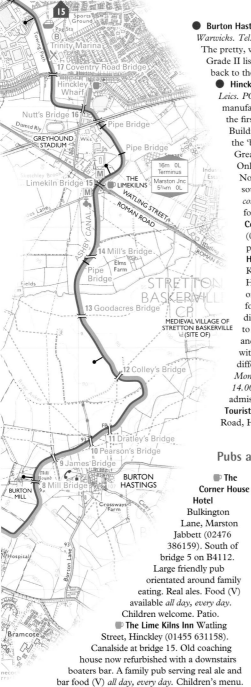

● **Burton Hastings**
Warwicks. Tel. A quiet village set on a hill in open farmland. The pretty, well-placed church dedicated to St Botolph is a Grade II listed building, parts of its construction dating back to the 14th C.

● **Hinckley**
Leics. PO, tel, stores, garage, station. A hosiery manufacturing town that can boast having installed the first stocking machine in Leicestershire, in 1640. Buildings of interest include St Mary's church with the 'bleeding' tombstone in the churchyard; the Great Meeting Chapel (1722) and the museum. Only the bailey and part of the moat remain of the Norman castle. There is a greyhound stadium south of bridge 16 with racing *Wed and Sat commencing at 19.30.* Telephone (01455) 634006 for further details.

Concordia Theatre Stockwell Head, Hinckley (01455 615005). Small local theatre with performances *all year round.*

Hinckley and District Museum Framework Knitters Cottages, Lower Bond Street, Hinckley (01455 251218). Established in a row of restored 17th-C thatched cottages once used for framework knitting, the museum houses displays on the town and area from prehistoric to medieval times. Also depicted are the hosiery and boot and shoe making industries together with annually changing exhibitions reflecting different aspects of local history. *Open Easter Mon–Oct, Sat and B Hol Mon 10.00–16.00, Sun 14.00–17.00.* Tearoom and cottage garden. Small admission charge.

Tourist Information Centre The Library, Lancaster Road, Hinckley (01455 635106).

Pubs and Restaurants

🍺 **The Corner House Hotel** Bulkington Lane, Marston Jabbett (02476 386159). South of bridge 5 on B4112. Large friendly pub orientated around family eating. Real ales. Food (V) available *all day, every day.* Children welcome. Patio.

🍺 **The Lime Kilns Inn** Watling Street, Hinckley (01455 631158). Canalside at bridge 15. Old coaching house now refurbished with a downstairs boaters bar. A family pub serving real ale and bar food (V) *all day, every day.* Children's menu. Canalside seating, garden and children's play area. Darts and crib. *Open all day.*

🍺 **The Wharf Inn** Hinckley (01455 615830). East of bridge 17, near Hinckley Wharf. Real ales dispensed in a pub dating back to the 1700s. Children's room and outdoor play area. Garden, darts, dominoes and crib. Dogs (on a lead) welcome. Summer barbecues *on Sat,* weather permitting. There are a variety of services close by including a good general stores, butcher's shop, PO, Indian restaurant, takeaway, newsagent and garage.

🍺✗ **The Watergate Restaurant** Trinity Marinas, Wharf Farm, Coventry Road, Hinkley (01455 896827; www.trinitymarinas. co.uk). Modern restaurant-cum-pub set in a marina complex, serving real ales, bar snacks (available *all day*) and an à la carte restaurant menu (V) *L and E (not Sun E),* prepared from local produce wherever possible. Children welcome when dining. Canalside decking and beer garden. Regular quiz and live entertainment.

Stoke Golding

The canal now runs fairly directly to Stoke Golding where there is one of the finest churches in Leicestershire. There are no locks, but the typical Ashby accommodation bridges occur regularly. The Ashby Canal is remote and rural, an ironic contrast to its *raison d'être*, the Ashby coalfields. After Stoke Golding the contours cause the canal to meander carelessly, passing Dadlington, heading in a northerly direction towards the Bosworth Battlefield Centre near Shenton. There is a community *post office* at the Almshouse Restaurant, Sutton Cheney, *open 09.00–13.00 Tue and Thur.*

Pubs and Restaurants

▣ ✕ **The Oddfellows Arms** Higham on the Hill (01455 212322). Real ale and food (V) served *L daily and E Wed–Sat.* Children welcome. Patio seating and family room. Pub games. Varied entertainment *every Fri and Sat.*

▣ **The Fox Inn** Higham on the Hill (01455 212241). Friendly country pub serving real ales, with home-made bar snacks (V) available *L Mon–Sat.* Children welcome during day. Beer garden. Quiz *Mon.*

▣ **The White Swan** Stoke Golding (01455 212313). Real ale dispensed in a homely village local with friendly staff. Bar snacks (V) available *L and E, daily.* Children and dogs welcome. Garden. Twice monthly quiz, pub games and *summer* barbecues. *Open 12.00–14.00 and 18.00–23.00 (Fri, Sat and Sun 16.30–23.00).*

▣ **The George & Dragon** Stoke Golding (01455 213268). Inexpensive, interesting and varied food (V) available *L and E, daily.* Real ale. Children welcome. Garden and children's play area. Book if eating *after 20.00.*

▣ ✕ **The Dog & Hedgehog** Dadlington (01455 212629). A most deceptive pub, tiny from the outside but able to seat upwards of 80 diners (V) *(L and E, daily)* in its air-conditioned, ex-malt-house dining room and minstrels gallery. Fresh

fish a speciality. A good selection of real ales available. Children well catered for, as are horses who have their own tethers and menu outside. No smoking dining room. The 2-acre gardens are an extravaganza of floral colour. Booking advisable *E and Sun L.*

▣ ✕ **The Hercules Inn** Sutton Cheney, Nr Market Bosworth, Nuneaton (01455 292591). Real ales and good-value bar meals and snacks (V) available *L and E, Tue–Sun and B Hol Mon* – booking advisable for *Sun L.* Children welcome. Patio. No food *Mon L or Sun and Mon E.* Quiz *twice a month.*

✕ ♆ **The Almshouse** Sutton Cheney, nr Market Bosworth, Nuneaton (01455 291050). Meals (V) *L and E,* and afternoon teas. Charming dining room, covered veranda and intimate garden seating. Barbecue area. Children catered for. B & B. Booking advisable.

▣ ✕ **The Royal Arms** Sutton Cheney, nr Market Bosworth, Nuneaton (01455 290263). An excellent range of real ales. Food (V) is available *L and E, daily,* served in the traditional pub restaurant. Children welcome. B & B.

WALKING & CYCLING
In Shenton Cutting, waymarked from Railway Bridge 34A, there is a wildlife walk and a bird-watching hide.

Boatyards

Ⓑ**The Barge** Hinckley Lane, Higham on the Hill, Nuneaton (01455 234213). Long-term mooring.

Ⓑ **Ashby Boat Company** The Canal Wharf, Stoke Golding, Nuneaton (01455 212671; www.ashbyboats.co.uk). 🚽 🛍 🔧 D E Pump out, narrowboat hire, gas, day-hire craft, overnight mooring, long-term mooring, winter storage, chandlery, books, maps and gifts, boat building and fitting out, boat sales and repairs, engine sales and repairs, tearoom, toilets, telephone. *Emergency call out.*

Ⓑ **Ashby Canal Centre** Willow Park Marina, Stoke Golding, Nuneaton (01455 212636). 🔧 Short and long-term moorings, winter storage, crane, slipway, covered wet dock, boat brokerage, boat building and fitting out, boat painting, engine sales, DIY facilities, boat and engine repairs, chandlery, solid fuel, boat surveys, books, maps, toilets.

BOAT TRIPS

Ashby Trip run a variety of public and charter boat trips on *nb Rose* and *nb Rosebud* throughout the year, based at Sutton Cheney Wharf beside bridge 34. These include afternoon cream tea cruises, lunch trips, candlelit dinners and supper cruises and Irish and 60s music nights. Telephone (01455) 213838/07778 734073 or visit www.ashbytrip.co.uk for further details.

35 Bradfields Bridge

SUTTON CHENEY

King Richard's Well

AMBION WOOD

34A

34 Sutton Wharf Bridge

BOAT TRIP

SUTTON CHENEY CP

33 Geary's Bridge

Wooden Top Bridge

31

Dadlington Wharf Bridge 30

32

Sutton Lane Bridge

Allotments Bridge 29

DADLINGTON

Dadlington Bridge 28

Off-line Mooring Basin

27 Foster's Bridge

Foxwell's Bridge 26

Crown Hill

Wharf Bridge 25

Stoke Golding Wharf

13m 0L
Terminus
Marston Jnc
8¾m 0L

STOKE GOLDING

STOKE GOLDING CP

23 Higham Bridge

Basin Bridge 22

21 Wykin Bridge

HIGHAM ON THE HILL

20 Frieston's Bridge

ASHBY CANAL

19 Barn Lane Bridge

17A Dodwell's Road Bridge

● **Higham on the Hill**
Leics. PO, tel, stores, garage. One mile west of bridges 21 and 23. Quiet village on a hill overlooking the canal. To the west is the huge proving ground used by the Motor Industry Research Association for testing new vehicles.

● **Stoke Golding**
Leics. PO, tel, stores. The church is very beautiful, full of original 13th- and 14th-C work. It is large, on a hill, and the spire dominates the landscape. There are good moorings between bridges 27 and 28 and an attractive canalside picnic area.

● **Dadlington**
Leics. PO box, tel. Village built around a green with much new development. The church dates from the 13th C.

Market Bosworth

Just before Shenton Aqueduct there are good moorings for the Battlefield Centre. Shenton Park is passed on an embankment, and then the aqueduct carries the canal over the road to Shenton village. It continues towards Congerstone, with Market Bosworth and Carlton away to the east. Beyond Congerstone the navigation crosses the River Sence.

● **Shenton**
Leics. Tel. Estate village clustered around the Hall, a house of 1629 much rebuilt in the 19th C.
Battle of Bosworth Field 22 August 1485 Ambion Hill, Sutton Cheney. The battlefield where Richard III, last of the Plantagenets, was killed by Henry Tudor who thus became Henry VII. 3/4 mile walk from Shenton Embankment to the **Bosworth Battlefield Visitor Centre** Sutton Cheney, Market Bosworth (01455 290429; www.leics.gov.uk). Award winning interpretation of the battle. Cafeteria (Battlefield Buttery 01455 291048), shop. Toilets. Visitor Centre *open Apr–Oct, Mon–Sat 11.00–17.00; Sun and B Hols 11.00–18.00; Nov and Dec, Sun 11.00–dusk, and Mar, Sat and Sun 11.00–17.00.* Charge. Footpaths *open all year in daylight hours.* Disabled access to Visitor Centre and Battlefield Trails.
Whitemoors Antique and Craft Centre Main Street, Shenton, Market Bosworth (01455 212250/ 212981). Craft and antique centre. Tearooms. *Open all year (except Xmas Eve and Xmas Day), daily 11.00–17.00.*

● **Market Bosworth**
Leics. PO, tel, stores, garage, chemist, bank. Almost a mile east of its wharf. Small market town remaining much as it was in the 18th C.
Battlefield Line Shackerstone Station, Shackerstone (01827 880754; www.battlefield-line-railway.co.uk). Preserved railway line. A ride can be linked in with a visit to the Bosworth Battlefield Visitor Centre. *See* page 19 for further details.

Bosworth Water Trust Market Bosworth (01455 291876; www.bosworth-water-trust. freeserve. co.uk). Just to the west of Bosworth Wharf Bridge 42. Large leisure park with a 20-acre lake for water pursuits. Wetsuits and craft for hire. Changing rooms, toilets, showers and snack bar *open during main season.* Site *open all year, daily 10.00–dusk.* Charge.
Cadeby Experience The Old Rectory, Cadeby, Nuneaton (01455 290462). South east of Market Bosworth. The museum houses the Boston Collection of model and miniature railways and agricultural road vehicles. *Open on some Sats, telephone to confirm.* Donations.
Snibston Discovery Park Ashby Road, Coalville (01530 278444). It is feasible to access this all-weather attraction by bus from Market Bosworth. Route no 179 *Mon–Sat five times daily,* terminating in Memorial Square, Coalville. Further details from Traveline 0870 608 2608.

● **Congerstone**
Leics. Tel. Scattered village of small interest.

Pubs and Restaurants

⬛ ✕ **The Black Horse** Market Place, Market Bosworth (01455 290278). Old-world country pub dispensing real ales. Snacks and meals (V) available *L and E, daily* in bar and restaurant. There is always a vegetarian dish of the day. Children welcome. Patio area.
✕ **Victorian Tea Parlour** Wheatsheaf Courtyard, Market Bosworth (01827 880669). Off the Market Place. Step back in time and enjoy a trip down memory lane together with teas, coffees, snacks and light lunches (V). Children welcome. Pretty garden. *Open daily 10.00–17.00.*
⬛ **The Dixie Arms** Market Bosworth (01455 290218; www.market-bosworth.com/dixiearms). 400-year-old hostelry in the town centre. Bar, restaurant and hotel *open all day, every day,* dis-

pensing real ales and food (V). Children and dogs welcome. Garden and big screen TV. Cellar tours.
⬛ **Ye Olde Red Lion Hotel** Market Bosworth (01455 291713; www.theredlion.dabsol.co.uk). Another 400-year-old hotel and public house in the town centre serving real ales. Home-made snacks and meals (V) available *L and E (not Sun and Mon E).* Children and dogs welcome. Patio. Jazz *first and third Thur in month.* Open fires and pub games. Open *all day Sat.* B & B.
⬛ **The Gate Hangs Well** Carlton (01455 291845). Small country pub with warm, cosy interior serving real ale and rolls and sandwiches *L (not Sun).* Children and dogs welcome. Regular entertainment *Wed and Sat.* Conservatory, garden and children's play area.

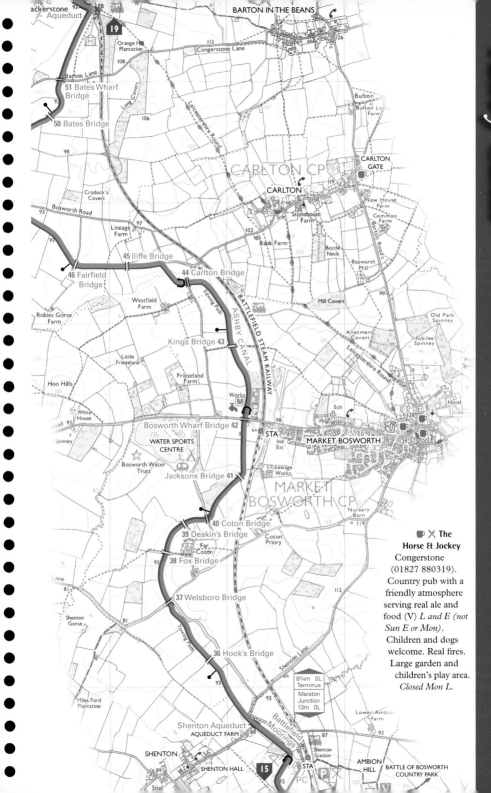

🍺 ✕ **The Horse & Jockey** Congerstone (01827 880319). Country pub with a friendly atmosphere serving real ale and food (V) *L and E (not Sun E or Mon)*. Children and dogs welcome. Real fires. Large garden and children's play area. *Closed Mon L.*

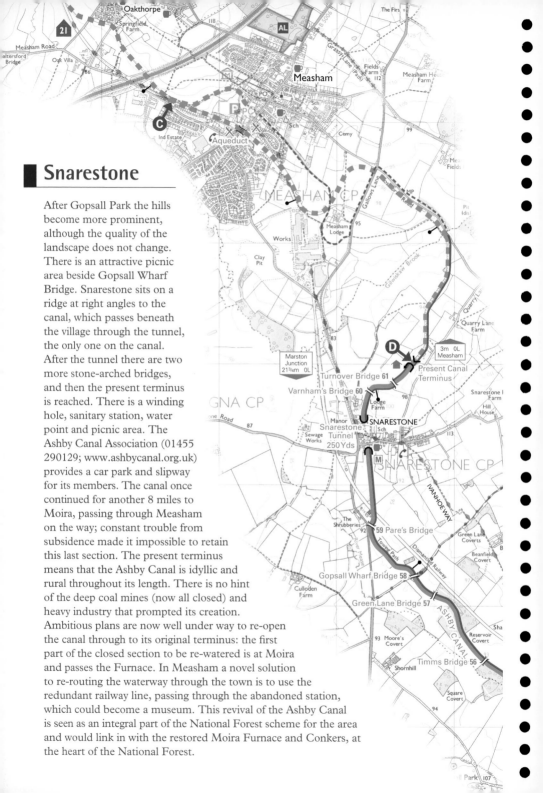

Snarestone

After Gopsall Park the hills become more prominent, although the quality of the landscape does not change. There is an attractive picnic area beside Gopsall Wharf Bridge. Snarestone sits on a ridge at right angles to the canal, which passes beneath the village through the tunnel, the only one on the canal. After the tunnel there are two more stone-arched bridges, and then the present terminus is reached. There is a winding hole, sanitary station, water point and picnic area. The Ashby Canal Association (01455 290129; www.ashbycanal.org.uk) provides a car park and slipway for its members. The canal once continued for another 8 miles to Moira, passing through Measham on the way; constant trouble from subsidence made it impossible to retain this last section. The present terminus means that the Ashby Canal is idyllic and rural throughout its length. There is no hint of the deep coal mines (now all closed) and heavy industry that prompted its creation. Ambitious plans are now well under way to re-open the canal through to its original terminus: the first part of the closed section to be re-watered is at Moira and passes the Furnace. In Measham a novel solution to re-routing the waterway through the town is to use the redundant railway line, passing through the abandoned station, which could become a museum. This revival of the Ashby Canal is seen as an integral part of the National Forest scheme for the area and would link in with the restored Moira Furnace and Conkers, at the heart of the National Forest.

● **Shackerstone**
Leics. Undeveloped and unchanged, Shackerstone is a farming village that reflects the pre-industrial feeling of the whole of the Ashby Canal. West of the village the canal flanks Gopsall Park; the house where Handel is reputed to have composed the *Messiah* was pulled down in 1951, and the park has since lost its original dignity and quality.
Battlefield Line Shackerstone Station, Shackerstone (01827 880754; www.battlefield-line-railway.co.uk). Although the railway line that follows the Ashby Canal is now closed, the former Shackerstone Junction station (near canal bridge 52) has come to life again as a small railway museum (*open Sat 12.00–17.30, Sun and B Hol Mon 10.30–18.00*) and a depot for preserved steam locomotives which run 9-mile round trips to Shenton, via Market Bosworth, on *Sun (Mar–Oct); Sat (Apr–Oct) and Wed (Jul and Aug)*. Diesel trains operate services on *Sat (Apr–Oct), Wed (May, Jun and Sep), Fri (Jun–Aug)*. Victorian tearooms and on-train catering with bar. Souvenir shop. Charge. Can be linked in with a visit to the Bosworth Battlefield Centre.

● **Snarestone**
Leics. Tel. An 18th-C farming village built over the top of the canal, which passes underneath through the crooked tunnel (250yds).

Snibston Discovery Park Ashby Road, Coalville (01530 278444). A unique mixture of science, the environment and history together with brief glimpses into the future in an all-weather setting. Visitors can discover the wonders of technology through over 30 hands-on experiments and experience Leicestershire's rich industrial heritage. Four galleries embrace transport, engineering, extractives and textiles and fashion. Colliery tours, led by ex-miners, explore nearby mine buildings. The site includes 100 acres of landscaped grounds with nature reserve, fishing lakes, sculpture trail and picnic areas (indoor and outdoor). Site railway, coffee and gift shops. *Open daily 10.00–17.00. Closed Xmas and Boxing Day.* Charge. Whilst the Discovery Park is not adjacent to the canal it can make a very worthwhile (wet-weather) day out and is accessible by bus from Hinckley, Market Bosworth, Snarestone and Measham. From Snarestone and Measham Arriva Buses (route no 97) run *in the morning Mon–Sat*, terminating in Memorial Square, Coalville – approx 800yds from the site entrance. Contact Traveline 0870 608 2608 (*open 07.00–22.30*) for further details. Bus details from Hinckley and Market Bosworth appear on previous pages.
Tourist Information Centre Snibston Discovery Park, Ashby Road, Coalville (01530 813608). Opening hours as per the Discovery Park.

Pubs and Restaurants

🍺 **Rising Sun** Shackerstone (01827 880215; www.therisingsun.cwc.net). A range of real ales served in a wood-panelled bar in this old village pub. Food (V) available *L and E, daily*. Children and dogs welcome. Conservatory and beer garden. Pool.

🍺 ✕ **Globe Inn** Main Street, Snarestone, Swadlincote (01530 270272). A good selection of real ales served in a relaxed and friendly atmosphere. Boaters are welcomed and reasonably priced meals and snacks (V) are available in both the bar and restaurant *L and E and all day Sat and Sun*. Children and dogs welcome (in the bar). Large garden and children's play area. Darts, dominoes and crib. *All day opening.*

NAVIGATIONAL NOTES

Headroom in Snarestone Tunnel decreases towards the northern portal.

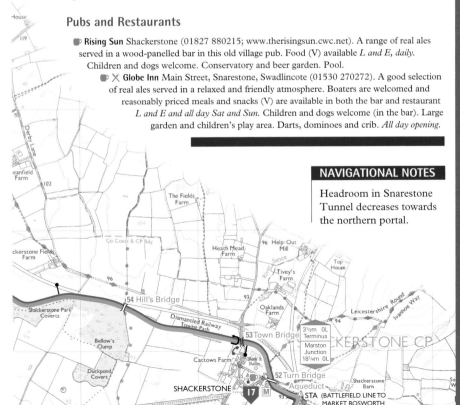

Moira

The 8-mile section of canal, beyond the present terminus at Snarestone, is under consideration for re-opening in three distinct sections; the most northerly, at Moira, being already completed. From the stop lock, the first length (C–D on the map) is already the subject of a Transport and Works Act Order and substantially follows the line of the original navigation. However, it deviates outside Measham to make use of the alignment of the disused railway, making an aqueduct crossing over the High Street a likely outcome. This length then terminates before reaching the A42, the major obstacle in the way of the second section (B–C). Once under this dual carriageway, the waterway can largely follow its old, meandering course through to Donisthorpe where it will meet the third and already re-watered section (A–B) leading past Moira Furnace and into the basin beside Conkers. The countryside between Snarestone and Moira is a mixture of rolling Leicestershire arable land and the residues of extensive coal mining and clay extraction which are now the focus for imaginative landscaping, re-development and afforestation.

● **Measham**
Leics. PO, stores, takeaway, garage, chemist.
Thriving industrial centre even before the arrival of the canal, with coal pits at Oakthorpe and clay deposits that led to the development of a pottery and sanitary ware industry. Famed for its pottery, much prized amongst boating families, Measham has more recently become a major motor auction centre. Boaters who have made the connection with the Great Train Robbery, whilst navigating the Grand Union north of Leighton Buzzard, will be intrigued to learn that the vehicles and effects of the Great Train Robbers were disposed of here.
Measham Museum 56 High Street, Measham (01530 273956). Follow the line of the old canal, from the present terminus at Snarestone, into Measham. Opposite St Lawrence's church. A uniquely personal history of a small community spanning 100 years as seen through the documents, artefacts and illustrations preserved by a former village doctor and his father. *Open Tue 10.00–12.00 and 14.00–17.00, Sat 10.00–12.00.* Donations appreciated.

● **Oakthorpe**
Leics. PO, stores, takeaway. One-time mining village beside the Ashby Woulds Heritage Trail (*see* Walking & Cycling).

● **Donisthorpe**
Leics. 19th-C Perpendicular style church, constructed of grey sandstone, dedicated to St John the Evangelist. Another ex-mining village, now at the start of the isolated length of the newly re-watered canal and close to the Saltersford Valley Picnic Area.

● **Moira**
Leics. Stores. Source of the majority of the coal exported along the canal to Oxford, London and the Home Counties. The name derives from the Moira Estates in Ireland, owned by Baron Rawdon who developed the colliery, foundry and furnace in the area. Saline springs in the area also produced health-giving water but potential visitors were put off 'taking the waters' by the proximity of the coal mines and it was transported to Ashby-de-la-Zouch for final consumption.
Ashby Woulds Heritage Trail Moira (0116 265 7061). A 3-mile local history and heritage trail for walkers and cyclists connecting Conkers to Measham and laid out along the old trackbed of the Ashby and Nuneaton Joint Railway Line. Access points link attractions and numerous country sites.
Conkers Rawdon Road, Moira (01283 216633; www.visitconkers.com). Ambitious project bringing the visitor close to nature in all its myriad forms. This hands-on experience, at the heart of the National Forest, offers a host of indoor and outdoor activities for all the family.
Cycle Hire National Forest Cycle Hire (seasonal), Conkers, Moira (01283 558084); Just Bikes, 8 The Green, Ashby-de-la-Zouch (01530 415021); City Cycles, 61 Meadow Lane, Coalville (01530 812727).
Moira Furnace Furnace Road, Moira (01283 224667; www.nwleicestershire.gov.uk). The furnace, completed in 1806, is a focus for a variety of hands-on exhibitions and outdoor attractions including a 150-year-old deciduous woodland plantation, lime kilns and a wildflower meadow, adventure playground, tea rooms and craft centre. The furnace itself had a short working life and so remains in superb condition today, providing an excellent means of accessing the industrial archaeology of this important area. Horse riding and cycling trails; regular special events and children's fun days; guided heritage walks. Furnace *open Apr–Aug, Tue–Fri 12.30– 17.00; Sat, Sun and B Hols 11.30–17.00 and Sep– Mar, Wed–Fri 12.30–16.00; Sat and Sun 11.30– 16.00.* Charge. *Site open all day, every day.* Free.

Traveline (0870 608 2608). Comprehensive bus information *07.00–22.30*.

● **Ashby de la Zouch**

Leics. All services (exception station). Ashby is mentioned in the Doomsday Book as a settlement of approximately 100 people largely situated round the present site of St Helen's church. In 1160 a Norman nobleman, Alain de Parrhoet la Zouch, became lord of the manor by marriage so bestowing the somewhat striking addition to the town's name. During the 15th C, Ashby Manor was gifted to Lord Hastings by Edward IV and the town became the main seat of the Hastings family. The noble lord converted the manor house into a castle and extensively rebuilt St Helen's church. The Grammar School was founded in 1567 against a backdrop of growth and general prosperity as skilled craftsmen – swordsmiths, gold beaters, pewter workers, clockmakers and silversmiths – set up in 'courts' in the area of Market Street. Inevitably it was a Royalist garrison that occupied the castle during the

Civil War under the command of Henry Hastings, later Lord Loughborough. It fell to the Parliamentarians in 1646 after a year-long siege and was all but destroyed. With the publication of Sir Walter Scott's classic romance in 1820, the castle regained something of its former prominence, this time as a romantic backcloth to Ivanhoe's victorious tournament and Robin Hood's arrow-splitting exploits. Two years later Ashby took on the mantle of Spa Town with the construction of the Ivanhoe Baths and the Royal (then Hastings) Hotel. Ironically enough, its fortunes were founded upon imported water, brought by canal from nearby Moira and discovered in the course of coal extraction. It was felt that mining was a somewhat less than salubrious companion to taking the waters! This was a relatively short-lived prosperity and following a steady decline, the Baths were closed in 1884. Today Ashby is both a centre for light industry and highly sought after as a residential area.

BOAT TRIPS

Joseph Wilks based at Moira Furnace operates trips along the newly restored section of canal. Trips go through the new lock *at weekends* and along the pound to Donisthorpe *during the week*. Telephone (01283) 224667 for further details.

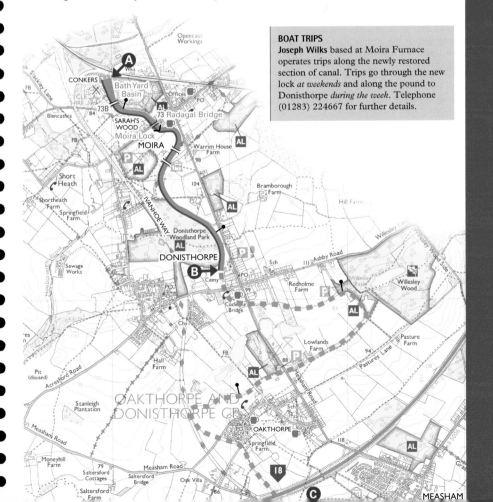

Ashby de la Zouch Museum North Street, Ashby de la Zouch (01530 560090). A permanent display of the history of Ashby and its environs, archives of its rich heritage and a model of the castle as it was during the year-long siege of the Civil War. *Open Easter–Sep, Mon–Fri 10.00–12.00 and 14.00–16.00, Sat 10.00–16.00, Sun 14.00–16.00.* Disabled access. Small charge.

Ashby Castle South Street, Ashby de la Zouch (01530 413343; www.english-heritage.org.uk). While some early remains date back to its 12th-C manor house origins, the most striking feature is the 75' Hastings Tower standing gaunt amongst the ruins. As the castle was designed to resist siege, this tower was connected by underground passage to the kitchens, which can still be explored today. *Open daily Apr–Sep 10.00–18.00; Oct 10.00–16.00; Nov–Mar, Wed–Sat 10.00–16.00.* Charge.

St Helen's Church South Street, Ashby de la Zouch. In Perpendicular style, this church was built by Lord Hastings in 15th C on the site of an earlier Norman building. Enlarged and restored in 1880, it contains much of interest including a rare finger pillory (said to be used in the punishment of those misbehaving in church), glass from Ashby Castle chapel and a series of windows portraying the life of Christ.

Tourist Information Centre North Street, Ashby-de-la-Zouch (01530 411767; www.nwleicester.gov.uk). *Open Mon–Fri 10.00–17.00 and Sat 10.00–15.00.*

● **Staunton Harold**
Leics. Tel. A hamlet of isolated farms, cottages and the Hall, two miles north of Ashby. There are early Saxon references to the manor of Staunton Harold which passed to the Normans following the Conquest of 1066. Later in the hands of the Ferrers family and subsequently held by the Shirleys. The Palladian style hall is now a Sue Ryder Home and is private.

Ferrers Centre for Arts and Crafts Staunton Harold, Ashby de la Zouch (01332 865408; www.ferrersgallery.co.uk). Stable block now home to a thriving and diverse selection of crafts men and women. Tea room and gift shop situated in the courtyard together with the Ferrers Gallery (01332 863337) who hold regular exhibitions and artist-led workshops. *Open Tue–Sun 11.00–17.00 (16.30 in winter).* Ground floor disabled access. Free.

Holy Trinity Church Staunton Harold, Ashby de la Zouch (01332 863822; www.nationaltrust.org.uk). One of the few churches to have been built during the Commonwealth Period, in 1653. It contains a splendid painted ceiling, fine panelling and still has the original hangings, cushions and pews. *Open Apr–Oct, Wed–Sat 13.00–17.00 (or dusk); Oct Sat and Sun only.* Coffee shop at the Hall.

Calke Abbey Ticknall, Nr Melbourne (01332 863822; www.nationaltrust.org.uk). An extraordinary establishment: on the face of it another Baroque mansion from the early 18th C surrounded by extensive park and woodlands. It is in fact a time capsule depicting a grand country house in decline, the clock having stopped with the death of Sir Vauncey Harpur-Crewe in 1924. Since then little has altered either inside, or outside within the 750 acres of park, the stable block or Gothic-style church. Shop and information room. Restaurant. Disabled access including buggy driven by volunteers for access around the grounds. *Open Apr–Oct from approx. 11.00–17.30. Closed Thur and Fri.* Telephone for precise opening times. Charge.

WALKING & CYCLING

Although there is still a long way to go before the Ashby Canal is fully complete between Marston Junction and Moira, this is nevertheless a paradise for the walker and cyclist wishing to enjoy the countryside free from the motor car. Starting at the present canal terminus at Snarestone, a portion of the old waterway route can be walked into Measham. Where a stream makes the path impassable, go down onto Bosworth Road to the right, turn left and proceed to the crossroads and then turn left again. Rejoin the canal on your right near Measham Lodge and follow it into the village. To reach Moira by foot (or bicycle) join the Ashby Woulds Heritage Trail (*see* details in text) in Measham. The Ashby Canal Restoration Project (01530 273956) publish an excellent free walking guide (number 5 in the series) which details a series of walks based on, or around, the northern section of the waterway – Snarestone–Moira. Also available from local TICs. *A Family Cycling Guide* (free) is published by North West Leicestershire District Council (www.nwleicestershire.gov.uk) and details a variety of local routes, together with publications that cover cycling further afield in north west Leicestershire. For the most part these are off-road cycleways or include substantial traffic-free sections. Another excellent leaflet from North West Leicestershire DC, this time for the walker, is *Exploring the Ashby Woulds – A Guided Walk and Things To Do*. Free.

Pubs and Restaurants

✕ **The Mustard Seed** High Street, Measham (01530 272784). Teas, coffees and home-made snacks and light meals (V) available *Mon–Sat (not Wed) 09.30–14.00.* Children welcome.

🍺 **White Hart** 13 Bosworth Road, Measham (01530 270459). Traditional and friendly pub serving real ale and bar snacks *Fri and Sat L.* Children welcome. Beer garden. Log fires; darts, pool, dominoes and large-screen TV.

🍺 **Swan Inn** High Street, Measham (01530 270518). Attractive pub serving real ale and food (V) *L and E.* Children welcome. Beer garden.

🍺 ✕ **Hollybush Inn** Main Street, Oakthorpe, Swadlincote (01530 270943). Large rambling establishment – the oldest building in the village – with a striking canal scene mural painted on an outside wall. This pub serves real ale and a wide and appetising range of English and continental food (V) *L and E (L weekends only).* Children and dogs (in bar) welcome. Garden and children's play area. Quiz *Thur.*

🍺 ✕ **Shoulder of Mutton** Chapel Street, Oakthorpe, Swadlincote (01530 270436). Friendly, village pub serving real ales and food (V) *L and E.* Children welcome.

🍺 **Mason Arms** 1 Church Street, Donisthorpe (01530 270378). An attractive exterior and a friendly welcome inside. This hostelry dispenses real ales and home-made traditional pub food (V) *L and E, daily.* Children and dogs (in bar) welcome. Garden and children's play area. Pool and pub games.

🍺 **Woodman** 1 Shortheath Road, Moira (01283 218316). Friendly local serving real ale and bar snacks (filled cobs) *L.* Children welcome *L only.* Beer garden.

🍺 **Railway** 3 Ashby Road, Moira (01283 217453). Small, welcoming local dispensing real ale and bar snacks *all day.* Children and dogs welcome. Patio seating. Quiz *at weekends.* Darts, dominoes, crib and pool.

✕ **Moira Furnace Tearooms** Furnace Lane, Moira (07773 383164). Serving a variety of home-made lunches, teas and snacks in a relaxed and friendly atmosphere. Children welcome. *Open Mon–Fri 09.30–17.00; Sat, Sun and B Hols 10.00–18.00.*

✕ **Conkers** Millennium Avenue, Rawdon Road, Moira (01283 216633; www. visitconkers.com). Traditional English fayre and snacks available in this fully licensed, lakeside restaurant. Children welcome. *Open daily 10.00–17.00 (later in summer).*

🍺 ✕ **Thirsty Miller** 8 Mill Lane Mews, Ashby de la Zouch (01530 411002). Real ales and a wide variety of good pub grub (V) served in generous portions *L and E, (Tue–Sat and 12.00–16.00 Sun.* Children welcome. Non-smoking restaurant. *Open all day,closed Mon.*

🍺 **Plough Inn** The Green, Ashby de la Zouch (01530 412817; www.the-plough-ashby.co.uk). Serves an excellent and ever-changing range of real ales together with good value, home-made food (V) available *L and E.* Pub games, no machines and open fires in *winter.* Outside seating and disabled access. Open all day. B & B.

✕ 🍷 **La Zouch** 2 Kilwardby Street, Ashby de la Zouch (01530 412536; www.lazouch.co.uk). A family run restaurant serving an English/ French style table d'hôte and a la carte menu *E,* together with morning coffee, snacks and light meals *L.* Also traditional *Sun* Roasts. Children welcome. Disabled access. *Open Tue-Sat 10.00–16.00 and 18.00–23.00, Sun 12.00–16.00. Closed Mon and B Hols.*

✕ **Tudor Court Tearooms** 51A Market Street, Ashby de la Zouch (01530 417610). Snacks, lunches and cream teas in a charming tearoom or outside under parasols in verdant surroundings. All food (V) is home-made.Children welcome. Non-smoking area and disabled access. *Open Mon–Sat 08.15–16.30; B Hols 10.00–16.30.*

🍺 **White Hart** 82 Market Street, Ashby de la Zouch (01530 414531). Unadulterated, 17th-C hostelry,complete with well and bear pit. Good selection of real ales and traditional, home-made food (V) *available Mon–Thur 12.00–20.00 and Fri–Sun 12.00–16.00. Sun roasts* a speciality. Children and dogs (on a lead) welcome. Patio (with heaters). Open fires in *winter.* Quiz *Tue,* soul and Motown *Thur,* live music *Sun. Open all day.*

🍺 **Smisby Arms** Main Street, Smisby, Nr Ashby de la Zouch (01530 412677). Set in a peaceful hamlet 2 miles north of Ashby. Traditional village local serving real ales and an appetising range of food (V) *L and E (not Sun E).* Young children not encouraged. Open fires in *winter.*

🍺 **Saracen's Head** Heath End Lane, Heath End (01332 862323). Traditional Victorian village local, well off the beaten track but handy for thirsty walkers trekking twixt Staunton Harold and Calke. Draught Bass dispensed from a jug. No machines. Pub games, open fires, quarry tile floors and scrubbed tables. Outside seating.

BIRMINGHAM CANAL NAVIGATIONS (BCN) – MAIN LINE

MAXIMUM DIMENSIONS
Length: 70'
Beam: 6' 10"
Headroom: 6' 6"

MANAGER
0121 506 1300
enquiries.tipton@britishwaterways.co.uk

MILEAGES

Birmingham Canal new main line
BIRMINGHAM Gas Street to:
SMETHWICK JUNCTION (old main line): $2^7/8$ miles
BROMFORD JUNCTION: $4^7/8$ miles
PUDDING GREEN JUNCTION (Wednesbury Old Canal): $5^5/8$ miles
TIPTON FACTORY JUNCTION (old main line): $8^3/4$ miles
DEEPFIELDS JUNCTION (Wednesbury Oak loop): 10 miles (Bradley Workshops: $2^1/4$ miles)
HORSELEY FIELDS JUNCTION (Wyrley & Essington Canal): 13 miles
Wolverhampton Top Lock: $13^1/2$ miles
ALDERSLEY JUNCTION (Staffordshire & Worcestershire Canal): $15^1/8$ miles
Locks: 24

Birmingham Canal old main line
SMETHWICK JUNCTION to:
SPON LANE JUNCTION: $1^1/2$ miles
OLDBURY JUNCTION (Titford Canal, 6 locks): $2^1/2$ miles
BRADESHALL JUNCTION (Gower Branch, 3 locks): $3^1/2$ miles
Aqueduct over Netherton Tunnel Branch: $4^3/8$ miles
TIPTON JUNCTION (Dudley Canal): $5^1/2$ miles
FACTORY JUNCTION (new main line): 6 miles
Locks: 9

Netherton Tunnel Branch
WINDMILL END JUNCTION to:
DUDLEY PORT JUNCTION: $2^7/8$ miles
No locks

Wednesbury Old Canal
PUDDING GREEN JUNCTION to:
RYDER'S GREEN JUNCTION: $5/8$ mile
No locks

Walsall Canal
RYDER'S GREEN JUNCTION to:
Ryder's Green Bottom Lock: $1/4$ mile
DOEBANK JUNCTION: $1^3/8$ miles
WALSALL JUNCTION: $6^7/8$ miles
Locks: 8

Walsall Branch Canal
WALSALL JUNCTION to:
BIRCHILLS JUNCTION (Wyrley & Essington Canal): $7/8$ mile
Locks: 8

Wyrley & Essington Canal
HORSELEY FIELDS JUNCTION to:
SNEYD JUNCTION: $6^1/4$ miles
BIRCHILLS JUNCTION (Walsall Branch Canal): 8 miles
PELSALL JUNCTION (Cannock Extension): $12^7/8$ miles
Norton Canes Docks: $1^1/2$ miles
CATSHILL JUNCTION: $15^3/8$ miles
OGLEY JUNCTION (Anglesey Branch): $16^3/8$ miles
Anglesey Basin and Chasewater: $1^1/2$ miles
No locks

Daw End Branch
CATSHILL JUNCTION to:
LONGWOOD JUNCTION (Rushall Top Lock): $5^1/4$ miles
No locks

Rushall Canal
LONGWOOD JUNCTION to:
RUSHALL JUNCTION: $2^3/4$ miles
Locks: 9

Tame Valley Canal
DOEBANK JUNCTION to:
RUSHALL JUNCTION: $3^1/2$ miles
Perry Barr Top Lock: $5^1/2$ miles
SALFORD JUNCTION: $8^1/2$ miles
Locks: 13

Currently a British Waterways T-shaped anti-vandal key is needed for Wolverhampton Locks. Other lock flights on the BCN are under review for similar treatment.

The Birmingham Canal Company was authorised in 1768 to build a canal from Aldersley on the Staffordshire & Worcestershire Canal to Birmingham. With James Brindley as engineer the work proceeded quickly. The first section, from Birmingham to the Wednesbury collieries, was opened in November 1769, and the whole $22^1/2$-mile route was completed in 1772. It was a winding, contour canal, with 12 locks taking it over Smethwick, and another 20 (later 21) taking it down through Wolverhampton to Aldersley Junction. As the route of the canal was through an area of mineral wealth and developing industry, its success was immediate. Pressure of traffic caused the summit level at Smethwick to be lowered in the 1790s (thus cutting out six locks – three on either side of the summit), and during the same period branches began to reach out towards Walsall via the Ryder's Green Locks, and towards Fazeley. Out of this very profitable and ambitious first main line there grew the Birmingham Canal Navigations, more commonly abbreviated to BCN.

As traffic continued to increase so did the wealth of the BCN. The pressures of trade made the main line at Smethwick very congested and brought grave problems of water supply. Steam pumping engines were installed in several places to recirculate the water, and the company appointed Thomas Telford to shorten Brindley's old main line. Between 1825 and 1838 he engineered a new main line between Deepfields and Birmingham, using massive cuttings and embankments to maintain a continuous level. These improvements not only increased the amount of available waterway (the old line remaining in use), but also shortened the route from Birmingham to Wolverhampton by 7 miles.

Railway control of the BCN meant an expansion of the use of the system, and a large number of interchange basins were built to promote outside trade by means of rail traffic. This was of course quite contrary to the usual effect of railway competition upon canals. Trade continued to grow in relation to industrial development and by the end of the 19th C it was topping $8^{1}/_{2}$ million tons per annum. A large proportion of this trade was local, being dependent upon the needs and output of Black Country industry. After the turn of the century this reliance on local trade started the gradual decline of the system as deposits of raw materials became exhausted. Factories bought from further afield and developed along the railways and roads away from the canals. Yet as late as 1950 there were over a million tons of trade and the system continued in operation until the end of the coal trade in 1967 (although there was some further traffic for the Birmingham Salvage Department), a pattern quite different from canals as a whole. Nowadays there is no recognisable commercial traffic – a dramatic contrast to the roaring traffic on the newer Birmingham motorways.

As trade declined, so parts of the system fell out of use and were abandoned. In its heyday in 1865, the BCN comprised over 160 miles of canal. Today just over 100 miles remain. However, all the surviving canals of the BCN are of great interest; excellent for leisure cruising, walking and cycling, they represent a most vivid example of living history and will reward exploration – one of the most important monuments to the Industrial Revolution.

Much has been done in recent years in landscaping waste land (as at the south end of Dudley Tunnel), dredging old basins (such as at the top of the Wolverhampton 21) and restoring disused buildings (such as the Pump House at Smethwick). The Birmingham Canal Partnership (British Waterways, Birmingham City Council, Groundwork Birmingham and various other departments and partners including European funds) is implementing a programme of improvements, having recognised the unique recreational potential of the canal system and its value as an area of retreat for the harassed city dweller and as a new area of exploration for the canal traveller.

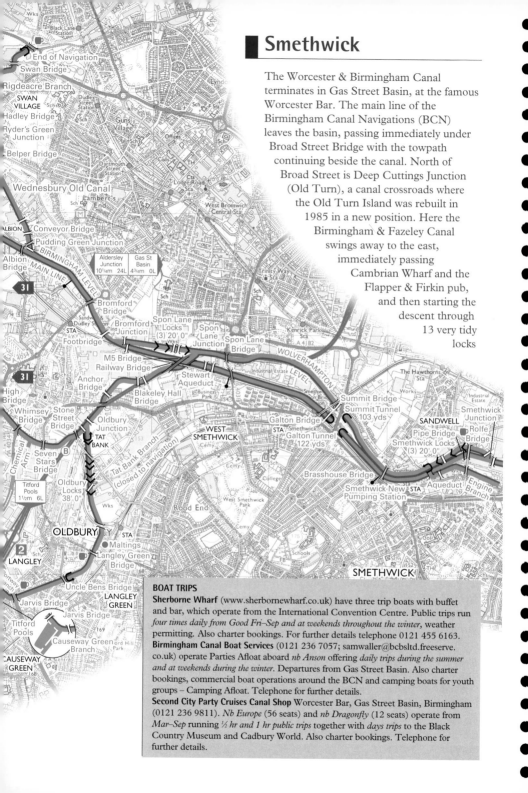

Smethwick

The Worcester & Birmingham Canal terminates in Gas Street Basin, at the famous Worcester Bar. The main line of the Birmingham Canal Navigations (BCN) leaves the basin, passing immediately under Broad Street Bridge with the towpath continuing beside the canal. North of Broad Street is Deep Cuttings Junction (Old Turn), a canal crossroads where the Old Turn Island was rebuilt in 1985 in a new position. Here the Birmingham & Fazeley Canal swings away to the east, immediately passing Cambrian Wharf and the Flapper & Firkin pub, and then starting the descent through 13 very tidy locks

BOAT TRIPS

Sherborne Wharf (www.sherbornewharf.co.uk) have three trip boats with buffet and bar, which operate from the International Convention Centre. Public trips run *four times daily from Good Fri–Sep and at weekends throughout the winter*, weather permitting. Also charter bookings. For further details telephone 0121 455 6163.
Birmingham Canal Boat Services (0121 236 7057; samwaller@bcbsltd.freeserve. co.uk) operate Parties Afloat aboard *nb Anson* offering *daily trips during the summer and at weekends during the winter*. Departures from Gas Street Basin. Also charter bookings, commercial boat operations around the BCN and camping boats for youth groups – Camping Afloat. Telephone for further details.
Second City Party Cruises Canal Shop Worcester Bar, Gas Street Basin, Birmingham (0121 236 9811). *Nb Europe* (56 seats) and *nb Dragonfly* (12 seats) operate from *Mar–Sep* running *½ hr and 1 hr public trips* together with *days trips* to the Black Country Museum and Cadbury World. Also charter bookings. Telephone for further details.

to Aston Junction (*see* page 36). The main line turns west at Farmer's Bridge, while the short Oozell's Street loop goes to the south, quickly disappearing behind old warehouses. This loop, which now houses a boatyard and moorings, and the others further along, are surviving parts of Brindley's original contour canal, now known as the Birmingham Canal Old Main Line. The delays caused by this prompted the Birmingham Canal Company to commission Telford to build a straighter line, the Birmingham Canal New Main Line. This was constructed between 1823 and 1838, and when completed reduced Brindley's old 22 1/2-mile canal to 15 miles. The Oozell's Street loop reappears from the south, and then, after two bridges, the Icknield Port loop leaves to the south. This loop acts as a feeder from Rotton Park Reservoir and rejoins after 1/4 mile at another canal crossroads – the Winson Green or Soho loop, which leaves the main line opposite the Icknield Port loop. This last loop is the longest of the three, running in a gentle arc for over a mile before rejoining the main line again. It is also the only loop to have a towpath throughout its length. At its eastern end is Hockley Port, formerly railway-owned but now used for residential moorings. There are houseboats, a community hall, dry docks and workshops. The main line continues towards Smethwick Junction. Here there is a choice of routes: Brindley's old main line swings to the right, while Telford's new main line continues straight ahead – the old line is the more interesting of the two. The two routes run side by side, but the old line climbs to a higher level via the three Smethwick Locks. Here there were two flights of locks side by side. Beyond the junction, Telford's new line enters a steep-sided cutting. This 40ft-deep cutting enabled Telford to avoid the changes in level of the old line and thus speed the flow of traffic. The two routes continue their parallel courses, the one overlooking the other, until the lower line passes under the Telford Aqueduct. This elegant single span cast iron structure carries the Engine Branch, a short feeder canal that leaves the old line, crosses the new line and then turns back to the south for a short distance. This arm is named after the first Boulton & Watt steam pumping engine to be bought by the Birmingham Canal Company.

This continued to feed the old summit level for 120 years. It was then moved to Ocker Hill for preservation and demonstrations, until the 1950s, when it was finally retired. The sides of the cutting are richly covered with wild flowers and blackberry bushes, and the seclusion of the whole area has turned it into an unofficial nature reserve. The old pumping station at Brasshouse Lane has been restored after years of disuse as part of the new Galton Valley Canal Park development. A Tangyes Engine has been installed to replace the original. The New Main Line continues through natural wilderness to Galton Tunnel. Telford's Galton Bridge crosses the cutting in one magnificent 150ft cast iron span. This bridge is preserved as an ancient monument. The old and the new Birmingham canal lines continue their parallel course, and soon the pleasant semi-rural isolation of the cutting ends, to be replaced by a complex meeting of three types of transport system. The M5 motorway swings in from the east, carried high above the canal on slender concrete pillars; the railway stays close beside Telford's new line; and the canals enter a series of junctions that seem to anticipate modern motorway practice. The new line leaves the cutting and continues in a straight line through industrial surroundings. It passes under Stewart Aqueduct and then reaches Bromford Junction. Here a canal sliproad links the old and the new lines via the three Spon Lane Locks, joining the new at an angle from the east. Note the unusual split bridge at Spon Lane top lock, which was rebuilt in 1986. The old line swings south west following the 473ft contour parallel to the M5, crossing the new line on Stewart Aqueduct. Thus canal crosses canal on a flyover. Spon Lane Locks, the linking sliproad, survive unchanged from Brindley's day and are among the oldest in the country. The old and the new lines now follow separate courses. The old line continues below the motorway to Oldbury Locks Junction. Here the short Titford Canal climbs away to the south via the six Oldbury Locks; this canal serves as a feeder from Titford Pools to Rotton Park Reservoir. After the junction the old line swings round to the north west and continues on a parallel course to the new line once again. After Bromford Junction the new line continues its straight course towards Wolverhampton. At Pudding Green Junction the main line goes straight on; the Wednesbury Old Canal forks right to join the Walsall Canal, which in turn joins the Tame Valley Canal at Doebank Junction.

WALKING & CYCLING

Much of Birmingham's 100-mile network of canals offers excellent opportunities for walkers and cyclists, and provides the chance to explore a side of the city well away from the obvious tourist attractions and close to the area's industrial roots. From a more formal approach, Birmingham is a crossroads for the National Cycle Network with Route 5 approaching from Kings Norton via Worcester & Birmingham Canal. Route 81 follows the Birmingham Level Main Line from the city to Wolverhampton, to eventually head into Mid Wales. Several excellent routes lead out from the city centre along traffic-free or contraflow cycle lanes. Further details are contained in *CycleCity's Birmingham Cycling Map – City Centre and Suburbs* and is available from Sustrans (0117 929 0888; www.sustrans.org.uk). Charge.

NAVIGATIONAL NOTES

Since the Titford Canal is the highest level on the BCN, it is advisable to telephone the BW Waterway Office (0121 506 1300) to check that there is adequate water before you visit the canal. You will need a water conservation key for Oldbury Locks in order to access this canal.

● The Titford Canal
Built in 1837 as part of the original Birmingham Canal scheme, acting as a feeder to Spon Lane, the Titford Canal served Causeway Green. This must have been a very busy canal in its heyday, with many branches, wharves and tramways connecting it to the surrounding mines and engineering works. Today it survives in shortened form and has the distinction of being the highest navigable part of the BCN, with a summit level above Oldbury Locks of 511ft. The locks are sometimes referred to as the Crow – a branch which left the canal above

the third lock and served the alkali and phosphorus works of a local industrialist and benefactor Jim Crow. The last surviving recirculatory pumphouse can be seen by the top lock. It is hoped that BW, in partnership with the local canal society, can raise funds for its restoration. The waterway now terminates at the wide expanse of water of Titford Pools

Tourist Information Centre *see* page 37.

Boatyards

Ⓑ **Sherborne Wharf** Sherborne Street Wharf, Birmingham (0121 455 6163; www. sherbornewharf.co.uk). On the Oozell's Street Loop. 🏠 🏠 🛒 D E Pump out, gas, day-hire boats, overnight mooring, long-term mooring, wet docks, winter storage, chandlery, boat repairs, engine sales and repairs, books, maps and gifts, DIY facilities, electrical hook-up, solid fuel, toilets, showers, laundrette, large supermarket nearby. *Emergency call out.*

Pubs and Restaurants

In a large city such as Birmingham there are many fine pubs and restaurants. As a result of the recent development of the area adjoining the canal, between Gas Street Basin and Cambrian Wharf, there are now approaching two dozen eating and drinking establishments. This choice is further expanded by walking south along Broad Street, from Broad Street Bridge, at Gas Street Basin. However beyond the canalside the enterprising boater (walker and cyclist) might like to seek out some of the City's more diverse hostelries:

🍺 **The Flapper & Firkin** Cambrian Wharf, Kingston Row (0121 236 2421). Real ale in a student-type pub, together with food (V) available *L and E*. Children welcome *until 19.00*. Outside terrace seating by the basin. Light music *most evenings. Open all day.*

🍺 **The Figure of Eight** 236-239 Broad Street (0121 633 0917). Sensibly priced real ale in a pub handy for Gas Street Basin. Food (V) available *all day, every day.* Outside seating and no smoking area. Disabled access. *Open all day.*

🍺 **The Fiddle & Bone** 4 Sheepcote Street, Ladywood (0121 200 2223; www.fiddle-bone. co.uk). Once an old school house, this two-storey canalside pub, with a strong musical theme, now dispenses real ales and an excellent range of food (V) *L and E (not Sun E)*. Patio seating. Disabled access. Mooring. *Open all day.*

🍺 **The Anchor** 308 Bradford Street (0121 622 4516). Edwardian pub tucked away behind the Digbeth coach station. Food (V) available *daily (until 18.00)* together with real ales, German and Belgian draught beers and real cider. Also an excellent range of bottled beers from far and wide. Outside seating. *Open all day.*

🍺 **The Woodman** 106 Albert Street, Digbeth (0121 643 1959). Friendly and very popular traditional pub that has survived the city's wholesale rebuilding programme. Real ales and food (V) available *L and E*.

🍺 **The Gunmaker's Arms** Bath Street (0121 236 1201). Comfortable, two-roomed pub serving real ales and food (V) *L and E, Mon–Fri.* Out- side seating. *Closed Sun E.*

🍺 **Darwins** 57 Grosvenor Street, Five Ways (0121 643 6064). Near Tesco's. Traditional two-roomed city pub, with a wide ranging clientele, dispensing real ales together with food *L and E, daily.* Children welcome *until 21.00.* Skittles, darts and pool. *Tue eves* entertainment.

🍺 **The Black Eagle** 16 Factory Road, Hockley (0121 523 4008). North of Hockley Port. Real ales and food (V) available *L and E (not Sun E).* Children welcome. Outside seating. Booking advisable for meals.

🍺 **The Olde Windmill** 84 Dudley Road, Winson Green (0121 455 6907). East of Lee Bridge, opposite the hospital. Real ales served in a compact, traditional old pub. Food available *L, daily.* Children welcome *until 16.00.* Beer garden and pub games. *Fortnightly Sat* musical entertainment. *Open all day.*

🍺 **The Finings & Firkin** 91 Station Road, Langley (0121 544 6467). A range of real ales dispensed in the old HP&D brewery tap. Friendly, welcoming atmosphere. Meals and bar snacks (V) available *L and E (until 20.00), daily.* Pub games, regular *weekday* quiz and *weekend* music. *Open all day.*

🍺 **The New Navigation** 156 Titford Road, Langley (0121 552 2525). Beside Jarvis Bridge. Canalside pub with a wide ranging clientele, serving food *L and E.* Children and dogs welcome. Outside seating. Mooring. *Weekend* quiz and musical entertainment.

🍺 **The Whiteheath Tavern** 400 Birchfield Lane, Whiteheath (0121 552 3603). Just west of Titford Pools, near M5 junction 2. Real ale in a pub close to Titford Pools. Children welcome at lunchtime. Traditional pub games.

Dudley

At Bradeshall Junction the Gower Branch links the two lines, descending to the lower level of the new line through three locks. To the south west of Tipton Junction is the branch leading to the Black Country Museum and the Dudley Tunnel. This branch connects with the Dudley Canal, the Stourbridge Canal, and thus with the Staffordshire & Worcestershire Canal. The old line turns north at the junction, rejoining the new line at Factory Junction. At Albion Junction the Gower Branch turns south to join the old line at Bradeshall. At Dudley Port Junction the Netherton Tunnel Branch joins the main line. The Netherton Tunnel Branch goes through the tunnel to Windmill End Junction; from here boats can either turn south down the old Dudley Canal to Hawne Basin, or west towards the Stourbridge Canal, and thus to the Staffordshire & Worcestershire Canal. North of Dudley Port the new line crosses a main road on the Ryland Aqueduct. Continuing its elevated course the new line reaches Tipton, where there are moorings with *shops* close by, and a small basin. The new line climbs the three Factory Locks and immediately reaches Factory Junction, where the old line comes in from the south.

Pubs and Restaurants

⚓ **The Old Court House** Lower Church Lane, Tipton (0121 520 2865). North east of Dudley Port Station. Real ales and food (V) available *L and E, daily* in a pub that used to be the holding cells for the police station across the road. Children and dogs welcome. Outside seating. Live bands *Tue* and karaoke *Fri*.

⚓ ✕ **The Bottle & Glass Inn** Black Country Living Museum, Tipton Road, Dudley (0121 557 9643). Real ale in a wonderful old pub, moved to the site. Cheese and onion cobs available *all day. Open 10.00–16.00*. More substantial refreshment available in the adjoining Stables Restaurant and 1930s fish & chip shop.

⚓ **The Port 'N' Ale** 178 Horsley Heath, Tipton (0121 532 2805). North east of Dudley Port railway station. One of the rare, genuine free houses left dispensing an excellent range of real ales and two traditional ciders. Children's room, outside seating and traditional pub games.

⚓ **The Rising Sun** 116 Horsley Road, Tipton (0121 530 9780). North of Dudley Port railway station. Real ale and a friendly welcome make this pub worth the walk. Also real cider. Food served *E (not Sun)*. Open fires in winter and traditional pub games. Camping.

⚓ **The Barge & Barrel** Factory Road, Tipton (0121 520 6962). A recently refurbished pub in a wine bar setting, serving real ale, and inexpensive bar meals (V) *L*. Children welcome. Karaoke *Thur and Sun*, DJ *Fri and Sat*.

⚓ **The Boat Inn** Coseley (01902 492993). Friendly, canalside pub serving real ales. Snacks and basket meals (V) available *L and E*. Children welcome. Garden seating and traditional pub games. Karaoke *Wed and Sat evenings*. Barbecue facilities available for patrons use.

Boatyards

Ⓑ **Oldbury Boat Services**
Oldbury Wharf, Stone Street
Bridge, Oldbury (0121 544 1795).
D Gas, long-term mooring, winter
storage, chandlery, maps, solid fuel.

Ⓑ **Caggy's Boatyard** Owen Street,
Tipton (07710 343773). 🚿 ♿ D
Pump out, day-craft hire, overnight
mooring, winter storage, crane,
slipway, boat repairs, engine
repairs, boatbuilding, boat fitting
out, dry dock, wet dock, DIY facilities, chandlery, books, maps, gifts,
toilets, showers, solid fuel.
Emergency call out.

BOAT TRIPS
Aaron Manby operates trips
from outside the Malthouse
Stables outdoor pursuits centre.
Telephone 0121 520 7861 for
further details.

● **Black
Country Museum**
Tipton Road, Dudley (0121
557 9643; www.bclm.co.uk). A
superb outdoor museum built around a
reconstructed canalside village, with a pub,
shops and an inland port. See demonstrations of
sweet-making, glass-cutting and metal-working, ride
on a tram or trolly bus, take a boat trip into Dudley
Tunnel or a coalmine tour. And if you have time, participate
in an old-time school lesson, ride on the fairground, watch an
old film and meet the horses and ponies. *Open Mar–Oct, daily
10.00–17.00 and Nov–Feb, Wed–Sun 10.00–16.00.* Charge.

Walsall Canal
Church Hill
Willingsworth Hall Bridge
Pipe Bridge
see Book 2
Monway Bridge
Metro Bridge
Wednesbury Parkway
GOSPEL OAK BRANCH
Wiggins Mill Bridge
Wednesbury Great Western Street Station
see Book 2
Leabrook Road Bridge
Rushall Jnc 3½m 0L
Tame Valley Canal
Doe Bank Bridge
Tame Valley Junction
Holloway Bank Bridge
Jones Bridge
OCKER HILL TUNNEL BRANCH
Pipe Bridge
Rail Bridge
OCKER HILL
BW Office
Aqueduct
Golds Hill Bridge
Ocker Hill Bridge
Golds Green
6½m 8L Birchills Jnc
Pudding Gr Jnc 2m 6L
Golds Hill
Moors Mill Lane Bridge
Harvills Hawthorn
Toll
Hempole Lane Bridge
Rail Bridge
GREAT BRIDGE
Aqueduct
Brickhouse Lane Bridge
Pipe Bridge
STA
Wellington Footbridge
Great Bridge Bridge
End of Navigation
Swan Bridge
BIRMINGHAM LEVEL MAIN LINE
HORSELEY HEATH
Ryder's Green Locks 45' 0"
RYDERS GREEN
Rigdeacre Branch
SWAN VILLAGE
Hadley Bridge
Pipe Bridge
Victoria Park
Sheepwash Urban Park
New Town
Ryder's Green Junction
Playing Fields
Aqueducts
Ryland Aqueduct
Dudley Port Junction
Belper Bridge
WOLVERHAMPTON LEVEL
Wednesbury Old Canal Works
Randall's Bridge
DUDLEY PORT
Dudley Port Bridge
Trading Estate
NETHERTON BRANCH
GREETS GREEN
Albion Junction
Conveyor Bridge
ALBION
Pudding Green Junction
Keir's Bridge
Tividale Aqueduct
TIVIDALE
Pipe Bridge
BURNT TREE
Netherton Tunnel 3027 yds
Gilbert's Bridge
Dudley Road West Bridge
Brades Locks (3) 20' 0"
GOWER BRANCH
Albion Bridge
SANDWELL
see Book 2
Fisher's Bridge
Bradeshall Junction
Aldersley Junction 10¼m 24L
Gas St Basin 4¾m 0L
26
BRADES VILLAGE
Pipe Bridge
Brades Bridge
ROUND'S GREEN
Civic Centre
26
High Bridge
Whimsey Bridge
Chemical Arm
Seven Stars Bridge

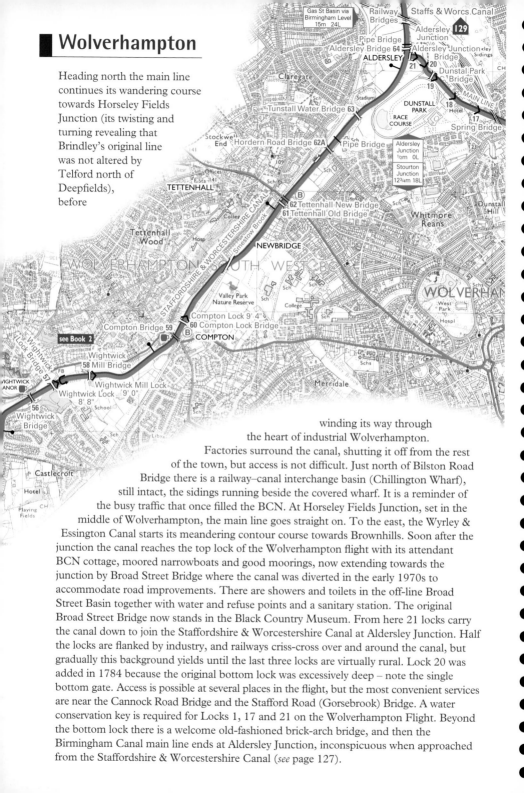

Wolverhampton

Heading north the main line
continues its wandering course
towards Horseley Fields
Junction (its twisting and
turning revealing that
Brindley's original line
was not altered by
Telford north of
Deepfields),
before

winding its way through
the heart of industrial Wolverhampton.
Factories surround the canal, shutting it off from the rest
of the town, but access is not difficult. Just north of Bilston Road
Bridge there is a railway–canal interchange basin (Chillington Wharf),
still intact, the sidings running beside the covered wharf. It is a reminder of
the busy traffic that once filled the BCN. At Horseley Fields Junction, set in the
middle of Wolverhampton, the main line goes straight on. To the east, the Wyrley &
Essington Canal starts its meandering contour course towards Brownhills. Soon after the
junction the canal reaches the top lock of the Wolverhampton flight with its attendant
BCN cottage, moored narrowboats and good moorings, now extending towards the
junction by Broad Street Bridge where the canal was diverted in the early 1970s to
accommodate road improvements. There are showers and toilets in the off-line Broad
Street Basin together with water and refuse points and a sanitary station. The original
Broad Street Bridge now stands in the Black Country Museum. From here 21 locks carry
the canal down to join the Staffordshire & Worcestershire Canal at Aldersley Junction. Half
the locks are flanked by industry, and railways criss-cross over and around the canal, but
gradually this background yields until the last three locks are virtually rural. Lock 20 was
added in 1784 because the original bottom lock was excessively deep – note the single
bottom gate. Access is possible at several places in the flight, but the most convenient services
are near the Cannock Road Bridge and the Stafford Road (Gorsebrook) Bridge. A water
conservation key is required for Locks 1, 17 and 21 on the Wolverhampton Flight. Beyond
the bottom lock there is a welcome old-fashioned brick-arch bridge, and then the
Birmingham Canal main line ends at Aldersley Junction, inconspicuous when approached
from the Staffordshire & Worcestershire Canal (*see page 127*).

Boatyards

Ⓑ **Associated Cruisers** Lock Street, Little's Lane, Wolverhampton (01902 423673). 🏠 🛠 Engine hoist, boat sales and repairs, engine sales and repairs, boat building and fitting out, wet dock, telephone, toilets.

NAVIGATIONAL NOTES

A water conservation key is needed to operate Tipton Factory Locks.

BOAT TRIPS

Nb Stafford is a 42-seat boat operating public trips *on first Sun of the month* and booked charter trips. Telephone (01902) 789522 for further details.

Ⓑ **Oxley Marine** The Wharf, Oxley Moor Road, Wolverhampton (01902 789522). 🏠 D Pump out, gas, overnight and long-term mooring, slipway, crane, boat and engine sales and repairs. Licensed bar *each evening*, snacks.

Ⓑ **Kingfisher Narrowboats** 3/3A, 16 Union Mill Street, Horseley Fields, Wolverhampton (01902 351311). Crane, boat and engine sales, boat repairs, boat building and fitting out, wet dock, DIY facilities, chandlery, solid fuel. *24hr emergency call out.* See Staffordshire & Worcester Canal, page 128 – for boatyards marked at Bridges 59 and 62.

Map labels

Gorsebrook Bridge, Pipe Bridge, Stour Valley Viaduct, Fox's Lane Bridge, Jordans Bridge, Wolverhampton Locks (21) 132′ 0″, Cannock Road Bridge, Springfield, Deans Road Bridge, Little's Lane Bridge, Broad Street Bridge, WOLVERHAMPTON, Mill Street Bridge, Horseley Fields Bridge, Rail Bridge, Walsall Street Bridge, Pipe Bridge, Chillington Wharf, Bilston Road Bridge, Pipe Bridge, Cable Street Bridge, Dixon Street Bridge, Pipe Bridge, Priestfield, Catchems Corner Bridge, Pipe Bridges, Jibbet Lane Bridge, Millfields Bridge, MILLFIELDS, LADYMOOR, Highfields Road Bridge, Deepfields Junction, SPRING VALE, Gas St Basin 10m 3L, 5m 21L Aldersley Junction, WOLVERHAMPTON LEVEL, MAIN LINE, Wyrley & Essington Canal, see Book 2, Wards Bridge, Nordley Hill, Pinfold Bridge, Church Bridge, Rookery Bridge, Wednesfield Junction, New Cross Bridge, HEATH TOWN, Heath Town Bridge, New Bentley Bridge, Site of Bentley Canal, Neachells, 8m 0L Birchills Jnc, Swan Garden Bridge, Horseley Fields Junction, MONMORE GREEN, Stow Heath, East Park, Speedway Stadium, Freezeland, 30, 72B

Pubs and Restaurants

In a town such as Wolverhampton there are many pubs to choose from. Below are a selection for the enterprising to seek out:

The Feathers Molineux Street, Wolverhampton (01902 426924). By the football ground. Small friendly local renowned for its garden. Real ale, and food *L Mon–Fri*. Children welcome. Pub games. Karaoke *Sat. Open all day Mon–Sat.*

The Clarendon Chapel Ash, Wolverhampton (01902 420587). A41, just to the west of the town centre. Refurbished, somewhat to its detriment, this pub offers real ale and food *L Mon–Fri*. Also breakfasts *08.00–L*. Children's room. Outside seating. *Open all day.*

The Combermere Arms 90 Chapel Ash, Wolverhampton (01902 421880). Real ale served in a terraced house look-alike: both cosy and intimate. Open fires and garden. Food *L Mon–Fri*. Children welcome. Disabled access.

The Great Western Sun Street, Wolverhampton (01902 351090. Real ale, railway memorabilia and good local cooking *L (not Sun)*. Children welcome at lunchtime if eating, dogs welcome in the evening. Garden and traditional pub games.

Posada 48 Lichfield Street, Wolverhampton (01902 711304). Grade ll listed building with its striking tiled frontage. A good range of real ales and snacks *L Mon–Fri* (together with tea and coffee) are always available. *Open all day except Sun.*

The Tap & Spile 35 Princes Street, Wolverhampton (01902 713319). An open bar and two snugs in a city centre pub dispensing an excellent range of real ales and home-made food (V) *L Mon–Fri*. Also real cider and traditional pub games. Disabled access. *Open all day, every day.*

Birmingham New Main Line at Winson Green (see page 27)

BIRMINGHAM & FAZELEY CANAL

MAXIMUM DIMENSIONS
Length: 70'
Beam: 7'
Headroom: 7' 6"

MILEAGE
FARMER'S BRIDGE JUNCTION
(Birmingham Canal) to:
  ASTON JUNCTION (Digbeth Branch):
  1¹/2 miles
SALFORD JUNCTION (Tame Valley
Canal): 3¹/4 miles
Minworth Top Lock: 6¹/4 miles
Curdworth Tunnel: 8¹/2 miles
Bodymoor Heath Bridge: 11¹/2 miles

FAZELEY JUNCTION (Coventry Canal):
15 miles
Hopwas: 17³/4 miles
Whittington Brook: 20¹/2 miles

Locks: 38

MANAGER
01283 790236
enquiries.fradley@britishwaterways.co.uk

The Birmingham & Fazeley Canal was authorised in 1784, after a great deal of opposition from the well-established Birmingham Canal Company (who very soon merged with it), as a link between Birmingham and the south east. Until then, London-bound goods from Birmingham had to go right round by the River Severn. Naturally, the canal was useless until the Coventry Canal had at least reached Fazeley, but the new Birmingham & Fazeley Company ensured – even before its enabling Act was passed – that the other canals important to its success were completed. Thus at Coleshill in 1782 the Oxford Canal Company agreed to finish its line to Oxford and the Thames; the Coventry Canal Company agreed to extend its line from Atherstone to Fazeley; the new Birmingham & Fazeley Company agreed to build its proposed line and continue it along the defaulting Coventry route from Fazeley to Whittington Brook; and the Trent & Mersey Company pledged to finish the Coventry's line from Whittington Brook to Fradley Junction on the Trent & Mersey Canal.

This rare example of cooperation among canal companies paid off when, in 1790, the great joint programme was finished and traffic immediately began to flow along the system. The Birmingham & Fazeley Company employed John Smeaton to build their canal: he completed it in 1789. The flights of narrow locks at Farmer's Bridge and Aston became very congested, especially after the Warwick canals had joined up with the Birmingham & Fazeley Canal at Digbeth; two new canals were built to bypass this permanent obstacle, one on each side. The Tame Valley Canal and the Birmingham & Warwick Junction Canal were opened in 1844, and traffic flowed more smoothly. After this the Birmingham & Fazeley Canal became more attractive to carriers and it continued to be an important link route. It still provides this link, but is now worthy of exploration in its own right.

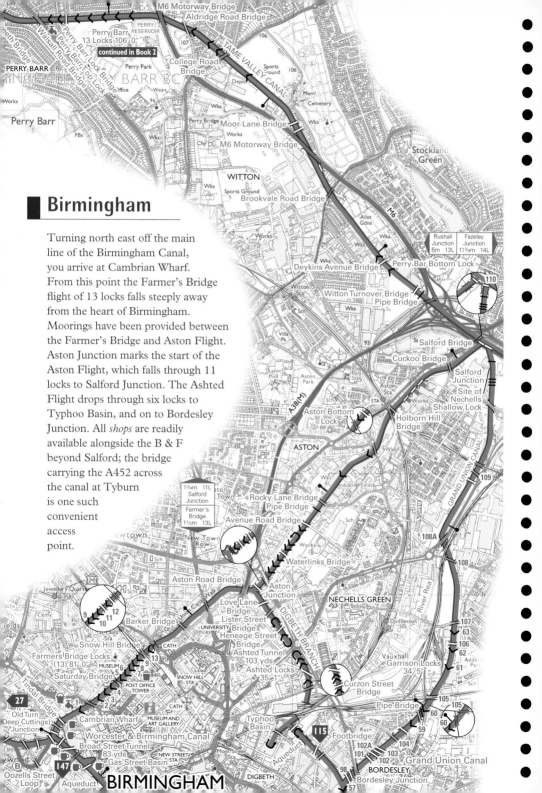

Birmingham

Turning north east off the main line of the Birmingham Canal, you arrive at Cambrian Wharf. From this point the Farmer's Bridge flight of 13 locks falls steeply away from the heart of Birmingham. Moorings have been provided between the Farmer's Bridge and Aston Flight. Aston Junction marks the start of the Aston Flight, which falls through 11 locks to Salford Junction. The Ashted Flight drops through six locks to Typhoo Basin, and on to Bordesley Junction. All *shops* are readily available alongside the B & F beyond Salford; the bridge carrying the A452 across the canal at Tyburn is one such convenient access point.

The Digbeth Branch This leaves the Birmingham & Fazeley main line at Aston Junction, and descends through six locks to Typhoo Basin, where it meets the former Warwick & Birmingham Canal, which became part of the Grand Union Canal when the GUC Company was formed in 1929. There was a stop lock – called Warwick Bar – at the junction by Bordesley Basin. One of the lesser-known tunnels on the canal system is on this branch – Ashted Tunnel. There is a narrow towpath through it, protected by railings and with a corrugated surface for the towing horses to get a good grip on.

Tourist Information Centre Birmingham Convention and Visitor Bureau, City Arcade (0121 643 2514).

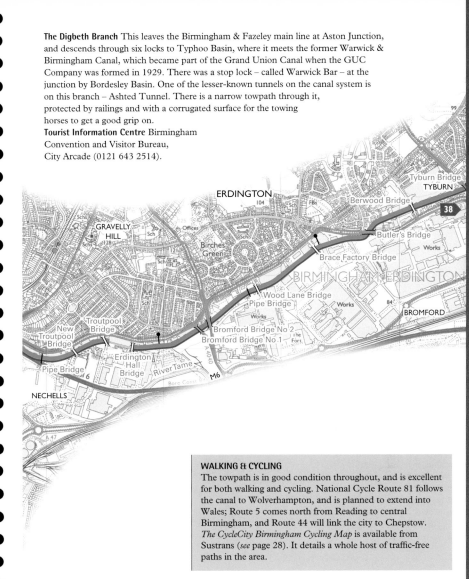

Birmingham & Fazeley Canal

Birmingham

WALKING & CYCLING

The towpath is in good condition throughout, and is excellent for both walking and cycling. National Cycle Route 81 follows the canal to Wolverhampton, and is planned to extend into Wales; Route 5 comes north from Reading to central Birmingham, and Route 44 will link the city to Chepstow. *The CycleCity Birmingham Cycling Map* is available from Sustrans (*see* page 28). It details a whole host of traffic-free paths in the area.

Pubs and Restaurants

Flapper & Firkin Cambrian Wharf, Kingston Row (0121 236 2421). Real ale in a student-type pub. Food (V) *L and E*. Children welcome *until 19.00*. Outside terrace seating by the basin. Light music *most evenings*. *Open all day*.

The Malt House Overlooking Deep Cuttings Junction (0121 633 4171). Friendly pub serving food (V) *12.00–20.00 daily*. Children welcome *until 19.00*. Outside seating, and a balcony. DJs *Fri and Sat evenings*.

The James Brindley Gas Street Basin, Bridge Street (0121 644 5971). Modern pub overlooking Gas Street Basin. Bar meals (V) served *L and E (not Sat E)*. There is outside seating, and a jazz band entertains *Sat and Sun L*.

Reservoir Cuckoo Bridge, Lichfield Road (0121 327 3336). Friendly pub undergoing refurbishment. Food. Children welcome. Disco *Fri and Sat*.

Curdworth

Most of the factories on this section ignore the canal, although the Cincinnati works are a laudable exception: landscaped lawns and gardens run down from the buildings to the water's edge. Minworth Locks start the descent towards Fazeley, and gradually the canal loses the industry that has accompanied it from Birmingham. Curdworth is passed in a tree-lined cutting: the church tower here has been visible for some time. The cutting continues beyond Curdworth Bridge, and enters a short tunnel (57yds), with the towpath alongside. From now until Fazeley the canal makes its passage in complete isolation through the empty fields, only the 11 locks falling down to Fazeley Junction breaking its journey. The lack of hedges in this area is very noticeable and only those by the towpath seem to have survived. As the canal swings north, hedges and trees thankfully reappear, and after Bodymoor Heath trees line the canal on both sides for two miles. By the bottom lock there is a swing bridge (kept open) which contributes to what is a pretty canal scene. Flooded gravel pits, and the bird life they attract, enliven the surroundings.

● **Tyburn**
Warwicks. PO, tel, stores. A mixture of factories and houses.

● **Minworth**
Warwicks. PO, tel, stores. A mainly residential area on the city outskirts, totally dominated by roads. There is a handy transport café close to Hansons Bridge.

● **Curdworth**
Warwicks. PO, tel, stores, garage. Now set in the shadow of the motorway, and not far from the sewage works, Curdworth still manages to cling to a village identity. The squat church is partly Norman, c. 1170; note the finely carved Norman font, with images of standing men, a monster and a lamb.

● **Bodymoor Heath**
Warwicks. Tel. A scattered village beyond which gravel pits, many flooded, break up the fields. Yet, amidst this broken landscape there are occasional 18th-C buildings, surviving as a

memory of the pre-industrial Midlands. The pub, the Dog & Doublet, is one such fine example.

Kingsbury Water Park Bodymoor Heath (01827 872660). A 600-acre landscaped park containing 30 lakes and pools, created from gravel pits worked over the last 50 years. Walks, nature trails, fishing, horse riding, sailing, power-boating and windsurfing. Visitor centre and coffee shop. Excellent programme of events *Apr–Sep* (modest charge per event). There is also a children's farm at Broomey Croft, with goats, sheep and ponies. Telephone 01827 873844 for details. Charge, tearoom.

Salford Junction	Fazeley Junction
3m 0L	8¾m 14L

Pubs and Restaurants

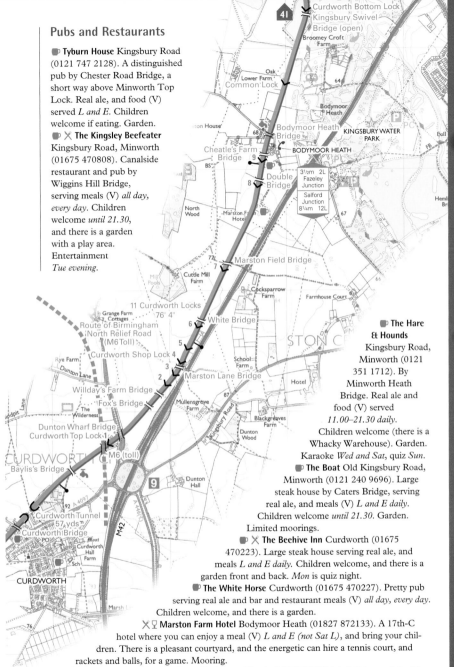

▶ **Tyburn House** Kingsbury Road
(0121 747 2128). A distinguished
pub by Chester Road Bridge, a
short way above Minworth Top
Lock. Real ale, and food (V)
served *L and E*. Children
welcome if eating. Garden.

▶ ✕ **The Kingsley Beefeater**
Kingsbury Road, Minworth
(01675 470808). Canalside
restaurant and pub by
Wiggins Hill Bridge,
serving meals (V) *all day,*
every day. Children
welcome *until 21.30*,
and there is a garden
with a play area.
Entertainment
Tue evening.

▶ **The Hare
& Hounds**
Kingsbury Road,
Minworth (0121
351 1712). By
Minworth Heath
Bridge. Real ale and
food (V) served
11.00–21.30 daily.
Children welcome (there is a
Whacky Warehouse). Garden.
Karaoke *Wed and Sat*, quiz *Sun*.

▶ **The Boat** Old Kingsbury Road,
Minworth (0121 240 9696). Large
steak house by Caters Bridge, serving
real ale, and meals (V) *L and E daily*.
Children welcome *until 21.30*. Garden.
Limited moorings.

▶ ✕ **The Beehive Inn** Curdworth (01675
470223). Large steak house serving real ale, and
meals *L and E daily*. Children welcome, and there is a
garden front and back. *Mon* is quiz night.

▶ **The White Horse** Curdworth (01675 470227). Pretty pub
serving real ale and bar and restaurant meals (V) *all day, every day*.
Children welcome, and there is a garden.

✕ ♀ **Marston Farm Hotel** Bodymoor Heath (01827 872133). A 17th-C
hotel where you can enjoy a meal (V) *L and E (not Sat L)*, and bring your children. There is a pleasant courtyard, and the energetic can hire a tennis court, and
rackets and balls, for a game. Mooring.

▶ ✕ **The Dog & Doublet** Dog Lane, Bodymoor Heath (01827 872374; info@dog-and-doublet.
com). Smart and handsome red-brick canalside pub by Cheatles Farm Bridge, serving real ale.
Varied menu and specials (V) *L and E*. Children welcome. Canalside garden with good views,
and a barbecue. A venue well worthy of its popularity. Mooring. B & B. Look out for George,
the 'car park ghost'.

Fazeley

Continuing north, the canal runs through quiet and attractive open farmland, flanked on both sides by oak trees, their roots often projecting into the water. The isolation of the canal ends at Drayton Bassett where the A4091 swings in to run parallel as far as Fazeley. By Drayton Bassett is a curious footbridge, a marvellous folly, and immediately after it a second swing bridge. These features make the Birmingham & Fazeley Canal pleasantly eccentric, allowing it to end with an unexpected flourish. The countryside then gives way to the outskirts of Fazeley, which are quickly followed by the junction with the Coventry Canal.

● **Drayton Bassett**
Staffs. PO, tel, stores, fish & chips. The village is set ¹/₂ mile to the west of the canal. The best feature is the charming and totally unexpected Gothic-style footbridge over the canal. Its twin battlemented towers would look quite commanding but for their ridiculously small size. This bridge is unique, and there seems to be no explanation for its eccentricity, thus greatly increasing its attraction.

Drayton Manor Family Theme Park Alongside the canal, off the A4091 at Drayton Manor Bridge. 24hr recorded information for general enquiries on (01827) 287979. Formerly the site of the house of Sir Robert Peel's father, built 1820–35. The now-vanished house was designed by Sir Robert Smirke and the garden, 15 acres of wood and parkland, was originally laid out by William Gilpin. It now has an extensive series of exciting rides, including Storm Force Ten, and amusements. *Open late Mar–Oct, 10.00–late afternoon.* Charge. Caravan & camping site.

● **Fazeley**
Staffs. PO, tel, stores, garage. Its importance as a road and canal junction determines the character of Fazeley; it is a small, industrial centre that has grown up around the communication network. From the canal the town appears more attractive than it really is. Useful as a supply centre.

● **Fazeley Junction**
Staffs. The Birmingham & Fazeley Canal joins the Coventry Canal here. Originally the Coventry Canal was to continue westwards to meet the Trent & Mersey Canal at Fradley; however, the Coventry company ran out of money at Fazeley, and so the Birmingham & Fazeley Canal continued on to Whittington (this section is covered within the Coventry Canal, for continuity). The Trent & Mersey Company then built a linking arm from Fradley to Whittington, which was later bought by the Coventry Company, thus becoming a detached section of their canal. The junction has been tastefully restored, with good moorings and a canalside seat made from a balance beam, overlooked by a fine navigation office. It was at Fazeley, in the 1790s, that Robert Peel, father of the prime minister, in partnership with Joseph Wilkes, transformed the area, building mills and wharves, chapels and watercourses, and making it a centre of industry that was to last until the depression of the mid-19th C. Just to the south of the canal junction is the Bourne Brook Cut, which has its source in reservoirs to the north of Watling Street and originally supplied the bleach and dye works here. A little further south of the junction, by the Birmingham & Fazeley Canal, is Fazeley Mill, built in 1886 as a tape mill and which has continued as such largely unaltered. Just beyond the next bridge, on the opposite side of the canal, is one of the best surviving mills of the Richard Arkwright pattern, built in 1791 with three storeys and 19 bays. In Coleshill Street a fine terrace of 20 workers' houses can still be seen.

Boatyards

Ⓑ **Fazeley Mill Marina** Coleshill Road, Fazeley (01827 261138; mail@fazeleymillmarina.co.uk). 🛢 🛢 ⚓ D Pump out, gas, overnight and long-term mooring, engine repairs, toilets and showers, solid fuel.

Ⓑ **Debbies Day Boats** Canal Wharf, Coleshill Road, Fazeley (01827 262042). ⚓ Gas, day-hire boats, long-term mooring, boat and engine repairs, toilet, solid fuel. *Emergency call out.*

Ⓑ **BW Fazeley** Peel's Wharf, Fazeley (01827 252000). 200yds west of the junction. 🛢 🛢 ⚓

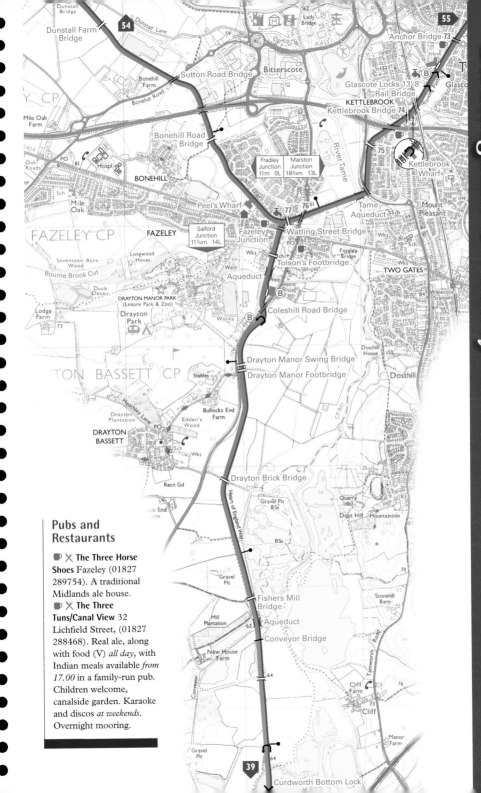

Pubs and Restaurants

🍺 ✕ **The Three Horse Shoes** Fazeley (01827 289754). A traditional Midlands ale house.

🍺 ✕ **The Three Tuns/Canal View** 32 Lichfield Street, (01827 288468). Real ale, along with food (V) *all day,* with Indian meals available *from 17.00* in a family-run pub. Children welcome, canalside garden. Karaoke and discos *at weekends.* Overnight mooring.

Cruising past Hartshill Yard (see page 50)

COVENTRY CANAL

MAXIMUM DIMENSIONS

Length: 70'
Beam: 7'
Headroom: 6' 6"

MILEAGE
COVENTRY BASIN to:
HAWKESBURY JUNCTION (Oxford Canal):
$5^1/2$ miles
MARSTON JUNCTION (Ashby Canal):
$8^1/4$ miles
Boot Wharf, Nuneaton: $10^1/2$ miles
Hartshill: 14 miles
Atherstone Top Lock: $16^1/2$ miles
Polesworth: $21^1/2$ miles

Alvecote Priory: $23^1/4$ miles
Glascote Bottom Lock: $25^1/2$ miles

FAZELEY JUNCTION (Birmingham & Fazeley Canal): 27 miles
Hopwas: $29^3/4$ miles
Whittington Brook: $32^1/2$ miles
Huddlesford Junction: 34 miles

FRADLEY JUNCTION (Trent & Mersey Canal): 38 miles

Locks: 13

MANAGER
01283 790236
enquiries.fradley@britishwaterways.co.uk

The Coventry Canal, whose enabling Act of Parliament was passed in 1768, was promoted by pit owners such as the Parrotts of Hawkesbury and the Newdigates of Arbury with two main objectives: to connect the fast-growing town of Coventry with the new trade route called the Grand Trunk, now the Trent & Mersey Canal; and to provide Coventry with cheap coal from Bedworth coalfield, 10 miles to the north. The first, long-term objective was not achieved for some years until the company had overcome financial difficulties, but – wisely – the stretch between Coventry and Bedworth was completed early on, so that the profitable carriage of local coal was quickly established along the canal, in 1769.

By the time the canal reached Atherstone in 1771, all the authorised capital had been spent and James Brindley, the original engineer of the canal, had been sacked. For these reasons – and because of the interminable wrangle with the Oxford Canal Company, whose scheme to link Coventry with southern England had followed hard upon the original Coventry scheme – the Coventry Canal did not reach Fazeley, nearly 12 miles short of its intended terminus at Fradley, until 1790.

By this time, the Birmingham & Fazeley Canal had been built, extending along the Coventry Canal's original proposed line to Whittington Brook, from where the Grand Trunk Canal Company carried it north to Fradley. The Coventry Company later bought this section back, which explains the fact that there is now a detached portion of the Coventry Canal from Whittington Brook to Fradley Junction.

In 1790, the Oxford Canal was also completed through to Oxford and thus to London via the Thames. The profits of the Coventry Canal rose quickly, and rose even higher when the Grand Junction Canal was completed in 1799, shortening the route to London by 60 miles. Other adjoining canals contributed to the Coventry Canal's prosperity: the Ashby, the Wyrley & Essington and the Trent & Mersey. The extension of the Grand Junction Canal via Warwick to Birmingham naturally dismayed the Coventry, but the numerous locks – and high tolls on the stretch of the Oxford Canal between Braunston and Napton Junctions – ensured that a lot of traffic to and from Birmingham still used the slightly longer route via the Coventry and Birmingham & Fazeley Canals, especially after the Oxford Canal was shortened by 14 miles between Braunston and Longford. The continuous financial success of the Coventry Canal could be attributed both to its being part of so many long-distance routes and to the continued prosperity of the coal mines along its way. It was certainly one of the most persistently profitable canals ever built in Britain, paying a dividend until 1947.

Coventry

The Coventry Canal begins at the large Bishop Street Basin, opened in 1769, near the town centre. It is an interesting situation on the side of a hill, overlooked by tall new buildings and attractive old wooden canal warehouses; the warehouses date from 1914, although there were, of course, earlier such buildings on the site. They once stored grain, food and cement, and were well restored in 1984. The old Weighbridge Office is now a shop and information centre, looking out over the basin towards the Vaults, which were used to store coal. The canal leaves the terminus through bridge 1, a tiny structure designed to be easily closed with a wooden beam each evening: indeed at one time no boats were allowed to stay in the basin overnight (it is now an excellent mooring). At one time there was a toll house here. To the west of this bridge is Canal House, built for the local trader Alderman Clarke. The canal company purchased the house in 1809 and it was used for successive canal managers until 1947, when the last manager of the Coventry Canal, John Kaye, purchased it upon his retirement. It is now owned by the City Council. The canal now begins to wind through what were busy industrial areas towards Hawkesbury: it is in places quite narrow, and often flanked by buildings. Just beyond bridge 2 are 'Cash's Hundred Houses', an elegant row of weavers' houses, where the living accommodation was on the lower two floors, with the top storey being occupied by looms, driven by a single shaft from a steam engine. There never were 100 houses: only 48 were built, and of these only 37 remain. The canal then, after various contortions, continues towards Hawkesbury, passing through the outskirts of Coventry. Before it ducks under the motorway, just beyond bridge 10, you will notice that the canal is wider: this was the site of the original junction between the Oxford and Coventry Canals. It was known as Longford Junction. Hawkesbury Junction, their present meeting, contains all the elements expected of such a notable place: plenty of traditional boats, interesting buildings including a fine engine house, a splendid pub and useful facilities for boaters. To the east of the junction is Hawkesbury Hall (private), at one time the home of mine owner and sponsor of the Coventry Canal, Richard Parrott. The towpath between Coventry and Hawkesbury is decorated with some excellent sculptures, as the Canal Art Trail (watch the lights come on at bridge 6!).

● **Coventry**
West Midlands. PO, tel, stores, garage, station, cinema, theatre. Recorded as Couentrev in the Domesday Book, Coventry's modern history begins with the foundation of a Benedictine priory by Leofric and his wife Godgyfu in 1043, but its fame came with Lady Godiva, who in legend rode naked through the streets, to divert Leofric's anger from the town. This episode is first recorded in the *Flores Historiarum* of 1235. Following the Norman invasion, the town became second in commercial importance to London. Largely destroyed during World War II, it is today a modern and well-planned city, although a restored row of medieval buildings can be visited in Spon Street, in the west of the city centre. The origin of the popular phrase 'to send to Coventry', meaning to cold-shoulder or ignore, is uncertain, but there is no reason to connect it with the present population, who seem generally warm and friendly.
Herbert Art Gallery & Museum Jordan Well (02476 832381). Graham Sutherland sketches for the design of the Coventry Cathedral tapestry.

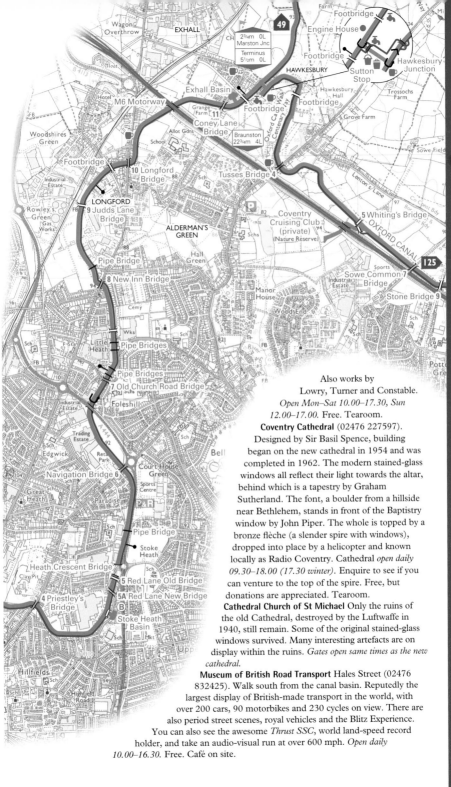

Also works by
Lowry, Turner and Constable.
*Open Mon–Sat 10.00–17.30, Sun
12.00–17.00.* Free. Tearoom.
Coventry Cathedral (02476 227597).
Designed by Sir Basil Spence, building
began on the new cathedral in 1954 and was
completed in 1962. The modern stained-glass
windows all reflect their light towards the altar,
behind which is a tapestry by Graham
Sutherland. The font, a boulder from a hillside
near Bethlehem, stands in front of the Baptistry
window by John Piper. The whole is topped by a
bronze flèche (a slender spire with windows),
dropped into place by a helicopter and known
locally as Radio Coventry. Cathedral *open daily
09.30–18.00 (17.30 winter).* Enquire to see if you
can venture to the top of the spire. Free, but
donations are appreciated. Tearoom.
Cathedral Church of St Michael Only the ruins of
the old Cathedral, destroyed by the Luftwaffe in
1940, still remain. Some of the original stained-glass
windows survived. Many interesting artefacts are on
display within the ruins. *Gates open same times as the new
cathedral.*
Museum of British Road Transport Hales Street (02476
832425). Walk south from the canal basin. Reputedly the
largest display of British-made transport in the world, with
over 200 cars, 90 motorbikes and 230 cycles on view. There are
also period street scenes, royal vehicles and the Blitz Experience.
You can also see the awesome *Thrust SSC*, world land-speed record
holder, and take an audio-visual run at over 600 mph. *Open daily
10.00–16.30.* Free. Café on site.

Tourist Information Centre Bayley Lane, Coventry, near the Cathedral and University (02476 227264).

● **Longford Bridge**

West Midlands. Stores, off-licence, chandlery. It was here, between 1769 and 1865, that members of the nearby Salem Baptist Chapel were baptised in the canal.

● **Hawkesbury Junction**

Hawkesbury Junction is also known as Sutton's Stop, after the name of the toll clerks here. It was always a busy canal centre, and remains so today, with plenty of narrowboats permanently moored at the junction. There are also other things to see:

a fine canal pub, a stop lock and a disused engine house. The latter used to pump water up into the canal from a well. Its engine was installed in 1821, having been previously employed for nearly 100 years at Griff Colliery, a few miles up the canal towards Nuneaton. This Newcomen-type atmospheric steam engine, called Lady Godiva, is now in Dartmouth Museum. It ceased work in 1913. Sephtons House and Boatyard once faced the junction: it was here, in 1924, that *nb Friendship* was built. This boat can now be seen at the Boat Museum, Ellesmere Port.

BOAT TRIPS

Nb Coventrian is a 38-seater boat, making trips from Coventry Basin *Easter–Sep, Sun and B Hols 15.15 and 17.15*. Also private charter. Details from (02476) 258864.

Boatyards

Ⓑ **Club Line Cruisers** Swan Lane Wharf, Swan Lane, Stoke Heath, Coventry (02476 258864; swanlanewharf@hotmail.com). 🚽 🚰 ♿ D Pump out, gas, narrowboat hire, long-term mooring, slipway, boat and engine repairs, toilets, books and maps.

WALKING & CYCLING
The towpath is in good condition for walkers throughout, and the stretch between Coventry and Hawkesbury is now enlivened as the Canal Art Trail. Cyclists will find parts of the towpath bumpy.

A. K. A. SUTTON'S STOP

Hawkesbury Junction was more commonly known to the boat people as Sutton's Stop. It took this name from a family called Sutton who, during the 1800s, were the toll clerks here. The Greyhound overlooks the junction now as it did then. Corn, oats and maize used to be stored around the back of the pub, as feed for the towing horses. It was often the children's job to bag this up for a trip, lowering the sacks down using a small hand crane.

Pubs and Restaurants

✕ **Buckinghams Tearooms** Canal Basin, Coventry (02476 633477). Excellent cooked breakfasts, light meals, coffee and tea. Outside seating. *Open daily 10.00–17.00.*

🍺 **The Admiral Codrington** St Columba's Close, Coventry (02476 258520). By the canal basin. Food is served *L and E (not Sun)*. Children welcome *until 19.00*. Garden. Karaoke and disco *every Sat.*

🍺 ✕ **The Royal Hotel** (02476 686152). Near bridge 7. Friendly local, serving snacks *L*. Children's room and garden.

🍺 ✕ **The Greyhound** Hawkesbury Junction (02476 363046). Fascinating pub beside the

junction, decorated with canal and rugby memorabilia, together with an immense collection of Toby jugs, warmed by log fires in *winter*. An imaginative selection of food (V), especially pies and salads, is served in the bar or restaurant *L and E*, and a choice of real ale is available. Canalside garden.

🍺 **The Boat Inn** Black Horse Road, Longford (02476 361438). A fine friendly pub with unspoilt rooms and a cosy lounge, all decorated with antiques, just a 3-minute walk north west of the junction. Real ale. Children welcome. Garden for the *summer* and a real fire for the *winter*.

Engine house at Hawkesbury

Nuneaton

Leaving Hawkesbury Junction, the canal passes through Bedworth in a long cutting: the town seems to be composed mainly of vast housing estates, but these make little impression upon the canal. At Marston Junction the Ashby Canal (*see* page 12) branches to the east through pleasant countryside, while the Coventry Canal bends due west for a short way before resuming its course towards Nuneaton to the north. There is a pleasant short stretch of open fields, giving a welcome breathing space, before the canal once again enters the suburbs, this time of Nuneaton. There are good moorings and easy access to the town by Boot Bridge (bridge 20). The canal takes a route around the town, marked by a succession of housing estates and allotments.

● **Nuneaton**
Warwicks. PO, tel, stores, garage, station, cinema.
A rather typical Midlands town with much industrial development. On the site of the Griff Colliery canal arm are the hollows said to be the origin of the Red Deeps in the *Mill on the Floss* by George Eliot, who was born here in 1819.
Nuneaton Museum & Art Gallery Riversley Park (02476 376158). Archaeological specimens of Nuneaton from prehistoric to medieval times, and also items from the local earthenware industry. Geological and mining relics, ethnography from Africa, Asia, America and Oceania. Paintings, prints and watercolours. Personalia collection of the novelist George Eliot. *Open Tue–Sat 10.30–16.30, Sun 14.00–16.30. Closed Mon except B Hols.* Free. Tearoom (*open daily*) on site.
Arbury Hall (02476 382804). Two miles south west of the canal off B4102. Originally an Elizabethan house, it was gothicised by Sir Roger Newdigate in 1750–1800 under the direction of Sanderson Miller, Henry Keene and Couchman of Warwick. Fine pictures, furniture, china and glass. The Hall is in a beautiful park setting. *Open Easter–last Sun in Sep, B Hol Sun and Mon only; house 14.00–17.00, gardens 14.00–18.00.* Charge.
Tourist Information Centre Nuneaton Library, Church Street, Nuneaton (02476 384027).

● **Chilvers Coton**
Warwicks. PO, tel, stores. A suburb of Nuneaton. Its church dates from 1946 and was designed by H. N. Jepson and built by German prisoners-of-war.

● **Bedworth**
Warwicks. PO, tel, stores. The most impressive parts of this town are its church by Bodley and Garner, 1888–90, and the almshouses built in 1840. Good shops.

Pubs and Restaurants

● ✗ **The Navigation Inn** Bulkington Road, Nuneaton (02476 311990). Canalside at bridge 14. Large pub with a comfortable lounge and an award winning garden with swings. Real ale, and a large varied menu (V) served *12.00–21.30 daily*. Children welcome. Mooring.

● **The Boot Inn** Boot Wharf, Bridge Street, Chilvers Coton (02476 385635). Real ale in a pub with a large bar and quiet lounge. The enclosed garden has toys for the children and barbecues are held in *summer*. Meals (V) available *L and E*. Post box outside. Live music *Tue*, and the *occasional weekend* disco.

● **The Fleur de Lys** Coventry Road, Chilvers Coton (02476 382366). Two minutes' walk down the hill from bridge 19a. There is a large bar and pleasant lounge in this friendly pub. Food *L and E*. Children welcome. Garden. Regular *weekend* live music.

● **The King William** Coton Road, Chilvers Coton (02476 348308). About ¼ mile north east from bridge 19a. Traditional pub serving real ale. There is a pets corner in the garden.

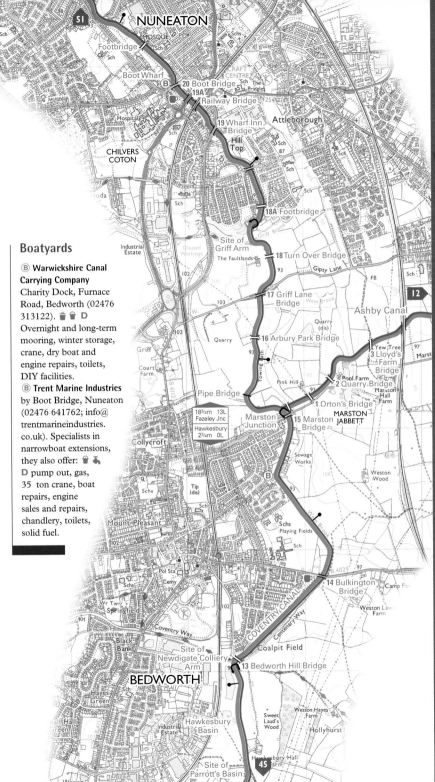

Boatyards

Ⓑ **Warwickshire Canal Carrying Company**
Charity Dock, Furnace Road, Bedworth (02476 313122). 🚻 🚮 **D**
Overnight and long-term mooring, winter storage, crane, dry boat and engine repairs, toilets, DIY facilities.

Ⓑ **Trent Marine Industries**
by Boot Bridge, Nuneaton (02476 641762; info@ trentmarineindustries. co.uk). Specialists in narrowboat extensions, they also offer: 🚻 ⚓
D pump out, gas, 35 ton crane, boat repairs, engine sales and repairs, chandlery, toilets, solid fuel.

NUNEATON

MOSQUE
Footbridge
Boot Wharf
20 Boot Bridge
19A
Railway Bridge
19 Wharf Inn Bridge
Hill Top
CHILVERS COTON
Attleborough

18A Footbridge

Site of Griff Arm
The Faultlands
18 Turn Over Bridge
Gipsy Lane
Ashby Canal
12

17 Griff Lane Bridge
Wem Brook

16 Arbury Park Bridge
Quarry (dis)
Yew Tree
3 Lloyd's Farm Bridge

Pipe Bridge
Pink Hill
2 Quarry Bridge
Pool Farm
Marston Hall Farm

18¾m 13L
Fazeley Jnc
Hawkesbury
2¾m 0L

Marston Junction
1 Orton's Bridge
15 Marston Bridge
MARSTON JABBETT

Collycroft

Sewage Works

Weston Wood

Tip (dis)

Playing Fields

14 Bulkington Bridge
Camp Hill
Weston Farm

COVENTRY CANAL

Centenary Way

Site of Newdigate Colliery Arm
BEDWORTH
13 Bedworth Hill Bridge
Coalpit Field

Hawkesbury Basin

Sweet Laud's Wood
Weston Hayes Farm
Hollyhurst

Site of Parrott's Basin
45

Hartshill

There is a *fish & chip shop*, and a *Chinese take-away* by bridge 21.
Continuing north west out of Nuneaton, the canal winds along the side of a hill into a landscape which is curiously exciting. What were once quarries and spoil heaps are now landscaped, with many transformed into nature reserves. The largest mountain of waste, built with spoil from the old Judkins Quarry, is known as Mount Judd. This distinctly man-made landscape is broken up with unexpected stretches of open countryside, with fine views away to the north across the Anker valley. The earth here has given the canal water a distinct rust colour. The canal passes below the town of Hartshill: the attractive buildings in the British Waterways yard are crowned by a splendid clock tower, and those travelling on the canal will want to slow right down to enjoy the mellow architecture and old dock. The canal then continues towards Mancetter, leaving the quarry belt and moving into open rolling country backed by thick woods to the west. The railway closes from the east as the canal approaches Atherstone.

Hartshill
Warwicks. PO, tel, stores, garage. Once a mining community, Hartshill has now been swallowed up by Nuneaton, and as such its interest lies mainly in its past. The Romans recognised its strategic importance. There is evidence that they settled here, as both kilns and fragments of pottery have been unearthed. Hugh de Hardreshull chose it as a site for his castle in 1125, the view from the ridge enabling him to see as far as the distant peaks of Derbyshire on a clear day. Below, on the plains, can be counted the towers and steeples of 40 churches. Hartshill's most famous claim is that it was the birthplace of the poet Drayton in 1563, a friend of both Ben Johnson and Shakespeare. Drayton's greatest work was *Polyolbion*, a survey of the country with a song for each county. He died in 1631 and was buried in Westminster. There are fine walks over Hartshill Green to Oldbury Camp, a Bronze Age hill-fort covering 7 acres. Hartshill's shops are a 15-minute walk from the canal.

Hartshill Yard Part of the yard contains a 19th-C carpenters' workshop and blacksmiths' forge. Visits are by appointment *for groups* only – telephone (01283) 790236 for details.

Mancetter
Warwicks. PO, tel, stores, garage. About 1/2 mile east of bridge 36. The church dates from the 13th C, but its best feature is the large collection of 18th-C slate tombstones displaying all the elegance of Georgian incised lettering. There are some almshouses of 1728 in the churchyard, and across the road another row with pretty Victorian Gothic details. The manor, south of the church, is rather over-restored. It was from this house, in 1555, that Robert Glover was led when the Bishop of Lichfield ordered his arrest. A victim of the reign of Mary Tudor, he was seized and taken to the stake, where he was executed alongside a poor cap-maker from Coventry.

Pubs and Restaurants

🍺 **Cock & Bear** Queens Road (02476 385875). Large local pub 300yds east of bridge 21, serving real ale. Garden. Entertainment *Fri and Sat.*

✕ 🍺 **Stag & Pheasant** (02476 393173) About a ½-mile walk up the lane behind Hartshill Yard, this family-run village-green pub has outside seating and a family room. Real ale. Restaurant food (V), *L and E,* features Italian specialities.

🍺 **The Anchor** Glascote Road, Glascote Village, Tamworth (01827 314905). Popular and friendly brick-built canalside pub by bridge 29, with a large garden. Look for the milestone painted on the wall. Real ale is served, along with good food (V) *L and E (not Sun or Mon E).* Children welcome. Entertainment *Wed and Sat.*

Boatyards

Ⓑ **Valley Cruises** Springwood Haven, Mancetter Road, Nuneaton (02476 393333; www.valleycruises.co.uk). 🚽 🛒 ⚓ D Pump out, gas, narrowboat hire, overnight and long-term mooring, narrowboat slipway, boat repairs, engine sales and repairs, boat fitting out, chandlery, toilets, solid fuel.

BW Hartshill Yard Clock Hill, Hartshill (02476 392489). ⚓

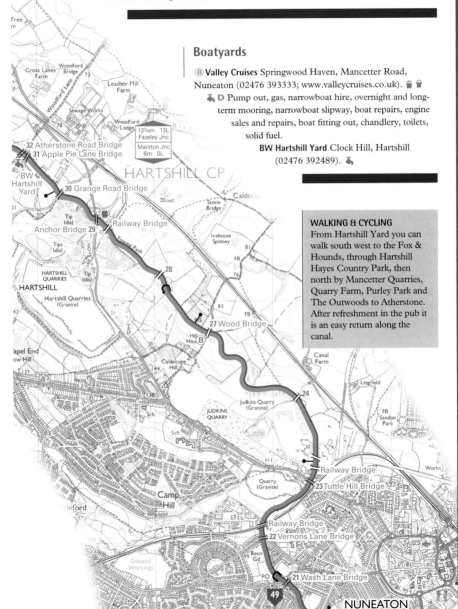

WALKING & CYCLING
From Hartshill Yard you can walk south west to the Fox & Hounds, through Hartshill Hayes Country Park, then north by Mancetter Quarries, Quarry Farm, Purley Park and The Outwoods to Atherstone. After refreshment in the pub it is an easy return along the canal.

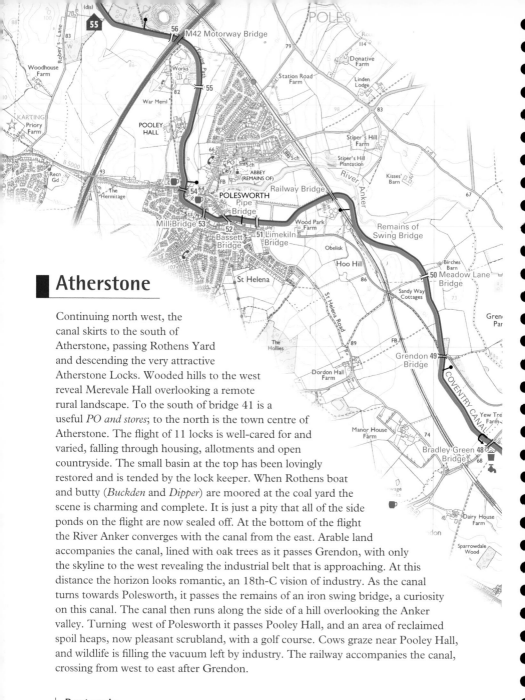

Atherstone

Continuing north west, the
canal skirts to the south of
Atherstone, passing Rothens Yard
and descending the very attractive
Atherstone Locks. Wooded hills to the west
reveal Merevale Hall overlooking a remote
rural landscape. To the south of bridge 41 is a
useful *PO and stores*; to the north is the town centre of
Atherstone. The flight of 11 locks is well-cared for and
varied, falling through housing, allotments and open
countryside. The small basin at the top has been lovingly
restored and is tended by the lock keeper. When Rothens boat
and butty (*Buckden* and *Dipper*) are moored at the coal yard the
scene is charming and complete. It is just a pity that all of the side
ponds on the flight are now sealed off. At the bottom of the flight
the River Anker converges with the canal from the east. Arable land
accompanies the canal, lined with oak trees as it passes Grendon, with only
the skyline to the west revealing the industrial belt that is approaching. At this
distance the horizon looks romantic, an 18th-C vision of industry. As the canal
turns towards Polesworth, it passes the remains of an iron swing bridge, a curiosity
on this canal. The canal then runs along the side of a hill overlooking the Anker
valley. Turning west of Polesworth it passes Pooley Hall, and an area of reclaimed
spoil heaps, now pleasant scrubland, with a golf course. Cows graze near Pooley Hall,
and wildlife is filling the vacuum left by industry. The railway accompanies the canal,
crossing from west to east after Grendon.

Boatyards

Ⓑ **A G & R A Rothen** Top Lock Wharf, Atherstone (01827 717884). **D** Coal and gas. Canal carrying.

● **Atherstone**
Warwicks. PO, tel, stores, garage, station, cinema.
A pleasant town, with a strong 18th-C feeling, especially in the open market place in front of the church.
Merevale A large battlemented house, high to the west, is Merevale Hall, an early 19th-C mock Tudor mansion. To the west are the remains of the 12th-C abbey and the very pretty 13th-C church which contains fine stained glass, monuments and brasses.

● **Grendon**
Warwicks. 1/2 mile north east of bridge 48. Grendon is just a small church set in beautiful parkland. The woods and rolling fields are a last refuge before the industrial landscape that precedes Tamworth.

● **Polesworth**
Warwicks. PO, tel, stores, garage, fish & chips, station. The splendid gatehouse and the clerestory are all that remain of the 10th-C abbey, where Egbert, first Saxon King of England, built a nunnery.

Pubs and Restaurants

🍺 **Old Red Lion Hotel** Long Street, Atherstone (01827 713156). Friendly residential hotel serving real ale. Bar snacks *L and E, daily*, restaurant meals (V) *E only*. Children welcome. B & B.

🍺 **The Kings Head** Old Watling Street, Atherstone (01827 717945). Real ale, along with bar and à la carte meals (V) *L and E*. Special meals for OAPs. Children welcome. Outside seating, mooring. Live music *once a month*.

🍺 ✕ **The Black Swan** Watling Street, Grendon (01827 713640). Real ale, and meals (V) from an English and Indian menu *L and E*. Children welcome, and there is Harry Hedgehog's Fun Factory – a soft toy activity centre for children. Garden, mooring.

🍺 **The Bulls Head** Tamworth Road, Polesworth (01827 893022). West of bridge 54. Real ale, and meals (V) *L and E (not Sun E or Mon)*. Children welcome if eating.

🍺 **Fosters Yard Hotel** 12 Market Street, Polesworth (01827 899313). South of bridge 53. Tall listed building, with oak beams, an open fire and a skittle alley, also incorporating an Indian restaurant. Real ale and meals (V) *L and E*. Children welcome. Live bands and karaoke *Sat*. Moorings 100yds away at the bridge.

🍺 **The Royal Oak** Grendon Road, Polesworth (01827 331025). South of bridge 52. Traditional pub offering real ale. Food (V) served *12.00–19.00 daily*. Children welcome, outside seating on the patio. Live music *Sat*, and the bowling club meets here.

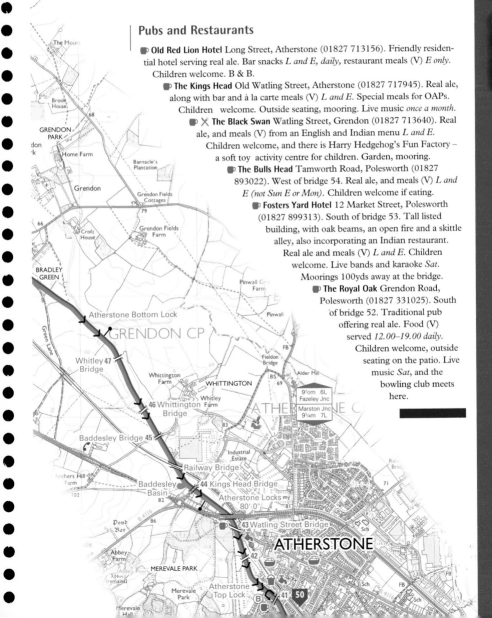

9½m 6L
Fazeley Jnc

Marston Jnc
9¼m 7L

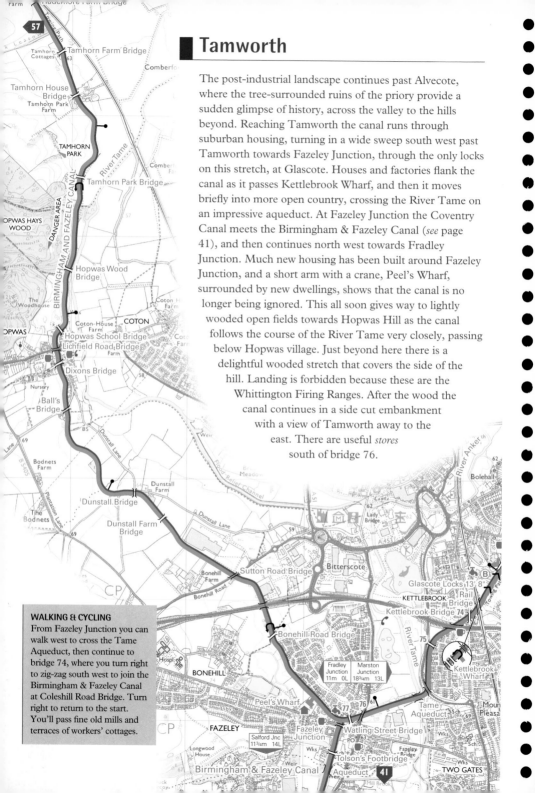

Tamworth

The post-industrial landscape continues past Alvecote, where the tree-surrounded ruins of the priory provide a sudden glimpse of history, across the valley to the hills beyond. Reaching Tamworth the canal runs through suburban housing, turning in a wide sweep south west past Tamworth towards Fazeley Junction, through the only locks on this stretch, at Glascote. Houses and factories flank the canal as it passes Kettlebrook Wharf, and then it moves briefly into more open country, crossing the River Tame on an impressive aqueduct. At Fazeley Junction the Coventry Canal meets the Birmingham & Fazeley Canal (*see* page 41), and then continues north west towards Fradley Junction. Much new housing has been built around Fazeley Junction, and a short arm with a crane, Peel's Wharf, surrounded by new dwellings, shows that the canal is no longer being ignored. This all soon gives way to lightly wooded open fields towards Hopwas Hill as the canal follows the course of the River Tame very closely, passing below Hopwas village. Just beyond here there is a delightful wooded stretch that covers the side of the hill. Landing is forbidden because these are the Whittington Firing Ranges. After the wood the canal continues in a side cut embankment with a view of Tamworth away to the east. There are useful *stores* south of bridge 76.

WALKING & CYCLING

From Fazeley Junction you can walk west to cross the Tame Aqueduct, then continue to bridge 74, where you turn right to zig-zag south west to join the Birmingham & Fazeley Canal at Coleshill Road Bridge. Turn right to return to the start. You'll pass fine old mills and terraces of workers' cottages.

- **Amington**
  Staffs. PO, tel, stores, garage. To the south of bridge 68 is the Canal Craft Shop, where you can have Buckby canalware painted to order.
- **Tamworth**
  Staffs. PO, tel, stores, garage, station, cinema. Tamworth was originally a Saxon settlement, although only earthworks survive from this period.
  Tamworth Castle off Castle Street (01827 709626). With a Norman motte, an Elizabethan timbered hall and Jacobean apartments, it is a splendid mélange of styles.

Open Apr–Oct, Tue–Sun 12.00–17.15 (restricted opening in winter). Charge.
Tourist Information Centre 29 Market Street, Tamworth (01827 709581).
- **Fazeley Junction**
  Staffs. PO and stores in Fazeley. The Coventry Canal joins the Birmingham & Fazeley Canal here.
- **Hopwas**
  Staffs. PO, tel, stores. A pretty and tidy village with a green, built on the side of a hill. Anyone walking should look out for the danger flags for Whittington Firing Ranges.

Boatyards

ⓑ **Narrowcraft** The Boatyard, Robey's Lane, Alvecote (01827 898585; www. narrowboat. co.uk). 🛢 🚽 🔧 D Pump out, gas, overnight and long-term mooring, winter storage, slipway, boat sales and repairs, engine repairs, chandlery, toilets, showers, solid fuel, DIY facilities, books and maps. Club house, bar and restaurant.

ⓑ **S M Hudson** Glascote Basin Boatyard, Basin Lane, Glascote (01827 311317). 🔧 D Gas, long-term mooring, winter storage, boat and engine sales and repairs, boat building.
ⓑ **BW Fazeley Office** Peel's Wharf, Fazeley (01827 252000). 200yds west of the junction. 🛢 🚽 🔧

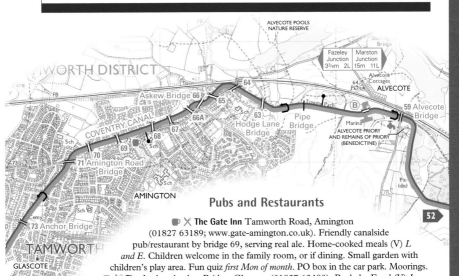

Pubs and Restaurants

🍺 ✕ **The Gate Inn** Tamworth Road, Amington (01827 63189; www.gate-amington.co.uk). Friendly canalside pub/restaurant by bridge 69, serving real ale. Home-cooked meals (V) *L and E.* Children welcome in the family room, or if dining. Small garden with children's play area. Fun quiz *first Mon of month.* PO box in the car park. Moorings.

🍺 ✕ **The Anchor** Anchor Bridge, Glascote (01827 63480). Real ale. Food (V) *L and E (not Sun or Mon E).* Children welcome in family room. Garden with moorings. Live entertainment *Sat,* quiz *Wed.*

🍺 **The Barge & Barrel** Tamworth Road, Kettlebrook (01827 284725) By bridge 74, next to Kettlebrook Basin. Real ale, and food (V) *L and E, daily (not Sun E).* Live entertainment *most weekends.* Children welcome *until 20.00* unless dining. Mooring.

🍺 ✕ **Three Tuns/Canal View** 32 Lichfield Street, (01827 288468). Real ale, along with food (V) *all day,* with Indian meals available *from 17.00* in a family-run pub. Children welcome, canalside garden. Karaoke and discos *at weekends.* Overnight mooring.

🍺 **The Tame Otter** Hints Road, Hopwas (01827 53361). Canalside pub serving real ale. Food (V) *all day, every day.* Children welcome. Garden and moorings.

🍺 **The Red Lion** Lichfield Road, Hopwas (01827 62514). A canalside pub with an extensive garden, offering real ale. Home-cooked food (V), with steaks a speciality, served *L and E.* Children welcome, and there is a play area.

Whittington and Fradley Junction

As the canal reaches Whittington and bridge 78, it changes back from being the Birmingham & Fazeley Canal to the Coventry Canal (*see* Introduction, page 43). A stone marks the actual point. At Huddlesford the remains of the eastern end of the Wyrley & Essington Canal, now referred to as the Lichfield Canal and presently used only for moorings, branches to the south west. This route, which extends west to Ogley Junction on the Anglesey Branch of the BCN, is the subject of an energetic and effective restoration campaign. Problems of possible obstruction by the new Birmingham Northern Relief Road seem to have been overcome, but much remains to be done. The Coventry Canal then runs northwards through flat, open country towards Fradley Junction. There are no locks, but a swing bridge announces your arrival at Fradley Junction. Here the Coventry Canal meets the Trent & Mersey Canal.

● **Fisherwick**
Staffs. Tel. A small hamlet overlooking the canal.
● **Whittington**
Staffs. PO, tel, stores, garage, chemist, Chinese takeaway, off-licence. The village centre is to the west of Whittington Bridge; shops are best approached from bridge 78.
● **Lichfield**
Staffs. PO, tel, stores, garage, cinema, station. Two miles south west along the A38. Although not on the canal, Lichfield is well worth a visit.
Art Gallery The Friary, Lichfield Library (01543 510700). *Open Mon, Wed and Fri 09.30–17.00, Tue and Thur 09.30–19.00 and Sat 09.00–13.00. Closed Sun.* Admission free.
Tourist Information Centre Donegal House, Bore Street, Lichfield (01543 308211).
● **Huddlesford**
Staffs. PO box. At Huddlesford Junction the

Wyrley & Essington Canal used to join the Coventry. Long abandoned, the first 1/4 mile is used for moorings and the remainder is scheduled for restoration, with much work already done.
● **Fradley**
Staffs. PO, tel, stores. A small village set to the east of the canal, and well away from the junction. It owed its prosperity to the airfield which is not used as such any more.
● **Fradley Junction**
Staffs. PO box, tel, garage. A long-established canal centre where the Coventry Canal joins the Trent & Mersey Canal. There is a boatyard, a British Waterways office and maintenance yard, BW moorings, a boat club and a popular pub – all in the middle of a five-lock flight.

Boatyards

Ⓑ **Streethay Wharf** Streethay Basin, Streethay, Lichfield (01543 414808; pat@streethaywharf. freeserve.co.uk). 🛉 🛉 🐾 D Pump out, gas, day-hire craft, overnight and long-term mooring, winter storage, wet dock, slipway, crane, boat and engine sales and repairs, boat building, telephone, toilets, showers, chandlery, solid fuel, laundrette, DIY facilities. *Emergency call out.*
Ⓑ **Tom's Moorings** Streethay Basin (01543 414808). 🐾 Pump out, gas, overnight and long-term mooring.

Ⓑ **BW Waterways Office** Fradley Junction (01283 790236). 🛉 🛉 🐾 Overnight mooring, long-term mooring, toilets.
Ⓑ **Swan Line Cruisers** Fradley Junction (01283 790332; info@swanlinecruisers.co.uk). 🐾 D Pump out (*not Sat*), gas, narrowboat hire, overnight mooring, boat and engine sales and repairs, chandlery, books and maps, gifts, groceries, laundry service.

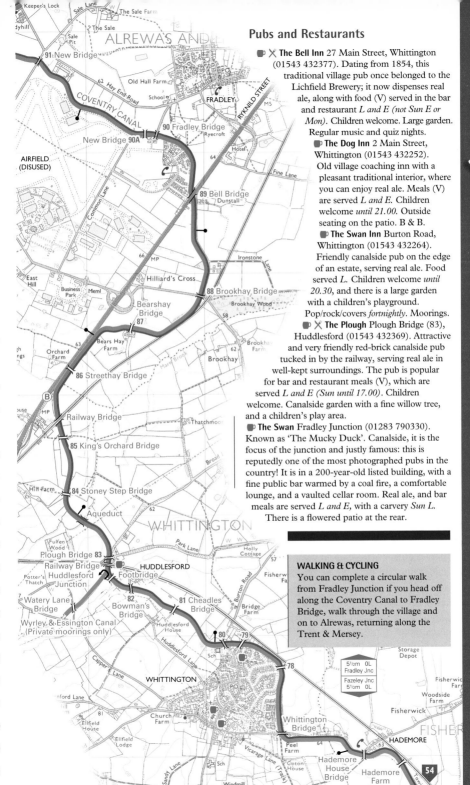

Pubs and Restaurants

🍺 ✕ **The Bell Inn** 27 Main Street, Whittington (01543 432377). Dating from 1854, this traditional village pub once belonged to the Lichfield Brewery; it now dispenses real ale, along with food (V) served in the bar and restaurant *L and E (not Sun E or Mon)*. Children welcome. Large garden. Regular music and quiz nights.

🍺 **The Dog Inn** 2 Main Street, Whittington (01543 432252). Old village coaching inn with a pleasant traditional interior, where you can enjoy real ale. Meals (V) are served *L and E*. Children welcome *until 21.00*. Outside seating on the patio. B & B.

🍺 **The Swan Inn** Burton Road, Whittington (01543 432264). Friendly canalside pub on the edge of an estate, serving real ale. Food served *L*. Children welcome *until 20.30*, and there is a large garden with a children's playground. Pop/rock/covers *fortnightly*. Moorings.

🍺 ✕ **The Plough** Plough Bridge (83), Huddlesford (01543 432369). Attractive and very friendly red-brick canalside pub tucked in by the railway, serving real ale in well-kept surroundings. The pub is popular for bar and restaurant meals (V), which are served *L and E (Sun until 17.00)*. Children welcome. Canalside garden with a fine willow tree, and a children's play area.

🍺 **The Swan** Fradley Junction (01283 790330). Known as 'The Mucky Duck'. Canalside, it is the focus of the junction and justly famous: this is reputedly one of the most photographed pubs in the country! It is in a 200-year-old listed building, with a fine public bar warmed by a coal fire, a comfortable lounge, and a vaulted cellar room. Real ale, and bar meals are served *L and E*, with a carvery *Sun L*. There is a flowered patio at the rear.

WALKING & CYCLING

You can complete a circular walk from Fradley Junction if you head off along the Coventry Canal to Fradley Bridge, walk through the village and on to Alrewas, returning along the Trent & Mersey.

EREWASH CANAL

MAXIMUM DIMENSIONS
Length: 72'
Beam: 10' 6"
Draught: 2' 6"
Headroom: 7' 4"

MILEAGE
TRENT LOCK to:
Sandiacre Lock: 3¹/₄ miles
Hallam Fields Lock: 5¹/₂ miles

LANGLEY MILL: 11³/₄ miles
Locks: 15

MANAGER
0115 973 4278
enquiries.sawley@britishwaterways.co.uk.

The Erewash Canal is one of five canals built towards the end of the 18th C to carry coal from the pits of the Nottinghamshire/Derbyshire coalfield to the towns of the East Midlands. The construction of the canal was supported by local merchants and landowners who were keen to profit from the coal deposits of the Erewash Valley, as were the local colliery owners who could see the financial benefits of widening their markets. Completed in 1779 at a cost of £21,000 by the engineer John Varley, the canal involved the construction of 14 locks which took the navigation up 109ft from Trent Lock to Langley Mill. Begun in 1778, its 11³/₄ mile course was open to navigation by the following summer. As £23,000 had been raised in £100 shares in order to finance the project, the capital outlay was low. Abundant trade from local collieries, brickworks and ironworks made the canal one of the most prosperous in the country. The monopoly that the company had over transport in the area along with the high demand for coal meant that the £100 shares had risen to an incredible £1300. The enormous success of the Erewash Canal encouraged the promotion and construction, during the following decade, of the Cromford, Nottingham, Derby and Nutbrook canals. However, by 1834 the Canal Company was in trouble. High tolls plus the competition presented by the railways were taking trade away from the navigation. The Company reduced its tolls in an attempt to regain trade, but the railway system was expanding rapidly in the area and the Canal Company was unable to compete. The surrounding canals were bought up by the railway companies which further added to the problems of the Erewash Canal. The railway companies were happy to see these neighbouring waterways fall into disuse, thus putting an end to through traffic. By 1932 the Erewash Canal Company admitted defeat and was bought up by the Grand Union Canal Company. Having also bought the Loughborough and Leicester navigations, it was their intention to revitalise the network by creating a through navigation from the coalfields of Derbyshire to London. Sadly their attempts failed. Nationalisation of the canals in 1947 brought the Erewash Canal under the administration of the British Transport Commission and in 1962 this body closed to navigation the upper section from Gallows Inn to Langley Mill. The need to supply water to the lower section for navigation and industry, however, meant that the upper section had still to be maintained and boats were allowed to navigate it upon application to the Commission and subsequently to its successor, the British Waterways Board. With the cessation of narrowboat carrying in 1963, such boats had been few, but the growing interest in pleasure boating resulted in more and more craft venturing up the canal from the popular River Trent. With increased use the canal gradually improved and the news that the major portion of it was to be designated a remainder waterway in the impending 1968 Transport Act was received locally with dismay. A public meeting led to the formation of the Erewash Canal Preservation and Development Association (ECPDA), a body consisting of representatives of boating and fishing interests, residents and local authorities. The need to convince local authorities of the value of the canal as an amenity was recognised at a very early stage and the association's efforts eventually met with success when, in 1972, Derbyshire and Nottinghamshire County Councils agreed to share the cost, with the British Waterways Board, of the restoration of the canal to cruising waterway standards. This ambition was achieved in February 1983 when the canal was upgraded and boaters can now enjoy the entire course of the waterway. Further improvements are already afoot due to the continued involvement of the Erewash Initiative, a joint project involving British Waterways, Erewash Borough Council and Groundwork Erewash.

Sandiacre Lock (see page 61)

Long Eaton

The Erewash Canal leaves the Trent Navigation at Trent Lock. There is a useful supermarket just above Dockholme Lock, on the offside. North of the big concrete bridge carrying the A52 at Sandiacre is a delightfully landscaped free overnight mooring.

NAVIGATIONAL NOTES

Trent Lock should always be left *full*, with the top gates open, except when there is much traffic about. This will ensure that any flotsam coming down the canal is able to escape over the bottom gates.

● **Trent Lock**
An important waterway junction and a long-established boating centre. Boats navigating the Trent in this rather complicated area should beware of straying too near Thrumpton Weir.

● **Long Eaton**
Derbs. All services.
Long Eaton Leisure Centre Wilsthorpe Road, Long Eaton (0115 946 1400). *Open daily until 20.00.* Charge.

Lock Cottage Sandiacre. The last remaining toll house on the Erewash Canal. *Open Sun 14.30–17.00 throughout the summer and on B Hols.*

● **Derby Canal**
The closure of the Derby Canal ended Derby's link with the navigable waterways which dated back to the time when the Danes sailed up the River Derwent to found the settlement of Deoraby.

WALKING & CYCLING

The towpath is in excellent condition throughout the whole navigation and is suitable for both walking and cycling. The Nutbrook Trail is an off-road cycleway that runs from Long Eaton to Shipley and makes use of both canal towpath and abandoned railway track.

Boatyards

ⓑ **Redhill Marine Ltd** Redhill Marina, Radcliffe on Soar, Nottingham (01509 672770; www.redhill-marina.co.uk). ⛽ 🔧 Gas, overnight and long-term mooring, winter storage, crane, slipway, hoist, boat sales and repairs, engine sales and repairs, boat refurbishment, chandlery, DIY facilities, toilets, café.

ⓑ **Sawley Bridge Marina** Above Sawley Locks (0115 973 4278; www.sawleymarina.com). ⛽ ⛽ 🔧 💧E Pump out, gas, narrowboat hire, day-hire boats, extensive moorings, two slipways, winter storage, 8-ton crane, chandlery,

boat sales and repairs, engine sales and repairs, boat building and maintenance, books, maps and gifts, groceries, toilet, showers, telephone, solid fuel, laundrette, café and pub.

ⓑ **Mills Dockyard** Trent Lock, Lock Lane, Long Eaton (0115 973 2595). Overnight and long-term mooring, winter storage, engine repairs, dry dock, wooden boat restoration and repairs, general boat maintenance, fitting out and repairs, houseboat construction.

ⓑ **Wyvern Marine** Wyvern Avenue, Long Eaton (0115 946 1752). Long-term moorings.

Pubs and Restaurants

Navigation Inn Trent Lock (0115 973 2984). Large, popular, family pub with a garden and play area. Real ale and a wide range of reasonably priced food (V) available *L and E, daily*. Moorings.

✕ **The Steamboat Inn** Trent Lock, on the Erewash Canal (0115 946 3955). Built by the canal company in 1791, when it was called the Erewash Navigation Inn, it is now a busy and popular venue. The bars have been handsomely restored and decorated with suitably nautical objects. Real ale and bar meals (V) available *L and E (not Sun E)*. Garden, animal farm and children's playground. Quiz *Sat*. Attached to the pub is Trattoria il Nautica.

The Old Ale House Long Eaton (0115 973 5265). Five real ales. Bar meals (V) available *Wed and Thur 12.00–15.00, Fri and Sat 12.00–17.00, Sun 12.00–14.00*. Children welcome. Outside seating. Live entertainment *Fri or Sat evening*. Skittle alley.

The Hole in the Wall Regent Street, Long Eaton (0115 973 4920). Two-roomed town local dispensing real ales, real ciders and food (V) *L, daily*. Children and dogs welcome. Garden, skittle alley and pub games. Barbecues.

BOAT TRIPS
Thompson Boat Company 336 Bennett Street, Long Eaton (0115 972 5373). Day-boat hire and narrowboat for short-term hire. Operates from Trent Lock/Sawley Marina.

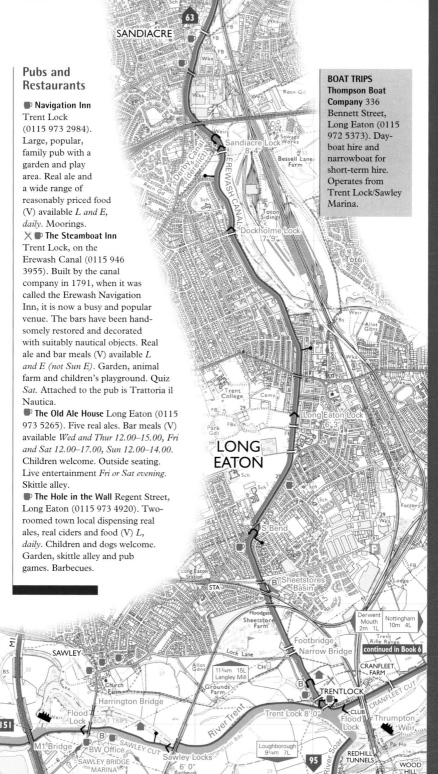

continued in Book 6

Ilkeston

At Stanton Gate the M1 motorway looms up and then crosses the canal on its way to
Sheffield. The outskirts of Ilkeston appear on the left side while, across the shallow
Erewash valley, the course of the disused Nottingham Canal appears from the east,
twisting along the contours of the hillside. Like the Erewash Canal, its course is
generally northerly, but the two waterways do not meet until Langley Mill. Meanwhile
the Erewash Canal passes extensive low-lying playing fields before reaching the pub at
Gallows Inn Lock with *PO, stores, takeaways, laundrette and garages to the west of the
navigation.* North of Gallows Inn Lock, the canal passes housing estates on one side
and water meadows and a main line railway on the other. The town of Ilkeston is on
the hillside on the west side of the canal. In spite of its proximity to these built-up
areas, the canal is relatively unspoiled and surprisingly rural.

● **Sandiacre**
*Derbs. PO, tel, stores, butcher, takeaway, garage,
bank.* Services are all conveniently near the canal,
but there is not much of interest in these outskirts, apart from the handsome Springfield Mill
by the canal and the church, which is set on a
rise called Stoney Clouds (clearly visible from the
canal at Pasture Lock). The mill was built by
Ernest Terah Hooley of Risley Hall in 1888. It
houses four separate spiral staircase towers, each
catering for an individual lace company. The
canal was used for the transportation of the raw
materials needed by the lace industry and for the
finished articles. There are fine views over the
industrial valley from the church which features
some original Norman work inside, including
carvings. Outside is an old tombstone bearing a
skull and crossbones. The font is 600 years old.

● **Ilkeston**
Derbs. All services. Cinema. A market and textile
town, with a compact main square.
Pedestrianised areas make this a pleasant place to
stroll. The parish church of St Mary dates from
1150 and has an unusual 14th-C stone screen.
The annual three-day funfair is held in the
Market Place in *Oct.*
Erewash Museum High Street, off East Street,
Ilkeston (0115 907 1141; www.erewash.gov.uk).
Set in a late 18th-C house, the museum tells the
story of the local and social history of the
Erewash area as well as housing permanent dis-
plays of an Edwardian period kitchen and wash
house and an exhibition of children's toys. *Open*
*Tue, Thur–Sat and B Hols 10.00–16.00. Closed
Xmas Day, New Year and Jan.* Free.

● **Cossall**
Notts. Tel. Cossall is a refreshing contrast to
Ilkeston, an attractive village built on top of a
hill, spreading gently down to the Nottingham
Canal. D.H. Lawrence used it as his background
for Cossethay in *The Rainbow.* A narrow street
winds among the houses, all of which seem to be
surrounded by pretty gardens. The little church
contains an oak screen made by village craftsmen; in the churchyard is a memorial to a soldier
killed at Waterloo. Next to the church is Church
Cottage, once the home of Louie Burrows to
whom Lawrence was engaged. She was the
model for the character of Ursula Brangwen.

● **Nutbrook Canal**
This little branch off the Erewash Canal used to
lead for 4¹/₂ miles almost parallel to the Erewash
Canal and slightly west of it. It still flows into the
Erewash Canal upstream from Stanton Lock
and parts of it are in water. The canal opened in
1795 at a cost of £22,800. Colliery owners
Edward Miller-Mundy and Sir Henry Hunloke
employed Benjamin Outram as engineer. It was
in fact mining subsidence which caused much
of the canal to be derelict by 1895 when it fell
into disuse. Two of the three reservoirs which
supplied the canal with water are still in
evidence at Shipley. The short section that
used to pass through the old Stanton
Ironworks was filled in in 1962 and is now quite
untraceable.

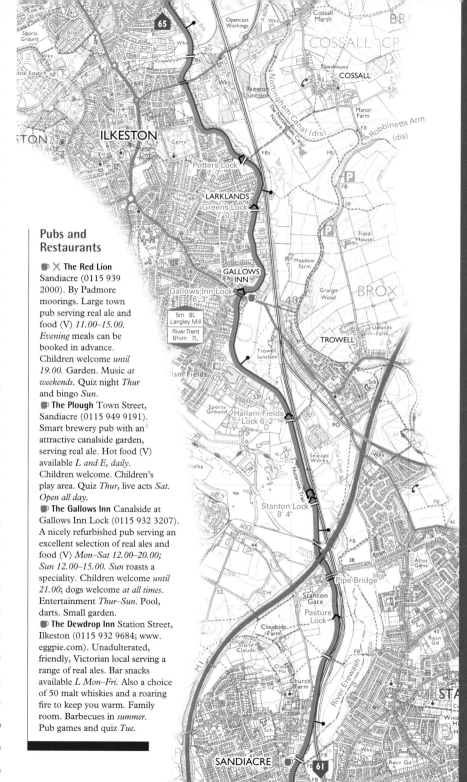

Pubs and Restaurants

The Red Lion Sandiacre (0115 939 2000). By Padmore moorings. Large town pub serving real ale and food (V) *11.00–15.00. Evening* meals can be booked in advance. Children welcome *until 19.00*. Garden. Music *at weekends*. Quiz night *Thur* and bingo *Sun*.

The Plough Town Street, Sandiacre (0115 949 9191). Smart brewery pub with an attractive canalside garden, serving real ale. Hot food (V) available *L and E, daily*. Children welcome. Children's play area. Quiz *Thur*, live acts *Sat. Open all day*.

The Gallows Inn Canalside at Gallows Inn Lock (0115 932 3207). A nicely refurbished pub serving an excellent selection of real ales and food (V) *Mon–Sat 12.00–20.00; Sun 12.00–15.00. Sun* roasts a speciality. Children welcome *until 21.00*; dogs welcome *at all times*. Entertainment *Thur–Sun*. Pool, darts. Small garden.

The Dewdrop Inn Station Street, Ilkeston (0115 932 9684; www. eggpie.com). Unadulterated, friendly, Victorian local serving a range of real ales. Bar snacks available *L Mon–Fri*. Also a choice of 50 malt whiskies and a roaring fire to keep you warm. Family room. Barbecues in *summer*. Pub games and quiz *Tue*.

Langley Mill

The northernmost section of the Erewash Canal is more isolated than the rest, and is definitely more rural and attractive. There are two splendid old canal buildings beside Shipley Lock – one was a stable and the other a slaughterhouse for worn-out canal horses. Just above the lock, the River Erewash creeps under the canal, which is carried above it on a very small aqueduct. Beyond the next pleasant rural stretch is Langley Mill, where the canal terminates at the Great Northern Basin beyond the final lock. Boatmen who have navigated the whole of the Erewash to this point are invited to call at *nb Ambergate* or Langley Mill Boat Company in order to obtain a head of navigation plaque or a certificate. See notice in the basin for further details.

● **Great Northern Basin**
This restored basin, officially reopened in 1973, once formed the junction of the Erewash, Cromford and Nottingham canals. A feeder enters here from Moorgreen Reservoir. Since it passed through a coalfield on its way to the basin, it brought down a lot of coal silt – which over the years filled up the Great Northern Basin. Now the Erewash Canal Preservation & Development Association has restored the basin and lock, so that boats may reach a good mooring site with an enjoyable pub beside it. The Nottingham and Cromford canals can never be restored here, for their closure was necessitated by mining subsidence – although substantial lengths of both canals are still in water, away from Langley Mill. The Cromford Canal was engineered by William Jessop and Benjamin Outram, its 14¹/₂ mile length being completed in 1793. One of its chief instigators had been Richard Arkwright who had come to Cromford in 1771 and built the world's first successful water-powered cotton spinning mill. The canal was used for transporting raw cotton and textile yarn as well as coal, iron, lead and building stone. Jessop was joined by James Green in engineering the Nottingham Canal. Running from Langley Mill to the River Trent at Nottingham, it involved 20 locks including a flight of 14 at Wollaton. The stretch from Langley Mill to Lenton had to be abandoned in 1937 but the remaining section through to the River Trent is still in use. Both canals pass through an interesting mixture of heavily industrial surroundings and quiet open countryside. The northern 5 miles of the Cromford Canal, from Ambergate to Cromford (a length still in water) is strongly recommended to all walkers, country lovers and especially industrial archaeologists. Explorers will find all kinds of exciting things, including two aqueducts and a fine old pumping station regularly in steam.

● **Langley Mill**
Derbs. PO, tel, stores, takeaway, station. Near the head of the Erewash Canal, with the little Erewash river going past it.

● **Eastwood**
Notts. PO, tel, stores, garage, bank. Up on the hill east of the Great Northern Basin, this mining town is best known as the childhood home of D.H. Lawrence. He was born at 8a Victoria Street, and the early part of *Sons and Lovers* is set in the town. The cemetery contains the Lawrence family graves. Lawrence's own headstone was brought from Vence in France and is now on display in the local library. A meeting at the Sun Inn in 1843, between local coal owners and iron masters, led to the construction of the Midland Railway. There are many mill shops in this area.

D.H. Lawrence Birthplace Museum 8a Victoria Street, Eastwood (01773 717353). Birthplace of the novelist, poet and playwright, David Herbert Lawrence. The house has been restored to reflect the lifestyle of a working-class Victorian family. There is also a video presentation of the author's Eastwood days. Also available from the museum is a leaflet entitled *The Blue Line Trail* which guides you around Eastwood's Lawrentian connections. *Open Sun and B Hols, Apr–Oct 10.00–17.00; Nov–Mar 10.00–16.00.* Charge.

Eastwood Library Wellington Place, Nottingham Road, Eastwood (01773 712209). The library houses a display of letters, books and first editions connected with D.H. Lawrence. Open *Mon, Tue, Thur 09.30–19.00, Fri 09.30–18.00, Sat 09.30–13.00. Closed all day Wed.* Free.

Heritage Centre Mansfield Road, Eastwood (01773 717353). Set in the mining company offices where Lawrence would have collected his wages. The displays tell you about Lawrence himself, the social history of the area and its changing community. *Opening times as per Birthplace Museum.* Charge.

American Adventure Theme Park Shipley (08453 302929; www.americanadventure.co.uk). 1¹/₄ miles south west of the canal. Leave the canal at Shipley Lock and after crossing the railway by the footbridge, follow the footpath to the A6007. Turn right towards Shipley and then follow the signs. Two hundred acres of parkland offering fun for the whole family. A chance to test your courage on some of the rides or unwind with a game of golf. *Open daily 10.00–17.00 during season with varying times out of season.* Charge.

Pubs and Restaurants

The Bridge 107 Awsworth Road, Ilkeston (0115 932 9903). Canalside pub with a large garden and adventure playground. Popular in season, this establishment has a warm, welcoming, friendly atmosphere and dispenses real ales. Filled cobs available *at weekends*. Children welcome *until 20.00*, dogs *until closing time*. Large garden with children's play area and bouncy castle. Moorings below Barker's Lock.

The Bridge Inn Bridge Street, Cotmanhay (0115 932 2589). Small canalside local serving real ale. Children and dogs welcome. Garden with swings. Traditional pub games. Moorings.

The Great Northern Langley Mill (01773 713834). At Great Northern Basin (the railway company was once owner of the canal). An excellent local pub serving real ale and traditional pub food (V) *L and E, daily*. Children and dogs welcome. Canalside garden. Quiz nights *Sun and Wed*, live music *Tue, Fri and Sat*, bingo *Sun*.

The Derby Arms High Street, Heanor (01773 713508). Real ale in a traditional drinkers pub. Children welcome. Garden and pub games.

**WALKING &
CYCLING**
The towpath is in excellent condition for both walking and cycling.

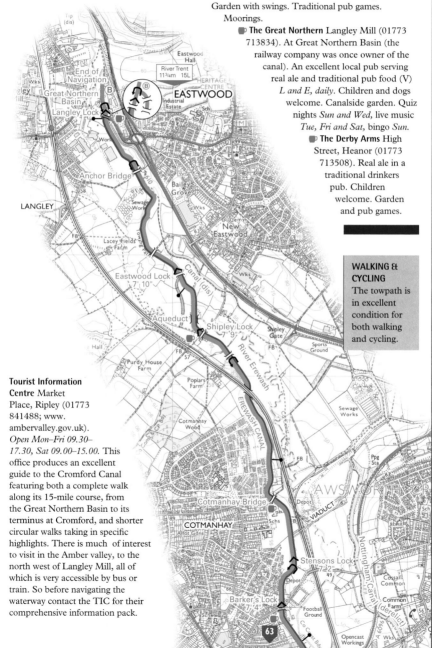

**Tourist Information
Centre** Market Place, Ripley (01773 841488; www. ambervalley.gov.uk). *Open Mon–Fri 09.30– 17.30, Sat 09.00–15.00.* This office produces an excellent guide to the Cromford Canal featuring both a complete walk along its 15-mile course, from the Great Northern Basin to its terminus at Cromford, and shorter circular walks taking in specific highlights. There is much of interest to visit in the Amber valley, to the north west of Langley Mill, all of which is very accessible by bus or train. So before navigating the waterway contact the TIC for their comprehensive information pack.

Boatyards

Ⓑ **Langley Mill Boat Co** Great Northern Basin, Langley Mill (01773 760758). 🚽 🎁 ♿ D Pump out, gas, overnight mooring, long-term mooring (by arrangement), winter storage, boat repairs, engine repairs, boat building and fitting out, dry dock, DIY facilities, solid fuel, toilets, laundrette. Ⓑ **ECPDA** (01773 779699). Moorings in Great Northern Basin.

GERMANS COTTON ON

Before the arrival of Richard Arkwright and his partners in August 1771, the area around Cromford was a scattered community of families who earned their livings in the lead mines. By Christmas of that year Arkwright was already utilising the waters of a local lead mine drain, the Cromford Sough, and of the Bonsall Brook, to power what was soon to become the world's first successful water-powered cotton spinning mill. By 1777 there were two mills in Cromford and further developments were soon to take place in Derby and Matlock Bath. New housing built to accommodate the workers in Cromford featured an additional upper storey which acted as a workroom. Visiting industrialists from New England were entertained in the new Greyhound Hotel. So impressed were they with the developments in Cromford that they returned to America and used Sir Richard's mills as a model for their own. By 1783 continental Europe was catching up with the rest of the world when its first water-powered cotton spinning mill was erected near Ratingen, Germany. Johann Gottfried Brägelmann created his very own cotton new town and named it Cromford in recognition of Arkwright's innovation.

*View of Foxton Locks (*see *page 75)*

GRAND UNION CANAL – LEICESTER SECTION AND THE RIVER SOAR

MAXIMUM DIMENSIONS

Norton Junction to Foxton Junction
Length: 72'
Beam: 7'
Headroom: 7' 6"

Market Harborough to Leicester
Length: 72'
Beam: 13'
Headroom: 7'

Leicester West Bridge to River Trent
Length: 72'
Beam: 14' 4"
Headroom: 7' 6"

MILEAGE

NORTON JUNCTION to:
Crick: 5 miles
Welford Arm: $15^1/2$ miles
Market Harborough Arm: $23^1/4$ miles

Blaby: 36 miles
Leicester West Bridge: $41^1/4$ miles
Cossington Lock: 49 miles
Barrow upon Soar: $53^1/4$ miles
Loughborough Basin: $57^1/4$ miles
Zouch Lock: $60^1/2$ miles
RIVER TRENT: $66^1/4$ miles

Locks: 59

MANAGER

Norton to Foxton (including the Welford Arm): 01788 890666
enquiries.braunston@britishwaterways.co.uk
Foxton to the Trent (including the Market Harborough Arm): 0115 973 4278
enquiries. sawley@britishwaterways.co.uk

The River Soar is a tributary of the River Trent and is approximately 40 miles long. It runs mainly through Leicestershire, rising at Smockington Hollow on the Warwickshire border. For most of the way from Aylestone (just south of Leicester) to the Trent, the Soar forms the Leicester section of the Grand Union Canal.

In 1634 Thomas Skipworth of Cotes attempted to make the River 'portable for barges and boats up to the town of Leicester' by means of a grant from King Charles I in return for 10 per cent of the profits. This scheme was a failure. But, after several other attempts, prominent citizens of Loughborough secured an Act of Parliament in 1776, and the River Soar Navigation (Loughborough Canal) was opened two years later, bringing great prosperity to the town. The continuation of the navigation up to Leicester (the Leicester Canal) was built under an Act passed in 1791. Its opening was marked by the arrival in Leicester of two boats loaded with provisions from Gainsborough on 21 February 1794. The engineers concerned with construction of the River Soar Navigation were John Smith and John May (Loughborough Canal) and William Jessop (Leicester Canal). With the completion of the Grand Junction Canal between Brentford and Braunston, a connection was soon established between this and the River Soar Navigation, built to the narrow gauge, thwarting the Grand Junction's scheme for a system of wide canals.

The Loughborough Navigation was one of the most prosperous canals in England, by virtue of its position in relation to the Nottinghamshire/Derbyshire coalfield and the Erewash Canal. However, railway competition took its usual toll, and although trade revived when the Grand Union Canal purchased the Loughborough and Leicester navigations in 1931, the improvement proved temporary. It remains a pretty, rural river and is much enjoyed by those on pleasure craft.

Norton Junction

Leaving Norton Junction there is a quiet, meandering mile through light woods and rolling fields before the motorway and railway take over; the canal passes the back door of the Watford Gap service area. The noise and bustle of the motorway and main railway line intrude, accentuating the sedate pace of those using the original of the three transport systems. The Watford Gap motorway service station (south of bridge 6) is by no means inaccessible from the towpath and could provide the boater with *24hr* sustenance and provisions. Otherwise the Leicester Section of the Grand Union Canal is very attractive, quiet and in no hurry to reach Foxton. It wanders through rolling, hilly country, riverlike with constant changes of direction that guide it gently north eastwards. It avoids villages and civilisation generally; only the old wharves serve as a reminder of the canal's function. The slow course of the canal, its relative emptiness and its original plan combine to make it very narrow in places; reeds, overhanging trees and shallow banks quite often do not allow two boats to pass. After negotiating Watford Locks and reaching the summit level of 412ft there is nothing strenuous to look forward to, as this level continues for the next $20^1/_2$ miles. Four of these locks form a staircase – adopt a 'one up, one down' procedure, and use both ground and side paddles when going either up or down. At Watford the canal swings east away from the M1 for good. The locks and Crick Tunnel with its wooded approaches offer canal excitement to contrast with the quiet of the landscape.

NAVIGATIONAL NOTES

1 Please consult the lock keeper before using Watford Locks which are *open daily: summer Mon–Thur 08.00–17.00, Fri–Sun 08.00–18.00; winter 08.00–15.30.*
2 Local branches of the IWA have produced a guide to the Leicester Arm obtainable from various lockside positions (using a BW key) or from 30 Lutterworth Road, Leicester, LE2 8PF.

● **Welton**
Northants. Tel. The village climbs up the side of a steep, winding hill, which makes it compact and attractive, especially around the church.

● **Watford**
Northants. PO, tel, stores. Set in the middle of wooded parkland, Watford gives the impression of being a private village. The church and Watford Court dominate, and luckily the M1 has made no impact. The 13th-C church contains some interesting monuments. The Court is partly 17th-C, although there are Victorian additions. The rich brown stone used throughout the village adds to the feeling of unity.

● **Crick Tunnel**
1528yds long, the tunnel was opened in 1814. All tunnels built in this area suffered great problems in construction. Quicksands caused the route of the tunnel to be changed and greatly affected work. Stephenson found similar difficulties when building the nearby Kilsby Tunnel for the London to Birmingham railway.

Pubs and Restaurants

● ✕ **The New Inn** Long Buckby Wharf (01327 842540; www.gillies-inns.com). Canalside, at Buckby Top Lock. Cosy alcoved free house, serving real ale and a range of inexpensive meals (V) and snacks *all day, every day*. Children welcome. Canalside seating and patio. Darts, dominoes and large screen TV. Moorings. *Open all day.*

● ✕ **The Stag's Head** Watford Gap (01327 703621). Award winning restaurant with a lovely canalside rose garden. An extensive menu – ranging from bar snacks to table d'hôte and a wide à la carte selection (V) – is available *L and E, daily*. The cuisine encompasses English, French and Portuguese dishes. Very much a family establishment with prices to match. Real ale. Occasional Portuguese food theme *eves in winter*. Moorings.

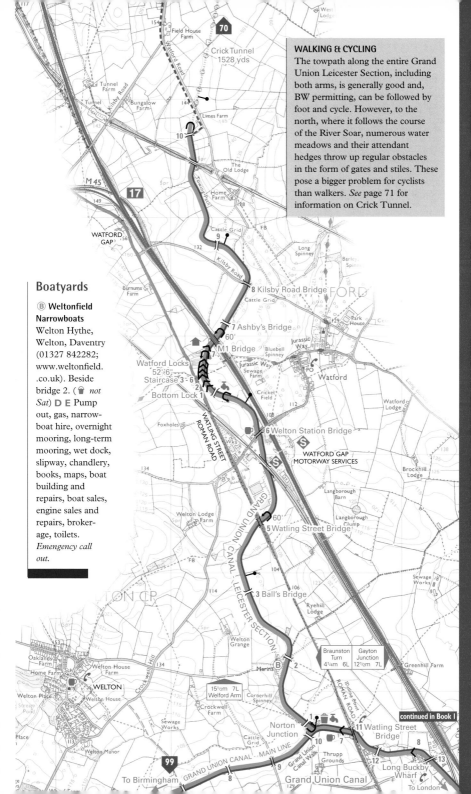

WALKING & CYCLING

The towpath along the entire Grand Union Leicester Section, including both arms, is generally good and, BW permitting, can be followed by foot and cycle. However, to the north, where it follows the course of the River Soar, numerous water meadows and their attendant hedges throw up regular obstacles in the form of gates and stiles. These pose a bigger problem for cyclists than walkers. *See* page 71 for information on Crick Tunnel.

Boatyards

Ⓑ **Weltonfield Narrowboats**
Welton Hythe, Welton, Daventry (01327 842282; www.weltonfield.co.uk). Beside bridge 2. (🛒 *not Sat*) **D E** Pump out, gas, narrowboat hire, overnight mooring, long-term mooring, wet dock, slipway, chandlery, books, maps, boat building and repairs, boat sales, engine sales and repairs, brokerage, toilets. *Emergency call out.*

Yelvertoft

Leaving Crick Tunnel the navigation bypasses the village and is soon alongside a smart, newly constructed marina. After skirting Crack's Hill, a curious tree-topped mound, the canal wanders to the east in a series of loops which cause it to miss both Yelvertoft and Winwick, the only villages in the section. Hills surround the course of the canal, encouraging its meandering. At one point it passes under the same road three times in under a mile. Occasional woods add to the pleasure of the isolation.

Pages Lodge Farm

72

30

Jurassic Way

Woodsi Farm

ELKIN

Cot

Heygate's Lodge **29**

Heygate Lodge

Elkington Bridge **28**
Elkington Farm Cottage

Farm

YELVERTOFT FIELDSIDE COVERT

27 Mountain Barn Bridge

Mountain Barn

26 Clay Barn Bridge

WINWICK MANOR FARM

Barn Ground Spinney

Bush Cl Spinn

Chester's Bridge **25**

YELVERTOFT

Larch Spinney

Skew Bridge **19**

20

24 Smart's Bridge

WINW

Flint Hill Farm
Pit (dis)

Darker's Bridge

New House Farm

23

ep Dip

18

21

GRAND UNION CANAL

Crick Road

16

17

22
Haddon Road Bridge

WINWICK GRANGE

Foxes Farm

15 Crackshill Farm

Flinthill

129

The Bungalow

CRACK'S HILL

Boatyards

14

Towing Path

13 Crick Lodge Bridge

Abattoir

Factory

CRICK

Marina

Crick Wharf

Nursery

12

Sch

PO

Cottage Farm

11

CP

10½m 0L
Welford Arm

Norton Jnc
5m 7L

Ⓑ **ABNB** Crick Wharf, West Haddon Road, Crick (01788 822115/07721 378653; www.abnb.co.uk). Boat sales.

Ⓑ **Crick Wharf** West Haddon Road, Crick (01788 822115; www.abnb.co.uk). ⚓ Long-term mooring, boat building and fitting out.

Ⓑ **Crick Marina** West Haddon Road, Crick (01788 824056). 🚿 🚽 ⚓ **D** (**E** by arrangement) Pump out, gas, solid fuel, overnight mooring, dry dock, boat repairs, long-term mooring, toilets, laundrette, telephone.

Ⓑ **Crick Dock** Hakuna Matata, Crick Wharf, West Haddon Road, Crick (01788 822384/07831 352812). 64ft covered wet dock, DIY.

Crick Tunnel
1528 yds

69

Field Hous Farm

After Winwick, a vague north east course is resumed, passing the long-abandoned village of Elkington. There are no locks, but a regular procession of brick-arched bridges serves as a reminder that it is still a canal.

● **Crick**
Northants. PO, tel, stores. A large village built around the junction of two roads. There are several attractive stone houses, and the large church has managed to escape restoration. It contains much decorative stonework and a circular Norman font. There is an intriguing second-hand shop *open Wed, Fri and Sat 14.00–18.00* that could well warrant a visit.

● **Yelvertoft**
Northants. PO, tel, stores, garage. Set back from the canal, the village is built round a wide main street, terminated in the east by the church. Sadly, many of the original thatched roofs have been replaced.

● **Winwick**
Northants. Tel. One mile south east of bridge 23. The 16th-C Manor House, built of richly decorated brick and with an ornamental Tudor gateway, is the major building in this neat, sleepy, village.

WALKING & CYCLING
Walkers and cyclists bypassing Crick Tunnel need to take the short track on the right of the tunnel mouth and, on joining the minor road, turn left. Follow this into the village and turn right down Boathorse Lane. When the road bends sharply to the left walkers may follow the footpath straight ahead (signposted to West Haddon), cross a field along the hedgerow (still following the waymarking to West Haddon) and, having negotiated the stile, bear left diagonally, downhill across the next field following the line of the drainage pits to the sign in the hedge, which is immediately above the northern tunnel cutting. Cyclists are advised to follow the road through the village, bearing right and rejoining the canal at bridge 12.

Pubs and Restaurants

Edwards of Crick Crick (01788 822517). Beside bridge 12. Restaurant and coffee house offering a wide-ranging menu from inexpensive snacks *L* through to a mouth-watering à la carte selection (V), available *all day*. Good value *Sun* lunch, children half-price. Everything home-made, including the bread. Excellent wine list and real ale. *Closed Sun E and Mon.*

The Red Lion Main Street, Crick (01788 822342). Real ale dispensed in a cosy, unadulterated pub with low ceilings and coal fires. Excellent home-cooked meals served with fresh vegetables (V) *L and E (not Sun E)*. Children *L only*. Dogs welcome. Patio seating.

The Wheatsheaf Main Street, Crick (01788 822284). Lively, friendly local dispensing real ale. Food (V) available *L and E and all day Sun*. Children welcome. Pool. Garden. *Open all day.*

The Royal Oak Church Street, Crick (01788 822340). Attractive old village local, with an unusual triangular, raised, wood-panelled bar area. Real ales. Bar snacks available *Fri, Sat and Sun*. Garden. Skittles, pool and darts. *Open Mon–Fri 16.30–23.00, Sat and Sun all day.* B & B.

The Knightly Arms Yelvertoft (01788 822401). Popular village local serving real ale. Home cooked food (V) available *L and E*. Traditional *Sun* lunch. Children and dogs welcome. Conservatory and large patio area. Garden. Table skittles, darts, dominoes and crib.

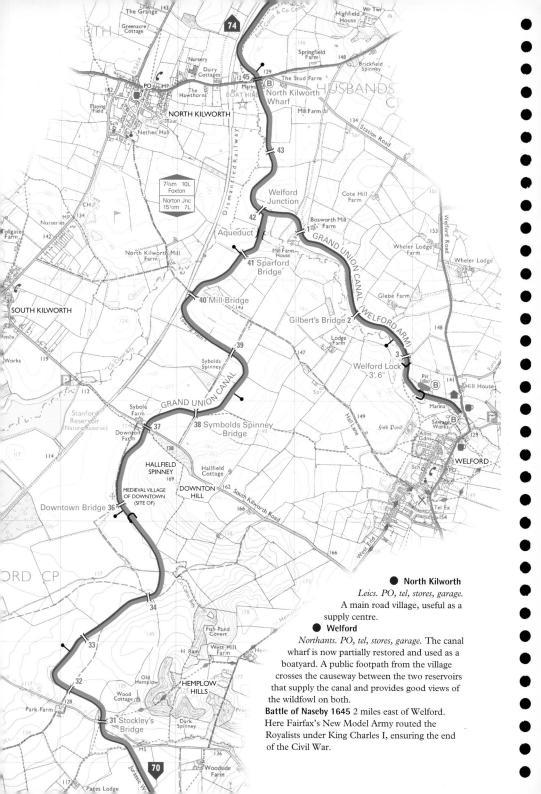

74

The Grange
Greenacre
Cottage
NORTH
Nursery
Dairy
Cottages
PO MP
The Hawthorns
Marina
BOAT HIRE
NORTH KILWORTH
The
Playing
Field
Sch
Nether Hall
Moat

45 129
North Kilworth
Wharf
The Stud Farm
Mill Farm

Highfield
House
Wr Twr
Springfield
Farm
Brickfield
Spinney
HUSBANDS
CP
Station Road

43

7¾m 10L
Foxton
Norton Jnc
15½m 7L

Welford
Junction

Bosworth Mill
Farm
Cote Hill
Farm

Wheler Lodge
Farm
Wheler Lodge

42

Aqueduct

Mill Farm
House

GRAND UNION CANAL

Glebe Farm

North Kilworth Mill
Farm

41 Sparford
Bridge

Gilbert's Bridge 2

Lodge
Farm

GRAND UNION CANAL (WELFORD ARM)

40 Mill Bridge

SOUTH KILWORTH

3

Welford Lock
3' 6"

Hill House

Works

39

Sybolds
Spinney

Pit
(dis)

Marina

Stanford
Reservoir
(Nature Reserve)

Sybole
Farm

GRAND UNION CANAL

Sewage
Works

37

Downtown
Farm

38 Symbolds Spinney
Bridge

Allot
Gdns

WELFORD

HALLFIELD
SPINNEY

Hallfield
Cottage

DOWNTOWN
HILL

Fish Pond

Sch

MEDIEVAL VILLAGE
OF DOWNTOWN
(SITE OF)

South Kilworth Road

Tel Ex

Downtown Bridge **36**

34

West End

Fish Pond
Covert

West Hill
Farm

33

ORD CP

32

Old
Hemplow

Wood
Cottage

HEMPLOW
HILLS

Park Farm

31 Stockley's
Bridge

Dark
Spinney

70

Woodside
Farm

Pages Lodge

● **North Kilworth**

Leics. PO, tel, stores, garage.
A main road village, useful as a
supply centre.

● **Welford**

Northants. PO, tel, stores, garage. The canal
wharf is now partially restored and used as a
boatyard. A public footpath from the village
crosses the causeway between the two reservoirs
that supply the canal and provides good views of
the wildfowl on both.

Battle of Naseby 1645 2 miles east of Welford.
Here Fairfax's New Model Army routed the
Royalists under King Charles I, ensuring the end
of the Civil War.

Welford

Continuing north east the canal wanders on through open fields, backed by wood-ed hills to the east. To the west there are splendid views over the Avon valley. The river passes under the canal before the Welford Arm. Beyond the valley the spires of South and North Kilworth churches can be seen for several miles. The Welford Arm, which was completed in 1814, branches away to the south east for 1 1/2 miles, linking the canal with the Welford and Sulby reservoirs, and reaches its terminus in a small basin; there is one shallow lock on the arm. Otherwise it is quiet and tree-lined, following closely the path of the Avon, whose source is just east of Welford. The arm was reopened to navigation in 1969, having been derelict for some years. The main line continues, entering the wooded cutting that announces Husbands Bosworth Tunnel. There are no locks, but many of the bridges are original, fine faded red brick, echoing the seclusion of the canal.

Stanford Hall Lutterworth (01788 860250; www.stanfordhall.co.uk). Two miles west of bridge 31. A William and Mary brick mansion (the south elevation is in stone), built in 1697–1700, with a Georgian stable block. Furniture, paintings, costume, motorcycle museum and a replica of the experimental flying machine built by Percy Pilcher in 1898. Walled rose garden and nature trail. Teas, shop and craft centre. *Open Easter–Sep, Sat, Sun, B Hol Mon and following Tue 13.30–17.30. Last admission 17.00. (Craft centre open Sun and B Hols.)* Charge.

Boatyards

Ⓑ **Welford Marina** Canal Wharf, Welford (01858 575995). 🚿 🚽 ⛽ D Gas, overnight mooring, long-term mooring, boat and engine repairs, boat fitting out, wet dock, dry dock, DIY facilities, solid fuel, toilets.

Ⓑ **Kilworth Wharf Leisure** Kilworth Marina, North Kilworth (01858 880484; kilworthwharf.leisure@ntlworld.com). By bridge 45. 🚿 🚽 ⛽ D E Pump out, gas, day-hire boats, overnight mooring, long-term mooring (up to 26ft only), winter storage, slip-way, wet dock, chandlery, boat sales and repairs, engine sales and repairs, boat fitting out, DIY facilities, books, maps and gifts, toilets, solid fuel. *Emergency call out.*

Pubs and Restaurants

🍺 ✕ **The Wharf Inn** Canal Wharf, Welford (01858 575075). Warm, friendly pub over 200 years old, popular with the locals, dispensing real ale and home-made food (V) *L and E (not Sun E)*. Carvery *Sun L*. Children and dogs welcome. Large, well-kept garden by the River Avon. Open-air theatre functions *during Aug*. B & B.

🍺 ✕ **The Elizabethan** 8 High Street, Welford (01858 575311; www.theelizabethan.co.uk). Country pub and restaurant serving real ale and food (V) *L and E*. Children and dogs welcome (dogs in bar area only). Garden. Live bands and discos *at weekends*. Large dance floor.

🍺 ✕ **The White Lion** Lutterworth Road, North Kilworth (01858 880260). Real ales and food (V) available *L and E (not Sun and Mon E)*. Children and dogs welcome. Garden and pub games. Disabled access.

🍺 ✕ **The Swan Inn** Lutterworth Road, North Kilworth (01858 880957). Real ales and bar snacks (V) *L and E (not Wed L)*. Traditional *Sunday* roasts. Children welcome.

Husbands Bosworth

Continuing north east, the canal enters a remote, but attractive stretch. There are no villages on the canal here, Husbands Bosworth being hidden by the tunnel. The A50 crosses over the tunnel and meets the A427 in Husbands Bosworth. The canal runs north east through fields to the top of Foxton Locks. It then falls 75ft to join the former Leicester & Northampton Union Canal. At the bottom of the locks the 5¹/₂ mile Market Harborough Arm branches off to the east.

NAVIGATIONAL NOTES

Foxton Locks are open daily as per Watford Locks, *see* page 68.

● **Husbands Bosworth**
Leics. PO, tel, stores, garage. Access from canal: walk up the lane from bridge 46.
Husbands Bosworth Tunnel 1166yds long, the tunnel was opened in 1813.
Foxton Locks The Foxton staircase was opened in 1812. There are two staircases of five locks each with a passing pound in the middle. Check each flight of five is clear before you enter.
Foxton Inclined Plane In 1900 an inclined plane was opened to bypass Foxton Locks. Two caissons carrying either two narrowboats or one barge moved sideways on rails up and down the plane. A steam-driven winch pulling an endless cable was used to start the caissons moving. The journey time was reduced from 70 to 12 minutes. Mechanical problems and high running costs, plus the fact that the planned widening of the Watford flight never took place, soon made the plane a white elephant. The cut leading to the bottom of the plane is still navigable, and the plane itself can still be traced, running at right angles to the east of the locks. Exploratory trail and museum *open Easter–Oct, daily 10.00–17.00; Nov–Easter, weekends 10.00–16.00 and some weekdays. Telephone for details.* Charge. Restoration is in the hands of **Foxton Inclined Plane Trust** Middle Lock, Foxton Locks, Foxton, Market Harborough (0116 279 2657; www.foxcanal. co.uk). There is a picnic site, car park and toilets (including disabled) at bridge 60, beside the Gumley road. Charge.

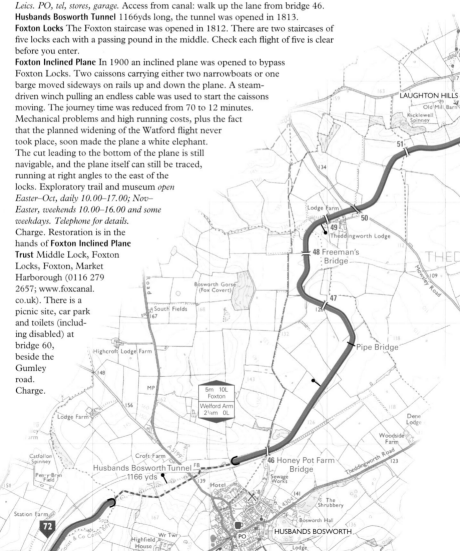

Boatyards

ⓑ **Foxton Boat Services** Bottom Lock, Foxton, Market Harborough (0116 279 2285). 🛁 🚿 ⚓ D Pump-out, gas, narrow boat hire, day-craft hire, overnight mooring, long-term mooring, winter storage, slipway, crane (20 tons), boat fitting-out, chandlery, boat sales and repairs, engine sales and repairs, wet dock, DIY facilities, telephone, toilets, showers, groceries, café and pub, laundrette, books, maps and gifts. Commercial boat hire. *24 hour emergency call-out.*

WALKING & CYCLING

Walkers and cyclists confronted with Husbands Bosworth Tunnel should take the track climbing up to the left of the tunnel mouth and follow it over the hill to the road on the outskirts of the village (A50). Cross this road and follow the track over the disused railway line, down a tree-lined glade, rejoining the waterway at the eastern tunnel portal.

Pubs and Restaurants

🍺 ✕ **The Bell Inn** Kilworth Road, Husbands Bosworth (01858 880246). Real ale and food available *L and E, daily*. Family room – children welcome. Garden. Live entertainment *Sat evening*.
🍺 **The Bell** Gumley (0116 279 2476).

Friendly, old village local serving real ale and real cider. Food (V) available *L and E (not Sun or Mon E)*. Children over 5 catered for. No-smoking restaurant, traditional pub games (no machines) and fires in winter. Garden.

BOAT TRIPS

Vagabond & Vixen Horse-drawn and motorised canal trips for casual visitors *on summer Sun afternoons and B Hols* from Foxton bottom lock; available for charter by parties any other day (minimum 20 passengers, maximum 51). Telephone 0116 279 2285 for details.

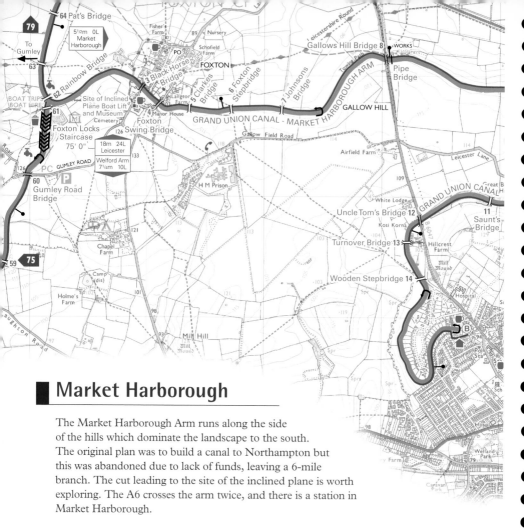

Market Harborough

The Market Harborough Arm runs along the side of the hills which dominate the landscape to the south. The original plan was to build a canal to Northampton but this was abandoned due to lack of funds, leaving a 6-mile branch. The cut leading to the site of the inclined plane is worth exploring. The A6 crosses the arm twice, and there is a station in Market Harborough.

● **Foxton**
Leics. Tel. A village built on the side of a hill, either side of the canal, in pretty countryside. There is an excellent information leaflet and village trail available from Foxton Boat Services and Market Harborough Tourist Information Centre.

● **Market Harborough**
Leics. PO, tel, stores, garage, banks, station. Established as a market town by 1203, Market Harborough still retains much of its rural elegance and local importance.
There is an antique and collectors market *every Sun* in the market hall (01604 882399).
Traveline (0870 608 2 608). For full details on bus travel to local (and not so local) attractions. *Open 07.00–22.30.*
Frank Haynes Gallery 50 Station Road, Great Bowden, Market Harborough (01858 464862; www.marketharborough.com/gallery). ¾ mile

north of the station. Two galleries with paintings and pottery from the region. Cards, etc. *Open Thur–Sun 10.00–17.00.* Free.
Harborough Leisure Centre Northampton Road, Market Harborough (01858 410115). The usual mix of swimming pool, child-enticing water features, fitness room, etc. Also bar, bistro and crèche.
Harborough Museum Council Offices, Adam and Eve Street, Market Harborough (01858 432468; www.harborough.gov.uk). Contains the Civic Society's own collection and illustrates local life from the earliest times. Relics of the Battle of Naseby, a reconstructed bootmaker's workshop and the Symington Collection of corsetry. *Open Mon–Sat 10.00–16.30 and Sun 14.00–17.00. Closed G Fri, Xmas Day and Boxing Day.* Free. Disabled access via council offices so contact staff in advance *on Sat, Sun and B Hols.*

Harborough Theatre Church Square, Market Harborough (01858 463673).

Market Harborough Canal Basin Significant as the site of the first Inland Waterways Association campaigning rally held in 1950 which, arguably, laid the foundations for a resurgence in canal interest that could easily be taken for granted by the contemporary pleasure boater. The canal basin has recently been extended and the surrounding area developed with apartments and facilities for craft units. There are new BW moorings together with a shower block, DIY pump out, toilets, etc. *(See* Navigational Notes on page 74.)

Parish Church of St Dionysius High Street. Built in the 14thC by Scropes and enlarged a century later.

Old Grammar School High Street. Founded by Robert Smyth. It stands on wooden carved pillars, and behind the arches was held the ancient butter market. The building was used as the grammar school until 1892 and is now a meeting hall.

Tourist Information Centre Council Offices, Adam and Eve Street, Market Harborough (01858 821010; www.harborough.gov.uk). *Open Mon–Fri 08.45–17.00, Sat 09.30–12.30.*

NAVIGATIONAL NOTES

A BW watermate key is required to operate Foxton Swing Bridge No 4.

WALKING & CYCLING

Brampton Valley Way runs for 14 miles along an old railway track and links Market Harborough with the northern outskirts of Northampton. It makes use of two old tunnels and passes a selection of old steam locomotives at Chapel Brampton.

Pubs and Restaurants

The Black Horse Main Street, Foxton (01858 545250). Family-run pub welcoming anyone who likes good food, drink (real ales) and lovely gardens. An excellent selection of home-made food (V) available *L and E, daily (not Sun E)*. (Bookings advisable *E in summer, and Sun L)*. Children and dogs welcome. No-smoking, conservatory dining area. Garden with animals for children. Jazz *Wed.* Crib, darts and skittle alley.

The Shoulder of Mutton Main Street, Foxton (01858 545666; haquasummer@aol.com). Real ales and food (V) available *L and E (not Mon in winter)* in a pub close to Foxton Locks. Children welcome. Large garden and patio seating. B & B.

The Union Leicester Road, Market Harborough (01858 433277). Family pub with a relaxed atmosphere. Real ales and a wide variety of food (V) available *L and E (not Sun E)*. Children welcome. Garden and children's play area. Regular music nights. B & B.

The Angel Hotel High Street, Market Harborough (01858 462702). Full à la carte restaurant menu through to bar meals (V), served *L and E, daily*. Patio. B & B.

Three Swans Hotel High Street, Market Harborough (01858 466644). Real ales and a comprehensive range of bar food (V) *L and E, daily*. The restaurant *(closed Sun E)* offers both table d'hôte and à la carte menus. Children welcome. Courtyard seating. B & B.

The Red Cow 58–59 High Street, Market Harborough (01858 463637). Real ale and food (V) available *L*. Pavement seating. *Sun night quiz.*

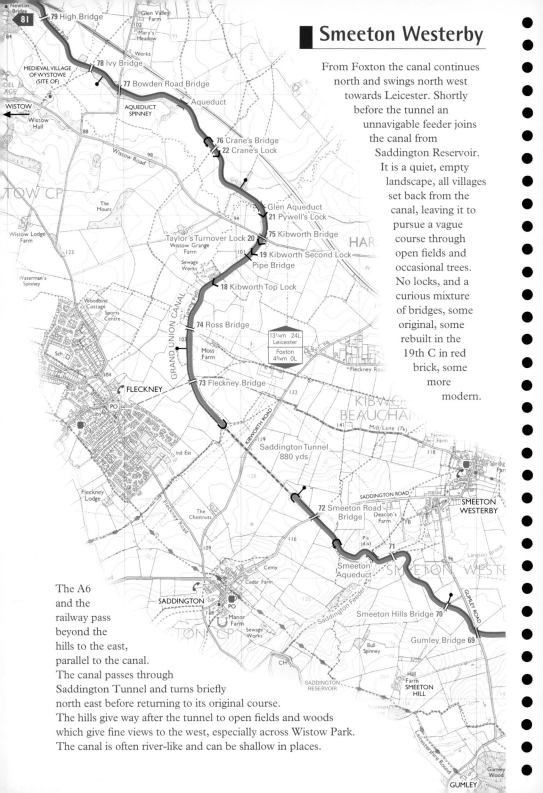

■ Smeeton Westerby

From Foxton the canal continues north and swings north west towards Leicester. Shortly before the tunnel an unnavigable feeder joins the canal from Saddington Reservoir. It is a quiet, empty landscape, all villages set back from the canal, leaving it to pursue a vague course through open fields and occasional trees. No locks, and a curious mixture of bridges, some original, some rebuilt in the 19th C in red brick, some more modern.

The A6 and the railway pass beyond the hills to the east, parallel to the canal. The canal passes through Saddington Tunnel and turns briefly north east before returning to its original course. The hills give way after the tunnel to open fields and woods which give fine views to the west, especially across Wistow Park. The canal is often river-like and can be shallow in places.

Gumley
Leics. PO box, tel. 1/2 mile west of bridge 63. Small village scattered among trees, set on a hillside high above the canal. The Italianate tower of Gumley Hall rises above the trees, overlooking the valley.

Saddington
Leics. Tel. Small village set back from the canal, with only the church tower breaking the skyline.

Smeeton Westerby
Leics. Tel. The village undulates over the hills to the east of the canal, built along the sides of the main street.

Saddington Tunnel 880yds long, the tunnel was completed in 1797, after great difficulties owing to its being built crooked. Naturalists enthuse about the bats that nowadays live in the tunnel.

Fleckney
Leics. PO, tel, stores. An industrial village just 10 minutes' walk from the canal. Very useful for its supermarket, fish & chip shop and Chinese takeaway.

Wistow
Leics. For a while the canal runs through woods and parkland to the west adjoining Wistow Park. Wistow itself has a church and a Hall, the church with Norman work but mostly 18th-C, including fine monuments. The Hall is Jacobean in principle but was largely rebuilt in the 19th C.

Pubs and Restaurants

⚓ ✕ **The Queens Head** Main Street, Saddington (0116 240 2536). A village centre pub with attractive gardens and a cosy restaurant, set in a tasteful extension with superb views over Saddington Reservoir. Real ale. A wide range of food from a full à la carte menu to tasty snacks and an extensive range of bar meals (V) *L and E (not Sun E)*. Children and dogs welcome. Booking advisable *especially at weekends.*

⚓ **The Kings Head** Smeeton Westerby (0116 279 2676). Unadulterated, village local offering a friendly welcome and real ale. Inexpensive food (V) available *L and E (not Mon L or Mon and Tue E)*. Children and dogs welcome. Small patio area. Darts, dominoes, crib.

⚓ **The Old Crown** Fleckney (0116 240 2223). West of bridge 73. Wide range of appetising snacks and nourishing main meals in this friendly, welcoming village pub. Food (V) is available *L and E, and all day Fri and Sat.* Real ale. Children welcome. Large garden with bouncy castle and children's play area. Patio, darts, dominoes and pool. Several of the walls are lined with a colourful array of books: bring a book and you are welcome to exchange it.

Boatyards

Ⓑ **Debdale Wharf Marina** Kibworth (0116 279 3034). 🚽 🛢 ⚓ D E Pump out, gas, overnight mooring, long-term mooring, winter storage, crane (30 tons), dry dock, wet dock, chandlery, boat lengthening, boat sales and repairs, engine sales and repairs, boat building and boat fitting out, DIY facilities, books and maps, solid fuel, general fabrication. *Emergency call out.*

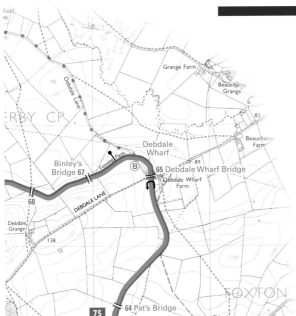

Wigston

Newton Harcourt breaks the unwritten rule of this navigation by being right beside it (other villages keep their distance). The tunnel, the bridges and the locks which begin the descent to Leicester provide plenty of canal interest although the amount of rubbish in the waterway begins to increase. The A6 and the main railway slowly encroach on the canal to the east. The navigation follows the north westerly course of the River Sence, bounded by low hills to east and west and still remote, until Kilby Bridge where indications of the city of Leicester begin with distant views of housing estates and factories. By Ervin's Lock at South Wigston the city seems to take over. The locks continue the steady fall, giving the stretch its individuality. A handcuff key is needed to operate the water saving gear between Kilby Bridge and Aylestone Mill. Keys are obtainable from boatyards and the Navigation pub at Kilby Bridge. Immediately to the north west of Leicester Road Bridge (98) is the original site of Pickfords Canal Carriers, established when they transferred their activities from horse and cart to the newly burgeoning canals. A little further west, before the navigation swings north, are the disused clay pits and derelict brickyard, once owned by the Union Canal Company; they produced the materials used to construct its locks and bridges.

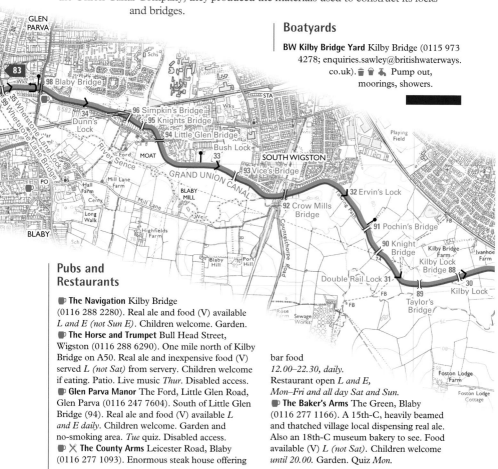

Boatyards

BW Kilby Bridge Yard Kilby Bridge (0115 973 4278; enquiries.sawley@britishwaterways. co.uk). Pump out, moorings, showers.

Pubs and Restaurants

The Navigation Kilby Bridge (0116 288 2280). Real ale and food (V) available *L* and *E (not Sun E)*. Children welcome. Garden.

The Horse and Trumpet Bull Head Street, Wigston (0116 288 6290). One mile north of Kilby Bridge on A50. Real ale and inexpensive food (V) served *L (not Sat)* from servery. Children welcome if eating. Patio. Live music *Thur*. Disabled access.

Glen Parva Manor The Ford, Little Glen Road, Glen Parva (0116 247 7604). South of Little Glen Bridge (94). Real ale and food (V) available *L and E daily*. Children welcome. Garden and no-smoking area. *Tue* quiz. Disabled access.

✕ The County Arms Leicester Road, Blaby (0116 277 1093). Enormous steak house offering

bar food *12.00–22.30, daily*. Restaurant open *L and E, Mon–Fri and all day Sat and Sun*.

The Baker's Arms The Green, Blaby (0116 277 1166). A 15th-C, heavily beamed and thatched village local dispensing real ale. Also an 18th-C museum bakery to see. Food available (V) *L (not Sat)*. Children welcome *until 20.00*. Garden. Quiz *Mon*.

Newton Harcourt

Leics. Scattered village bisected by the railway in a cutting. The Hall is 17th-C, with later rebuilding; it has a fine gateway. Newton Harcourt is a well-known Leicester beauty spot, popular on *Sun afternoons*.

Traveline (0870 6082608). For full details on bus travel to local (and not so local) attractions. Open *07.00–22.30 daily*.

Brocks Hill Country Park & Environment Centre Washbrook Lane, Oadby (0116 271 4514; www.oadby-wigston.gov.uk). Unique environment centre built to demonstrate wind and solar power, photovoltaics, rainwater recycling and sewerage composting. Set in 67 acres of newly planted Country Park with woodland, meadowland and an arboretum. Café and disabled access. Park *open all year* and Centre *open Mon–Fri 10.00–17.00; Sat, Sun and B Hols 10.00–16.00*. Free. Although a 2½ mile walk north along footpath from Clifton Bridge (85) and then via A5199 and B582, a visit to the Centre makes a very worthwhile day out.

Kilby Bridge

Leics. PO, tel.

Wistan Le Dale Model Village Wistow Garden Centre, Wistow, nr Great Glen (0116 259 2009). Take the footpath south from Ivy Bridge (78) to the church. Acclaimed model village (setting for the children's storybook *Tales from Old Wistan*), ¹⁄₁₈th scale, mid-Victorian period. Village railway. Also craft shop, artists' studios, teashop serving lunches, teas and coffee, garden centre and village store. *Open daily except Tue.*
    Donations to Rainbow, a children's hospice charity.

South Wigston

Leics. PO, tel, stores, garage. Wigston is now part of Leicester, but traces of its earlier independence can still be found. Much of the handsome church dates from the 14th C, especially the interior, while the cottages in Spa Lane, with their long strips of upper window, indicate an old Leicester industry, stocking making. At Wigston Parva there is a tiny Norman church and a monument to the Roman town of Veronae. Unfortunately, only housing estates and a school can be seen from the canal, but exploration is worthwhile.

Wigston Framework Knitters Museum 42/44 Bushloe End, Wigston (0116 288 3396). About ½ mile north of Kilby Bridge (87). Heritage award winning 18th-C knitters house and workshop. Demonstrations. Refreshments. *Open every Sun, first Sat of month and B Hol Mon (except Xmas and New Year) 14.00–17.00.* Charge.

Blaby

Leics. PO, tel, stores, garage. The church is partly 14th-C, with a fine 18th-C gallery unsuited to the Blaby of today. The County Arms, a monumental 1930s roadhouse beside bridge 98, is more in keeping.

WALKING & CYCLING
The navigation from Blaby into Leicester runs through a linear country park and mostly parallels the off-road cycleway along the old Grand Central trackbed. It is covered in three sections by a detailed series of leaflets, entitled *Discover Leicester's Riverside Park*, and available from Tourist Information Centres in the area. Both the towpath and the cycleway offer excellent walking and cycling opportunities. Throughout the city itself there is a series of well-marked cycle routes using coloured banding.

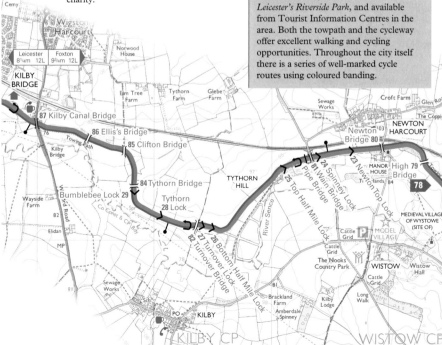

Aylestone

Following the River Sence to its junction with the Soar, the canal makes a wide swing around Glen Parva and then flows north into Leicester along the Soar valley. After Glen Parva the buildings suddenly cease, and there follows a mile of pleasant rural canal, lightly wooded to the east, and the extensive water meadows of the Soar to the west. The river and canal flow side by side separated only by the towpath; inevitably in winter this can cause flooding, *and anyone intending to navigate this stretch after heavy rainfall should check the state of the water before proceeding.* Only the pylons and the distant views of Braunstone and Aylestone reveal the closeness of Leicester. The canal and the Soar meet by the old gasworks where there is a huge weir; care is needed during times of flood. The canal enters Leicester along a pleasant cutting. A variety of buildings line the banks and there is a fine canalside walk under the ornamental bridges that lead straight into the town centre by West Bridge. These factors combine to make the canal entry to Leicester outstanding among large towns. The A46 and A426 run parallel to the canal, but the railway which follows it, the old Great Central line, is now closed.

NAVIGATIONAL NOTES

The canal and the River Soar meet just above Freeman's Meadow Lock, where there is an enormous unprotected weir. Care is needed, especially in time of flood. KEEP WELL OVER TO THE TOWPATH SIDE.

Glen Parva
Leics. Suburb of Leicester inseparable now from the main town. Curiously enough there was a Saxon cemetery in the town from which 6th-C grave ornaments have been excavated.

Aylestone
Leics. PO, tel, stores, takeaways, chemist, bank, garage. A Leicester suburb coming down to the east bank of the canal. The church contains an interesting stained-glass window of 1930. To the west of the canal the Soar is crossed by an old stone packhorse bridge of eight low arches, perhaps dating from the 15th C. This area still retains the feel of a country village, at least in the area sandwiched between the main Rugby road and the navigation. Narrow streets, bordered by pretty brick cottages, isolate the walker from the bustle of what is otherwise a busy suburb of Leicester. Aylestone Hall and its surrounding gardens and recreational park is a particular haven of peace. On the west of the waterway Aylestone Meadows is now a nature reserve stretching for 1¹/2 miles along the canal and Great Central Way (once the route of the Great Central Railway and now a cycle route and footpath). There are waymarked circular walks along a network of paths together with excellent illustrated interpretation boards. The nature reserve is operated by Leicester City Council who employ rangers who patrol the riverside on motorcycles and can provide advice and assistance. Access for shops and the Union Inn is east from Freestone Bridge (106). There is also a useful farm shop between Packhorse Bridge (105) and the railway bridge.
Traveline (0870 6082608). For full details on bus travel to local (and not so local) attractions. *Open 07.00–22.30 daily.*
Gas Museum National Gas Museum Trust, 195 Aylestone Road, Leicester (0116 250 3190). Situated in the Victorian gatehouse of one of the city's gas works: the first museum to tell the story of the impact of gas on our lives from 19th-C lighting to a gas hairdryer and radio. *Open Tue–Thur 12.00–16.30 (closed Xmas–New Year's Day).* Free. Disabled access to ground floor.
Raw Dykes Ancient Monument Aylestone Road, Leicester (0116 247 3021). A large earthwork near to the canal and River Soar; presumed to be a Romano-British aqueduct. Viewing area *open at all times.* Disabled access.

TO DYE – THE DEATH

For nearly two decades the appearance of the combined River Soar and canal skirting Aylestone – and along the Mile Straight, bordering the city itself – was of an inky, opaque blackness far removed from the image of a burbling, infant stream. This off-putting and unnatural phenomenon served only to reinforce the perception that Leicester was not a city to linger in. In reality the cause was trade effluent from several dye works, established in Wigston since the year dot, passing straight through the local sewerage treatment works. New legislation, however, imposed colour conditions on discharges amounting to full colour removal: a real challenge for the fledgling Environment Agency's hard-pressed chemists. Yet what remained was the puzzle of the problem's relatively recent origins. One plausible explanation lay in the changing nature of the fashion industry. Once, ostensibly, buyer-led (we responded to the length of a skirt or the cut of a suit) our sartorial whims became firmly orchestrated by the industry itself, colour consistently being its key device. In unison went a definite movement towards man-made fibres and their reactive dye processes; bright colours predominated in wardrobes, their turgid residues lingered in rivers.

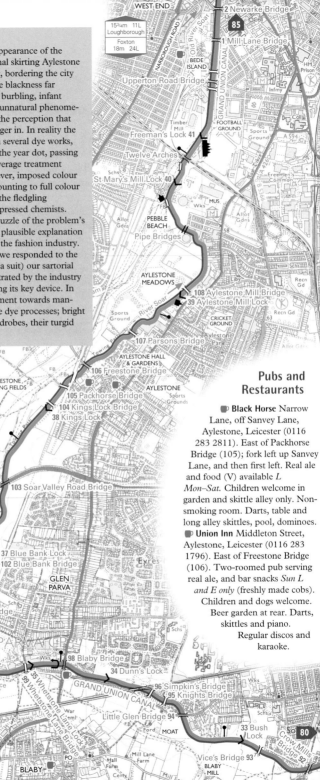

Pubs and Restaurants

🍺 **Black Horse** Narrow Lane, off Sanvey Lane, Aylestone, Leicester (0116 283 2811). East of Packhorse Bridge (105); fork left up Sanvey Lane, and then first left. Real ale and food (V) available *L Mon–Sat*. Children welcome in garden and skittle alley only. Non-smoking room. Darts, table and long alley skittles, pool, dominoes.

🍺 **Union Inn** Middleton Street, Aylestone, Leicester (0116 283 1796). East of Freestone Bridge (106). Two-roomed pub serving real ale, and bar snacks *Sun L and E only* (freshly made cobs). Children and dogs welcome. Beer garden at rear. Darts, skittles and piano. Regular discos and karaoke.

Leicester

For almost all of its journey through the city of Leicester, the navigation pursues a course quite separate from the river, the navigation having been rebuilt towards the end of the 19th C as part of Leicester's flood prevention scheme. For more than 1/2 mile south of West Bridge, the navigation, a section known locally as the Mile Straight, is like a formal avenue, tree-lined and crossed by several ornamental iron bridges, but where it curves under the old Great Central Railway it begins to follow a less public course through the nether regions of Leicester. A combination of locks, once-derelict canal basins (some now restored for moorings), tall factory buildings and a substantial stretch of parkland adds up to a stretch of urban canal that offers a greater variety of interest than exists in most other cities. At Belgrave Lock the canal joins the Soar, which proceeds to meander carelessly through the city's outskirts. The city centre is remarkably compact, and there are some gems amongst the façades jostled together along its main thoroughfares, with everything surprisingly close to the moorings at Castle Gardens. As is the case with all large towns, if you moor at an unprotected site make sure your boat is securely locked if you leave it unattended. Birstall provides a useful mooring and place to shop to the north of the city: tie up near the lock and walk up beside the White Horse.

NAVIGATIONAL NOTES

It is worth remembering that the River Soar may flood at any time, so boaters travelling after heavy rainfall should enquire about the navigational conditions in advance in order to avert the risk of running aground in the middle of a water meadow.

● **Leicester**
All services. A prosperous city with two universities. Fortunes were founded on the hosiery and the boot and shoe trades, but now a variety of light industries flourish in Leicester. There are a great many things to see, for this was the Roman town of Ratae and there is plenty of evidence of the Roman buildings, plus a castle that dates from 1088, with the delightful church of St Mary de Castro next to it. The travel agent Thomas Cook started business in Leicester; in 1841 he organised the first publicly advertised excursion by train. It was a great success, and Cook made the organising of such trips a regular occupation. Leicester has a particularly good selection of museums, and it is fortunate that most of these are near the Grand Union Canal which forms the western boundary of Castle Park. The city should be commended, both for the comprehensive manner in which it markets its copious wealth of attractions and for promoting its cultural diversity in such a positive fashion. The opportunities to sample Asian cuisine, produce, jewellery, cloth, faith and festivals must be second to none outside the Indian sub-continent and could, alone, fill this page. With the provision of secure visitor moorings at Castle Gardens boaters have no reason to ignore a city that has so much to offer.

Abbey Park Abbey Park Road, Leicester. All that remains of the abbey is a mansion built from the ruins and the old stone wall surrounding the grounds. Cardinal Wolsey was buried here in 1530. The park itself, very much in the Victorian mould, has a boating lake, Chinese garden, bandstand and riverside café and is the setting for music festivals and fairs. There is a landing stage in Abbey Park Basin. *Open daily.*
Abbey Pumping Station Corporation Road, Abbey Lane, Leicester (0116 252 7258). Dating from 1891 this refurbished site features the Victorian steam-powered beam engines that used to pump the city's sewerage to the nearby treatment plant. Also a unique public health exhibition and the manager's house c. World War II. *Open Mon–Sat 10.00–17.30, Sun 14.00–17.30. Closed G Fri, Xmas Day and Boxing Day.* Free. Partial disabled access. Moorings.
Belgrave Hall and Gardens Church Road, Belgrave, Leicester (0116 266 6590; www. leicestermuseums.ac.uk). Three-storey Queen Anne house dating from 1709 with attractive period and botanical gardens, and 18th- and 19th-C room settings including kitchen, drawing room and nursery. *Open Mon–Sat 10.00–17.30, Sun 14.00–17.30. Closed G Fri, Xmas Day and Boxing Day.* Free. Disabled access to gardens and ground floor only. Moorings.

Boatyards

Ⓑ **Nimbus Narrowboats** (Mill Lane Boatyard), Thurmaston (0116 269 3069). 🚽 🚻 ♿ D Slipway, gas, boat sales and repairs, overnight mooring, chandlery, engine sales and repairs, boat fitting out, DIY facilities, books, maps and gifts, toilets.

Ⓑ **Raynsway Marine** Pinfold Road, Thurmaston, Leicester (0116 260 6166). 🚽 🚻 ♿ D E Pump out, gas, overnight mooring, long-term mooring, slipway, crane, boat repairs, solid fuel, laundrette, toilets, showers. *Emergency call out.*

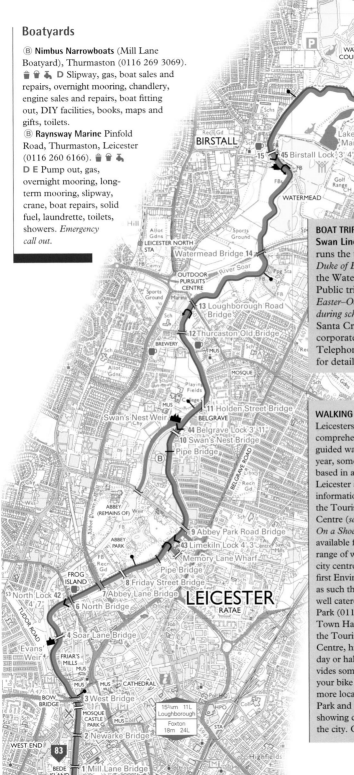

BOAT TRIPS

Swan Line Cruisers Ltd runs the trip boat *The Duke of Bridgewater* from the Waterside Centre. Public trips *Sun, Easter–Oct; Tue and Thur during school holidays.* Also Santa Cruises in Dec and corporate/private events. Telephone 0116 2512334 for details.

WALKING & CYCLING

Leicestershire offers a comprehensive range of guided walks throughout the year, some of which are based in and around the Leicester area. Further information is available from the Tourist Information Centre (*see* page 87). The *On a Shoestring* leaflet (also available from TIC) details a range of walks close to the city centre. Leicester was the first Environment City and as such the cyclist is very well catered for. The Bike Park (0116 299 1234) in Town Hall Square, opposite the Tourist Information Centre, hires bicycles by the day or half day and also pro-vides somewhere to leave your bike while you explore more locally. Both the Bike Park and the TIC have maps showing cycle routes around the city. Charge.

Castle Gardens & Castle Motte Riverside between St Nicholas Circle and The Newarke. Once a low-lying marshy area of reeds and willows, it was drained in the late 19th C as part of the city's flood alleviation scheme and initially used as allotments. The public gardens were established in 1926. The raised mound, or motte, dates from the 11th C and would originally have been surmounted by a timber fortification. Garden *open daily during daylight hours and as an access for boaters to secure moorings.*

Cathedral Guildhall Lane, Leicester (0116 210 9893). Originally the parish church of St Martin's, it was extended in the 14th and 15th C, restored in the 19th C and became the cathedral in 1927. *Open daily.* Donations. Disabled toilets.

De Montfort Hall Granville Road, Leicester (0116 233 3111). Prime venue for touring opera and ballet companies and for orchestras and soloist alike.

Eco House Western Park, Hinckley Road, Leicester (0116 285 6675/4047). Environment-friendly show home featuring energy-efficient, sustainable living with emphasis on renewable energy, organic garden, water conservation and health. Playground, shop and refreshments. *Open all year, Wed–Fri 14.00–17.00, weekends 10.00–17.00.* Free. Buses every 10 mins from High Street – numbers 16, 63, 64, 152, 153, 157, 158.

Golden Mile An area centred on Belgrave Road, to the north of the city centre, where the focus lies on the superb range of Asian cultural delights and cuisine, reflecting Leicester's status as a truly cosmopolitan city. Excellent guide entitled *A Taste of Asia* available from Tourist Information Centre (*see* page 87). Free.

Guildhall Guildhall Lane, Leicester (0116 253 2569). Built by the Guild of Corpus Christi and dating from the 14th C, it contains fine oak panelling and an elaborately carved chimney-piece from 1637. It includes the Old Town Library, 19th-C police cells and a Great Hall with civic murals. *Open Mon–Sat 10.00–17.30, Sun 14.00–17.30. Closed G Fri, Xmas Day and Boxing Day.* Free. Disabled toilets.

Guru Nanak Gurdwara & Sikh Museum 9 Holy Bones, Leicester (0116 262 8606). An impressive Sikh Temple in a transformed hosiery factory. Also spectacular models of shrines, manuscripts, paintings, coins, photographic portrayal of the part played by Sikh soldiers in both World Wars in a museum depicting the history of the Sikh nation. *Open to devotees daily.* Museum *open Thur 13.00–16.00. Other times by appointment.* Free.

Haymarket Theatre Belgrave Gate, Leicester (0116 253 9797). Venue for hit shows bound for the West End, with the emphasis on musicals. Also hard-hitting modern drama and the classics. **Studio Theatre** is home to more avant garde productions. Café and bar.

Jain Centre 32 Oxford Street, Leicester (0116 254 3091). A fine example of traditional Indian architecture in the western world and a place of pilgrimage for Jains. Shrines of white marble, hand-carved pillars, stained glass, mirror walls, a dome and ceilings in sandstone. *Open Mon–Sat 09.00–20.00.* Donations appreciated.

Jewry Wall Museum St Nicholas Circle, Leicester (0116 247 3021). Collection of the county's archaeology from early times through to the Middle Ages overlooking the Jewry Wall, a small portion of which remains. This is thought to have been part of a basilica or Roman baths dating from the 2nd C. Two Roman mosaic pavements can be seen *in situ. Open Mon–Sat 10.00–17.30, Sun 14.00–17.30. Closed G Fri, Xmas Day and Boxing Day.* Free. Disabled access (and toilet) via entrance in Holy Bones.

Little Theatre Dover Street, Leicester (0116 255 1302; www.thelittletheatre.net). Amateur dramatics, social activities and theatre workshops.

Markets Market Place, Leicester (0116 252 6776). The Food Hall, selling fresh meat, poultry, dairy produce and fish from all over the world, is *open Tue–Sat 06.30–18.00.* The retail market, composed of over 300 covered stalls, is *open Mon–Sat 07.00–18.00.*

New Walk Museum & Art Gallery New Walk, Leicester (0116 255 4100). Italian, Spanish and Flemish old masters. 18th–20th C English paintings. Also French Impressionists and German Expressionists, ceramics, silver, archives, natural history and geology. *Open Mon–Sat 10.00–17.30, Sun 14.00–17.30. Closed G Fri, Xmas Day and Boxing Day.* Free. Disabled access.

National Space Centre Exploration Drive, Leicester (0870 6077223; www.spacecentre.co.uk). The opportunity to explore many facets of space travel, to meet the furthest reaches of our universe face to face and to interact with both science fact and science fiction. Boosters Restaurant and Satellite Bar. Full disabled facilities. *Open Tue–Sun and B Hols 09.30–16.30; Mon 12.00–16.30 during school holidays only.* Charge. Frequent bus service (no 54) to Abbey Lane.

Newarke Houses Museum The Newarke, Leicester (0116 247 3222; www.leicestermuseums.ac.uk). The social history of the area from 1500 to the present day. Locally made clocks and a clockmaker's workshop. Also shows the history of the hosiery, costume and lace industries. There is a reconstructed Victorian street scene. *Open Mon–Sat 10.00–17.30, Sun 14.00–17.30. Closed G Fri, Xmas Day and Boxing Day.* Free. Disabled access difficult.

Phoenix Arts Centre Newarke Street, Leicester (0116 255 4854). Cinema and live performances of contemporary dance, mime, jazz and folk. Café serving a varied menu *L and E.*

Royal Infirmary Museum Knighton Street Nurses Home, Royal Infirmary, Leicester (01858 565532). History of the Infirmary from 1771 including medical and surgical equipment. *Open Tue and Wed 12.00–14.00.* Donations appreciated.

Shires Shopping Centre High Street, Leicester (0116 251 2461). All the usual big name (and not so big) stores under one high, glass-arched roof plus cafés, pizzeria and gelateria. *Open Mon, Tue, Thur and Fri 09.00–17.30, Wed 09.00–20.00, Sat 09.00–18.00, B Hols 10.00–17.00.* Disabled access.

St Martins Square & Loseby Lane Between Cank Street and Silver Street, Leicester (0116 253 8247). Speciality shopping centre in the heart of the city. Food, fashion, wine and flowers amongst which to browse placidly, take in some street entertainment or simply unwind. Most shops *open Mon–Sat 09.00–17.00.*

St Mary de Castro Castle Yard, Leicester. Founded in 1107 with excellent examples of Norman glass, stone and wood carving. Henry VI was knighted here in 1426 and Geoffrey Chaucer was probably married here.

St Nicholas Church St Nicholas Circle, Leicester. The oldest church in the city, dating back to Anglo-Saxon times, and retaining examples of Saxon construction and Roman brickwork in the tower. *Open for services.*

Wygston's House Museum of Costume 12 Applegate, St Nicholas Circle, Leicester (0116 247 3056).

'Y' Theatre YMCA East Street, Leicester (0116 255 6507). A mixed programme of largely local productions.

Tourist Information Centre Every Street, Town Hall Square, Leicester (0116 299 8888; www.discoverleicester.com). *Open Mon 10.00–17.30, Tue–Fri 09.00–17.30, Sat 09.00–17.00, B Hols and Sun during summer 10.00–16.00.* Leicestershire also offers a comprehensive range of guided walks throughout the year, some of which are based in the Leicester area. Contact the TIC for further details.

● **Thurmaston**
Leics. PO, tel, stores, garage. This unexciting suburb stretches along the Roman road, the old Fosse Way, now bypassed by a dual carriageway. However, the opportunity thus afforded to Thurmaston has not been exploited. Evidence of Roman habitation was discovered in 1955, when excavation of an Anglo-Saxon cemetery brought to light 95 urns dating from 50 years after Julius Caesar's invasion.

Pubs and Restaurants

In a large city such as Leicester there is a wide range of pubs and restaurants to choose from; those listed are close to the waterway.

🍺 **The Vaults** 1 Wellington Street, Leicester (0116 255 5506; www.the-vaults.co.uk). Friendly, welcoming cellar bar dispensing a wide and ever-changing range of real ales from micro-breweries. Also a range of real ciders. No children. Live music *Sat and Sun.*

🍺 **The Hat & Beaver** 60 Highcross Street (off High Street), Leicester (0116 262 2157). Close to the Shires shopping centre, a basic and friendly pub serving real ale and good bar snacks *L Mon–Sat.* Children welcome. Beer garden and pub games.

🍺 **Voodoo Bar** 29 Market Street, Leicester (0116 255 6877). Bar with a James Bond theme serving real ale and food (V) *12.00–18.00 (not Sun).* Also a downstairs bar *open until midnight.* No children. Outside seating. Guest DJs *Thur–Sat.*

🍺 **The Salmon** 19 Butt Close Lane, Leicester (0116 253 2301). Near to St Margaret's bus station, a friendly brewery pub serving real ale and food *L, daily.* Children welcome. Beer garden.

🍺 **The Northbridge Tavern** 1 Frog Island, Leicester (0116 251 2508). Canalside at North Lock. Busy, wood-panelled bars dispensing real ale. Food (V) *all day, every day.* Children and dogs welcome. Beer garden and pub games.

✕♀ **Altoco** St Martins Square, Leicester (0116 253 3977). Stylish pizza and pasta house offering good value meals. *Open Mon–Sat L 12.00–14.30 and E 18.00–22.30 (closes 23.00 Fri–Sat). Closed Sun.*

✕♀ **Golden Mile** Consult *A Taste of Asia* (see opposite under Golden Mile) for a wide-ranging selection of excitingly different and authentic eating experiences. This is a detailed and comprehensive selection numbering nearly 30 establishments.

🍺 **The White Horse** White Horse Lane, off Front Street, Birstall, Leicester (0116 267 4490). Large, friendly, riverside pub serving real ale. A wide variety of grills, snacks and meals (V) available *L and E (not Sun E).* Children welcome in eating areas. Garden. Quiz *Tue* and karaoke *fortnightly, on Sat.* Darts, dominoes and cards. Moorings. Close to Watermead Country Park.

Mountsorrel

North of Thurmaston the canal leaves the river and heads north through an area scarred by busy gravel workings. Just beyond the boatyard, the River Wreake flows in from the north east; the name of the nearby boatyard and the next lock hints at the significance of this little river. The River Soar rejoins the canal by Cossington Lock. The villages of Cossington and Rothley are one mile away from Cossington Lock, on opposite sides of the Soar. The Rothley Brook joins the canal north of the lock. At Sileby Lock is another water mill. There has been a mill here since 1608 and the present building has been restored as a private residence. From here it is a short distance to Mountsorrel. The lock here is very much a waterways showplace, and the extensive moorings and lockside pub make it a busy one.

● **Rothley**
Leics. PO, tel, stores, garage. Lies in the valley of the Rothley Brook which runs to the south of the village and through the grounds of Rothley Temple, once a preceptory for the Knights Templar. In the churchyard is a tall Anglo-Saxon cross, thought to be over 1000 years old.

● **Cossington**
Leics. Tel. A mile east of Cossington Lock, this is a pretty village with wide, well-kept grass verges and plenty of trees.

● **Sileby**
Leics. PO, tel, stores, takeaways, garage, chemist, bank, station. Once a thriving community based around hosiery manufacture, this large village is much swollen by dormitory housing for neighbouring Leicester and Loughborough.

● **Mountsorrel**
Leics. PO, tel, stores, takeaway, off-licence, garage. It is but a few yards from the lock here to the centre of the village with its long main street. **Traveline** (0870 6082608). *Open 07.00–22.30.* For full details on bus travel to local (and not so local) attractions.

The Melton Mowbray Navigation & the Oakham Canal This waterway was opened in 1797 as a broadlocked river navigation from the canal north of Syston to Melton Mowbray, 15 miles away to the east. Beyond Melton the Oakham Canal, constructed in 1802, extended the navigation as far as Oakham, in Rutland. When the railways were built the two waterways could not compete and the Oakham Canal was closed as early as 1841. More than a century later, some lengths still hold water; in other places the former canal bed is only a faint depression. The Melton Mowbray Navigation was closed to traffic in 1877.

Stonehurst Family Farm and Museum Loughborough Road, Mountsorrel (01509 413216; www.farm18.fsnet.co.uk). A chance to see a working farm, a museum of memorabilia and old cars, and for children to cuddle and stroke small animals. Teashop serving light lunches and cream teas. Farm shop selling fresh produce, home-made bread and preserves. *Open daily 09.30–17.00.* Charge. Shop and tearoom *open all year.* Disabled visitors telephone for assistance.

Boatyards

Ⓑ **L.R. Harris & Son** Old Junction Boatyard, Meadow Lane, Syston (0116 269 2135). 🛶 🏠 ⛽ Gas, overnight and long-term mooring, chandlery and extensive spares, slipway, winter storage, boat sales and repairs, boat building and fit outs, inboard and outboard engines sales and repairs, welding specialists, toilets and showers. *Emergency call out.*

Ⓑ **Sileby Mill Boatyard** Mill Lane, Sileby (01509 813583; www.silebymill.co.uk). 🛶 🏠 ⛽ D E Pump out, gas, narrowboat hire, day-craft hire, overnight mooring, long-term mooring, winter storage, slipway, boat sales and repairs, engineering, welding and structural repairs, wooden boat repair specialists, chandlery, engine sales and repairs, solid fuel, books, maps and gifts, ice creams, toilets, showers.

Ⓑ **Meadow Farm Marina** Huston Close, Barrow upon Soar (01509 812215/816035) 🛶 🏠 ⛽ D Pump out, gas, free visitor moorings, long-term mooring (20–60ft boats), slipway, crane, boat sales, toilets, showers. Private club for moorers. Disabled facilities.

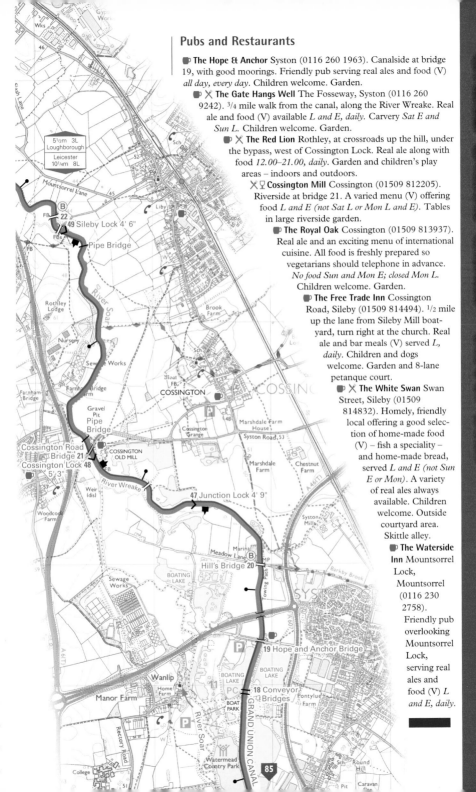

Pubs and Restaurants

🍺 **The Hope & Anchor** Syston (0116 260 1963). Canalside at bridge 19, with good moorings. Friendly pub serving real ales and food (V) *all day, every day*. Children welcome. Garden.

🍺 ✕ **The Gate Hangs Well** The Fosseway, Syston (0116 260 9242). ³/₄ mile walk from the canal, along the River Wreake. Real ale and food (V) available *L and E, daily*. Carvery *Sat E and Sun L*. Children welcome. Garden.

🍺 ✕ **The Red Lion** Rothley, at crossroads up the hill, under the bypass, west of Cossington Lock. Real ale along with food *12.00–21.00, daily*. Garden and children's play areas – indoors and outdoors.

✕ ♀ **Cossington Mill** Cossington (01509 812205). Riverside at bridge 21. A varied menu (V) offering food *L and E (not Sat L or Mon L and E)*. Tables in large riverside garden.

🍺 **The Royal Oak** Cossington (01509 813937). Real ale and an exciting menu of international cuisine. All food is freshly prepared so vegetarians should telephone in advance. *No food Sun and Mon E; closed Mon L*. Children welcome. Garden.

🍺 **The Free Trade Inn** Cossington Road, Sileby (01509 814494). ¹/₂ mile up the lane from Sileby Mill boat-yard, turn right at the church. Real ale and bar meals (V) served *L, daily*. Children and dogs welcome. Garden and 8-lane petanque court.

🍺 ✕ **The White Swan** Swan Street, Sileby (01509 814832). Homely, friendly local offering a good selection of home-made food (V) – fish a speciality – and home-made bread, served *L and E (not Sun E or Mon)*. A variety of real ales always available. Children welcome. Outside courtyard area. Skittle alley.

🍺 **The Waterside Inn** Mountsorrel Lock, Mountsorrel (0116 230 2758). Friendly pub overlooking Mountsorrel Lock, serving real ales and food (V) *L and E, daily*.

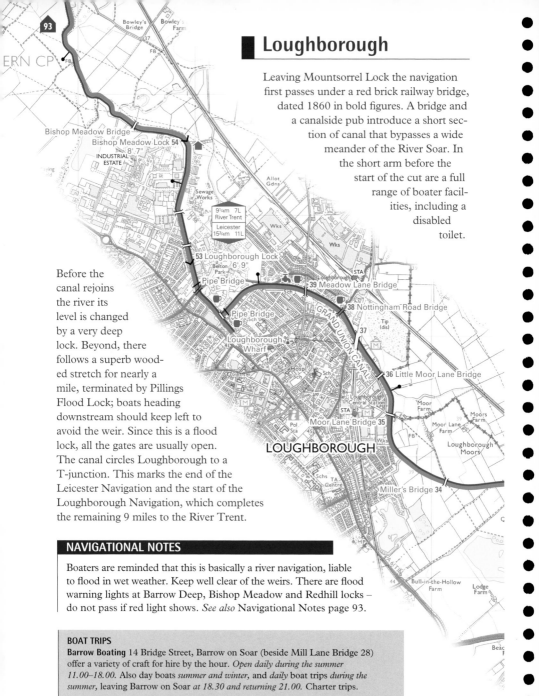

Loughborough

Leaving Mountsorrel Lock the navigation first passes under a red brick railway bridge, dated 1860 in bold figures. A bridge and a canalside pub introduce a short section of canal that bypasses a wide meander of the River Soar. In the short arm before the start of the cut are a full range of boater facilities, including a disabled toilet.

Before the canal rejoins the river its level is changed by a very deep lock. Beyond, there follows a superb wooded stretch for nearly a mile, terminated by Pillings Flood Lock; boats heading downstream should keep left to avoid the weir. Since this is a flood lock, all the gates are usually open. The canal circles Loughborough to a T-junction. This marks the end of the Leicester Navigation and the start of the Loughborough Navigation, which completes the remaining 9 miles to the River Trent.

NAVIGATIONAL NOTES

Boaters are reminded that this is basically a river navigation, liable to flood in wet weather. Keep well clear of the weirs. There are flood warning lights at Barrow Deep, Bishop Meadow and Redhill locks – do not pass if red light shows. *See also* Navigational Notes page 93.

BOAT TRIPS
Barrow Boating 14 Bridge Street, Barrow on Soar (beside Mill Lane Bridge 28) offer a variety of craft for hire by the hour. *Open daily during the summer 11.00–18.00. Also day boats summer and winter, and daily boat trips during the summer,* leaving Barrow on Soar *at 18.30 and returning 21.00.* Charter trips.

● **Loughborough**
Leics. All services (including laundrette). A busy industrial town. There is a bric-a-brac market held in the Queens Hall, Granby Street *every Fri.*

Bell Foundry Museum Freehold Street, Nottingham Road, Loughborough (01509 233414; www.taylorbells.co.uk). South of bridge 38. Gift shop. Partial disabled access. *Open*

Tue–Sat 10.00–12.30 and 13.30–16.30. Tour of works first Sun of month 14.00 (advanced bookings only). Charge.

Carillon & War Memorial Queens Park, Loughborough (01509 634704). *Open daily Good Fri–Sep 14.00–18.00.* Carillon recitals *Sun and B Hols 15.30, and Thur 13.00.* Charge.

Charnwood Museum Queen's Park, Granby Street, Loughborough (01509 233754; www.leicestershire.gov.uk/museums). Find out how different groups of people have contributed to life in Charnwood over the past 4000 years; discover more about the area's natural world; how the land has nurtured its inhabitants and how they, in turn, have earned a living. Gift shop and café with outdoor patio. *Open Mon–Sat 10.00–16.30, Sun 14.00–17.00.* Free. Full disabled access.

Great Central Railway Great Central Road, Loughborough (01509 230726; www.gcrailway. co.uk). South of bridge 36. 8 miles of preserved main line taking you back to the days of express steam haulage. *Open weekends and B Hols throughout the year and daily Jun–Sep.* Charge. Telephone for details of special events.

Tourist Information Centre John Storer House, Wards End, Loughborough (01509 218113; www.leicestershire.gov.uk).

Pubs and Restaurants

🍺 **The Navigation** Mill Lane, Barrow on Soar (01509 412842). Traditional, canalside country pub, with a copper-topped bar made from old pennies and halfpennies, dispensing real ales and home-cooked food (V) *L, daily.* Well-behaved children and dogs welcome.

🍺 **The Soar Bridge Inn** Barrow on Soar (01509 412686). Near Barrow Deep Lock. Real ale and food (V) available *L and E, daily.* Children welcome. Garden. Pianist or jazz band *Sun L.*

🍺 ✕ **The Riverside** Barrow on Soar (01509 412260). Riverside, below Barrow Deep Lock. A selection of real ales and food (V) served *L and E, daily.* Pizzas and pasta are specialities. Children and dogs welcome. Large lawn and children's play area.

🍺 **The Boat** Meadow Lane, Loughborough (01509 214578). Real ale and food (V) served *L and E, daily.* Children welcome *before 21.00.* Canalside seating. Quiz *Sun. Shops, takeaway, station and PO nearby.*

🍺 **The Swan in the Rushes** 21 The Rushes, Loughborough (01509 217014). A genuine, real ale pub with a friendly atmosphere serving home-made food (V) prepared from fresh ingredients *L and E (not Sat and Sun E).* An excellent combination of British and international cuisine. Draught cider. Children and dogs welcome. Non-smoking dining room. Outside seating. Skittle alley. Folk club *fortnightly on Sun.* Open-mike acoustic night *every other Thur.* Disabled access. B & B.

🍺 **The Three Nuns** 30 Churchgate, Loughborough (01509 611989; www.threenuns.co.uk). Warm, friendly traditional pub serving a range of real ales and home-made food (V) *L and E Mon–Thur.* Breakfast available *Sat 09.00–11.00.* Children welcome. Outside seating. Classic rock music *Sat.* Disabled access.

🍺 **The Albion Inn** Canal Bank, Loughborough (01509 213952). 1/4 mile north of Loughborough Wharf. Traditional, unspoilt canalside pub serving real ale and home-made food (V) *L and E (18.00–20.00) daily.* Well-behaved children and dogs welcome. Canalside seating and pub games.

Kegworth

The Loughborough Navigation has the same physical characteristics as the Leicester Navigation. It continues the fall towards the Trent with the same pattern of meandering river reaches and the occasional canal cut, with locks bypassing the weirs. Normanton on Soar is visible some way away because of its prominent church steeple; on approaching, one finds the church is only a matter of yards from the river bank. However the inhabitants of Normanton guard their waterfront jealously, making it extremely difficult to get ashore. Below Normanton is the settlement of Zouch which has a certain weary and less conventional charm, easier access and more facilities. At Devil's Elbow boats heading downstream should keep right to stay in the main navigation channel. At the point where the A6 and the Soar almost touch there is a riverside pub and a boatyard. North of the pub a willow-lined reach leads to a stone mansion with spreading lawns where the channel divides. To the left (nearer Kegworth) is a maze of shallow and weedy backwaters, weirs and a water mill; boats should keep to the right for Kegworth Deep Lock where a new lock has been constructed beside the old as part of a flood prevention scheme. After another sharp swing to the north the channel divides again, and northbound boats should once more bear right for Kegworth Shallow Lock.

- **Whatton House**
Visible from the river near the Devil's Elbow, this mansion was built about 1802, damaged by fire and restored in 1876. Its fine 25-acre gardens are *open summer, Sun 14.00–18.00.* Charge.
- **Normanton on Soar**
Notts. A quiet and carefully preserved village with wide grass verges and some discreetly pretty buildings. The cruciform church has a central tower and spire, rare in so small a church. On the east wall of the nave there are some excellent stone carvings; the centre one is an elaborate coat of arms with a quizzical lion in the middle. The plain glass windows make the church enjoyably light. A ferry here once again links Nottinghamshire to Leicestershire.
- **Kegworth**
Leics. PO, tel, stores, chemist, takeaways. Kegworth has an attractive situation up on a wooded hill

that is crowned by the church spire, but although it is close to the river, access is easy only from Kegworth Shallow Lock.
Kegworth Museum 52 High Street, Kegworth (01509 672886; www.leicestershire.gov.uk/museums). Award-winning displays include Victorian parlour, local school, saddlers, knitting industry, Royal British Legion war memorabilia and local transport history. *Open Easter–Sep, Sun, Wed and B Hol Mon 14.00–17.00.* Small charge.
- **Kingston on Soar**
Notts. Tel. Situated east of the railway embankment, this is a small quiet estate village which looks much as it must have done 50 years ago. The church, still very much the focus of the village, is a pretty building dating from 1900.

Boatyards

- Ⓑ **East Midlands Boat Services** London Road, Kegworth (01509 672385). 🚿 ⚓ D Pump out, gas, overnight mooring, long-term mooring, slipway, winter storage, boat sales and repairs, engine sales and repairs, chandlery, DIY facilities. *Emergency call out.*
- Ⓑ **Bridgefields Boatyard** Bridgefields, Kegworth (01509 672084/07779 997024;

johnlillie@btinternet.com). ⚓ D Long-term mooring, boat repairs, engine repairs and sales, boat fitting out. Incorporating Riverview Narrowboats – boat building.
- Ⓑ **Kegworth Marine** Kingston Lane, Kegworth (01509 672300). ⚓ D Day-hire craft, gas, long-term mooring, covered slipway, boat and engine repairs, DIY facilities, wet dock (60ft).

Pubs and Restaurants

🍺 ✕ **The Plough** Normanton on Soar (01509 842228; www. probablythebestpubsintheworld.com). High-class pub and restaurant with both traditional British and Mediterranean influences, serving food *all day, every day*. Real ale. Children and dogs (not in restaurant) welcome. Waterside seating. Moorings.

🍺 **The Rose & Crown** Zouch (01509 842240). Canalside at Zouch Road Bridge. Family-run canalside pub serving a selection of real ales, good wines and home-made food (V) *L and E (all day in summer)*. Children and dogs (in the bar) welcome. Ad hoc music nights and speciality food nights including pig roasts and barbecues. Canalside seating. Mooring outside.

🍺 ✕ **The Otter** London Road, Kegworth (01509 680921). South of the village. Riverside pub serving real ale and traditional English food (V) *all day, 12.00–22.00*. Children welcome. Water-side garden and patio area. Theme nights throughout the year. Overnight moorings (with electricity) available by arrangement.

🍺 **The Anchor** Kegworth (01509 672722). Near Kegworth Shallow Lock. Traditional pub serving real ales and food (V) *L and E (not Sun–Wed E)*. *Sunday* lunches. Children and dogs (in bar only) welcome. Open fires and outside seating.

🍺 **The Cap & Stocking** Borough Street, Kegworth (01509 674814). Peaceful, comfortable village local featuring a very attractive summer garden and an interesting, international cuisine (V) served *L and E, daily*. Children and dogs welcome. Sun-trap conservatory and pétanque piste. Dominoes and cribbage.

🍺 **The Red Lion** High Street, Kegworth (01509 672466). Traditional village community pub dispensing a range of real ales, real cider and food (V) *L and E until 20.00 (not Sat E or Sun L and E)*. Children welcome *until 20.30* unless dining. Dogs welcome in bar. Large garden with play area. Log fires, garden, children's play area and traditional pub games.

✕ 🍷 **Cottage Restaurant** Kegworth (01509 672449). 500-year-old thatched cottage: one of the oldest buildings in the village. Freshly prepared food (V), inexpensively priced, together with a good wine selection. Children welcome. *Closed Sat L and all day Mon.*

NAVIGATIONAL NOTES

For boats heading north there is a new flood mooring scheme in operation at Normanton on Soar. If a red marker board and flashing light are displayed boats should tie up to the mooring dolphins ¼ mile south east of Zouch Road Bridge.

Ratcliffe on Soar

From Kegworth Shallow Lock to the Trent the navigation is somewhat more isolated, but two notable landmarks are the spire of Ratcliffe on Soar church and the eight cooling towers and vast chimney of the Ratcliffe Power Station that totally dominate the landscape for miles around. The navigation skirts round the west side of Red Hill. The last lock here has a well-painted bridge on which are shown the flood levels for 1955 and 1960, explaining the necessity for the flood prevention works. A few hundred yards below Red Hill Lock the Soar flows into the River Trent and loses its identity in this much bigger waterway.

NAVIGATIONAL NOTES

Boats negotiating the junction of the rivers Soar and Trent should keep well away from Thrumpton Weir, which is just east (downstream) of the big iron railway bridge. Navigators are reminded that the main line of the Trent Navigation is the Cranfleet Cut. This begins 200yds upstream of the mouth of the Soar, right by the large, wooden building which houses one of the many sailing clubs on the Trent. The entrance to the Erewash Canal is also here, marked by a lock and a cluster of buildings. If the warning light at Redhill Lock shows red – do not pass.

● **Ratcliffe on Soar**
Notts. Tel. A tiny village with a spired church dating from the 13th C. The interior of the nave is pleasantly uncluttered and rather spartan. There is no stained glass to darken it, and the white-washed walls accentuate the bold and ancient arches. In the chancel, on the other hand, there is a profusion of stone effigies and wall memorials, many of them to the Sacheverell family.

● **Trent Lock**
A busy and unusual boating centre at the southern terminus of the Erewash Canal (*see* page 61). There is a boatyard and two pubs here.

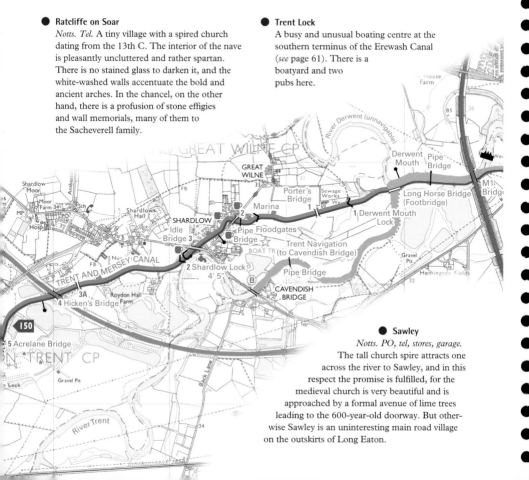

● **Sawley**
Notts. PO, tel, stores, garage.
The tall church spire attracts one across the river to Sawley, and in this respect the promise is fulfilled, for the medieval church is very beautiful and is approached by a formal avenue of lime trees leading to the 600-year-old doorway. But otherwise Sawley is an uninteresting main road village on the outskirts of Long Eaton.

61

Toton

Weir

Allot Gdns

Co Const

Wk's

Wilsthorpe

Trent College

Cemy

FB

EREWASH CANAL

Long Eaton Lock
6' 3"

LONG EATON

West Park
(Recn Gd)

Sch

Sch

Factory

P

Home Farm

FB

S Bend

P

Long Eaton Station

STA

Sheetstores Basin

New Sawley

Poplars

Derwent Mouth
2m 1L

Nottingham
10m 4L

Floodgate Sheetstore Farm

Trent Rifle Range

Cranfleet Lock 7' 9"

Footbridge

Narrow Bridge

CRANFLEET FARM

continued in Book 6

SAWLEY

Lane

CH

11¾ 15L
Langley Mill

TRENTLOCK

CRANFLEET CUT

Thrumpton

Church Farm

Grounds Farm

B

HARRINGTON BRIDGE

Trent Lock 8' 0"

SAILING CLUB

Weir

THRUMPTON PARK

Flood Lock

BOAT TRIPS

Lock

SAWLEY CUT

B

BW Office

Sawley Bridge Marina

Sawley Locks 6' 0"

Midshires Way

Earthwork

Const Bdy

Loughborough
9¼ 7L

Flood Lock

Thrumpton Weir

River Soar

REDHILL TUNNELS

RED HILL

WOOD HILL

POWER STATION

Lockington Grounds Farm

59 Redhill Lock
(floodlock)

B

Redhill Farm

Midshires Way

Grounds Farm Cottages

RATCLIFFE ON SOAR CP

Mason's Barn

CH

Warren Lane

Warren Farm

Ratcliffe Lane

58 Ratcliffe Lock

Weir

RATCLIFFE ON SOAR

24a

Barn Farm

Manor Farm

93

Sawley Cut

In addition to a large marina and a well-patronised BW mooring site, the Derby Motor Boat Club have a base on the Sawley Cut. All kinds of boats are represented here: canal boats, river boats and even seagoing vessels. It is certainly no place to be passing through on a *summer Sunday late-afternoon,* for there will be scores of craft queuing up to pass through the locks after spending the weekend downstream. There are windlasses for sale at Sawley Lock, as well as the more conventional facilities.

Boatyards

Ⓑ **Redhill Marine** Redhill Marina, Ratcliffe on Soar, Nottingham (01509 672770; www. redhill-marina.co.uk). 🛉 🔧 Gas, overnight and long-term mooring, winter storage, crane, slipway, hoist, boat sales and repairs, engine sales and repairs, boat refurbishment, chandlery, DIY facilities, toilets, café.

Ⓑ **Sawley Bridge Marina** Above Sawley Locks (0115 973 4278; www.sawleymarina.com). 🛉 🛒 🔧 ▫E Pump out, gas, narrowboat hire, day-hire boats, extensive moorings, two slipways, winter storage, 8-ton crane, chandlery, boat sales and repairs, engine sales and repairs, boat building and maintenance, books, maps and gifts, groceries, toilet, showers, telephone, solid fuel, laundrette, café and pub.

Ⓑ **Mills Dockyard** Trent Lock, Lock Lane, Long Eaton (0115 973 2595). Overnight and long-term mooring, winter storage, engine repairs, dry dock, wooden boat restoration and repairs, general boat maintenance, fitting out and repairs, houseboat construction.

WALKING & CYCLING

Once the River Trent is reached the towpath comes to an abrupt halt and there is no right of way along the south bank of the river. Originally there would probably have been a bridge here; more recently there was certainly a ferry. Walkers and cyclists will have to retrace their steps and make a detour (¼ mile north west of Ratcliffe Lock take the footpath south west and join the Midshires Way, meeting the Trent at Sawley Marina) if they wish to follow the waterways system further. This is a pity, as it is the only break in an otherwise continuous path linking London to Nottingham and the Humber estuary to the north east and Burton on Trent, and ultimately Manchester, in the north west.

Pubs and Restaurants

▫ ✕ **Chandlery Restaurant** Sawley Marina (0115 946 0300). Part of the marina complex this café/restaurant serves food (V) *L (not Mon),* specialising in large portions at low prices. Children and dogs welcome.

▫ **Plank & Leggit** Tamworth Road, Sawley (0115 972 1515; www.tomcobleigh.com). A new pub 200yds south of Sawley Cut, behind the marina, serving real ale. A wide ranging, inexpensive menu, majoring on healthy eating, is available *all day* as are inexpensive children's and special menus (wide V choice). Indoor and outdoor children's play areas, outside seating and summer barbecues. Dogs welcome on outdoor patio area.

▫ ✕ **Harrington Arms** Sawley (0115 973 2614; www.harringtonarms.co.uk). North of the flood lock. A 400-year-old, heavily beamed pub, ¼ mile from Sawley Marina, serving an extensive (and ever-changing) international à la carte menu (V) with food available *all day.* Excellent real ale selection. No children or dogs. Large garden and patio area. Real fires.

▫ **Nag's Head** Sawley (0115 973 2983). Village local serving real ale and sandwiches *L (not Sun).* No children or dogs. Darts and skittles. *Monthly quiz.*

▫ ✕ **White Lion** Sawley (0115 973 3961). North of the flood lock. Skittles, darts, pool and real ale. Children welcome. Garden. Karaoke *Sat.*

▫ **Navigation Inn** Trent Lock (0115 973 2984). Large, popular, family pub with a garden and play area. Real ales and a wide range of reasonably priced food (V) available *L and E, daily.* Moorings.

▫ ✕ **Steamboat Inn** Trent Lock, on the Erewash Canal (0115 946 3955). Built by the canal company in 1791, when it was called the Erewash Navigation Inn, it is now a busy and popular venue. The bars have been handsomely restored and decorated with suitably nautical objects. Real ale and bar meals (V) available *L and E (not Sun E).* Garden, animal farm and children's playground. Quiz *Sat.* Attached to the pub is Trattoria il Nautica.

GRAND UNION CANAL – MAIN LINE

MAXIMUM DIMENSIONS

Norton Junction to Camp Hill
Top Lock (Birmingham)
Length: 72'
Beam: 7'
Headroom: 7' 6"
Craft up to 12' 6" beam are permitted between Norton Junction and Camp Hill but all craft of this size must seek advice before proceeding. Permission must be obtained from BW for passage through the tunnels.

Camp Hill to Aston Junction and Salford Junction
Length: 70'
Beam: 7'
Headroom: 6' 6"

MILEAGE

NORTON JUNCTION to:
Braunston Turn: 4^{1}/4 miles
Napton Junction: 9^{1}/4 miles
Kingswood Junction: 31 miles
Bordesley Junction: 45^{1}/2 miles
Salford Junction: 48 miles

Locks: 68

MANAGERS

Norton Junction to Napton: 01788 890666
enquiries.braunston@bw.co.uk
Napton to Camp Hill: 01564 784634
enquiries.lapworth@britishwaterways.co.uk
Camp Hill to Salford Junction: 0121 506 1300
rherrington@britishwaterways.co.uk

The whole length of the Grand Union Canal is unique among English canals in being composed of at least eight separate canals, linking London with Birmingham, Leicester and Nottingham. Up to the 1920s all these canals were owned and operated by quite separate companies: five between London and Birmingham alone.

The original – and still the most important – part of the system was the Grand Junction Canal, constructed at the turn of the 18th C to provide a short cut between Braunston on the Oxford Canal and Brentford, west of London on the Thames. Previously, all London-bound traffic from the Midlands had to follow the Fazeley, Coventry and Oxford canals down to Oxford, there to tranship into lighters to make the 100-mile trip down river to Brentford and London. The new Grand Junction Canal cut this distance by fully 60 miles, and with its 14ft-wide locks and numerous branches to important towns rapidly became busy and profitable. The building of wide locks to take 70-ton barges was a brave attempt to persuade neighbouring canal companies – the Oxford, Coventry and the distant Trent & Mersey – to widen their navigations and establish a 70-ton barge standard throughout the waterways of the Midlands. Unfortunately, the other companies were deterred by the cost of widening, and to this day those same canals – and many others – can only pass boats 7ft wide. The mere proposal of the building of the Grand Junction Canal was enough to generate and justify plans for other canals linked to it. Before the Grand Junction itself was completed, independent canals were built linking it in a direct line to Warwick and Birmingham, and a little later a connection was established from the Grand Junction to Market Harborough and Leicester, and thence via the canalised River Soar to the Trent. Unfortunately, part of this line was built with narrow locks, thereby sealing the fate of the Grand Junction's wide canals scheme.

These canals made up the spine of southern England's transport system until the advent of the railways. When, in this century, the Regent's Canal Company acquired the Grand Junction and others, the whole system was integrated as the Grand Union Canal Company in 1929. In 1932 the new company, aided by the Government, launched a massive programme of modernisation: widening the 52 locks from Braunston to Birmingham. But when the grant was all spent, the task was unfinished and broad beam boats never became common on the Grand Union Canal.

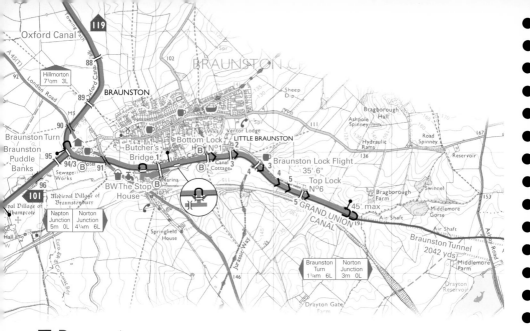

Braunston

From Norton Junction to Braunston the canal runs westward through hills and wooded country, then into a wooded cutting which leads to Braunston Tunnel. There is a good track over the top of the hill, which passes the brick tops of the ventilation shafts. A cutting follows the tunnel, and then the landscape opens out although the hills stay present on either side. Long rows of moored craft flank the canal, but there is usually plenty of space to moor, and a fine selection of old buildings at Braunston. Note especially the iron side-bridge and the 18th-C dry dock. The arm in fact was part of the old route of the Oxford Canal before it was shortened by building a large embankment (Braunston Puddle Banks) across the Leam Valley to Braunston Turn. The entrance to this arm was thus the original Braunston Junction. The Waterway Office in the Stop House was originally the Toll Office between the Oxford Canal and the Grand Junction Canal.

Boatyards

The Boat Shop (01788 891310). Started on board a boat moored at Braunston Turn, this is now a shop by Braunston Bottom Lock selling basic chandlery, coal, groceries, fruit and vegetables and canal ware, brass ware and much more. *Open mid Mar–mid Oct 08.00–20.00; rest of the year 08.00–18.00.*

ⓑ **Braunston Boats** Bottom Lock, Braunston (01788 891079). Long-term mooring.

ⓑ **Union Canal Carriers** Canalside at Braunston Pump House, Dark Lane (01788 890784; www.unioncanalcarriers.co.uk). 🛢 D Pump out, gas, narrowboat hire, day-boat hire, dry dock, engine sales, boat and engine repairs.

ⓑ **Braunston Marina** The Wharf, Braunston (01788 891373; www.braunstonmarina.co.uk). Through the fine bridge dated 1834 and into an historic canal wharf. 🚽 🚿 🛢 D E Pump out, gas, overnight and long-term mooring, dry and wet dock, chandlery, boat building sales and repairs, engine repairs, limited chandlery, toilets, showers, public telephone, gift shop selling books and maps, laundrette, coal, DIY facilities. There are also boatbuilders, fitters, fender makers and furnishers at the marina.

NAVIGATIONAL NOTES

Braunston Tunnel: two boats of 7ft beam can pass in this tunnel, but wide beam boats *must get permission from BW* on (01788) 890666 to arrange a passage.

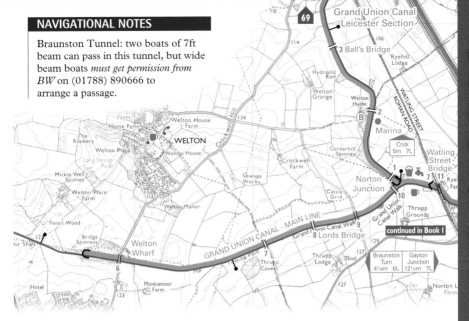

continued in Book 1

● **Welton**
Northants. Tel. The village climbs up the side of a steep hill, which makes it compact and attractive, especially around the church.

● **Braunston Tunnel**
Opened in 1796, to bore through the Northamptonshire heights, the tunnel is 2042yds long. Its construction was hindered by quicksands, and a mistake in direction whilst building has given it a slight S bend.

● **Braunston**
Northants. PO, tel, stores, butcher, fish & chips. Set up on a hill to the north of the canal. The village is really a long main street a little separate from the canal, with houses of all periods. A well-known canal centre, it is no less significant today than when the Oxford and Grand Junction canals were first connected here. British Waterways reopened the Stop House as the local Waterway Office in 1990, and there is a small information room and gift shop within.

WALKING & CYCLING
A footpath south west of bridge 91 crosses the sites of the medieval villages of Braunstonbury and Wolfhampcote.

Pubs and Restaurants

⚓ ✕ **The White Horse Inn** High Street, Welton (01327 702820). ³/₄ mile from the canal at bridge 6. A 400-year-old public house serving real ale. A wide range of bar and restaurant food (V) is served *all day, every day.* Large garden. Children welcome.

⚓ ✕ **The Admiral Nelson** Dark Lane, Little Braunston (01788 890075). A haunted country pub by lock 3. Real ale. Food, including excellent cod & chips, *L and E (not Sun E).* Canalside seating. Cottage crafts are sold nearby.

⚓ **The Wheatsheaf** The Green, Braunston. A locals' pub with a warm atmosphere. Real ale. Meals (V), including traditional *Sunday* lunch, are served *L Tue–Fri, and E Wed–Mon.* Children welcome *until 21.00.* Garden with a barbecue. Live music *Fri and Sat.*

⚓ ✕ **The Old Plough** 82 High Street, Braunston (01788 890000). A fine village pub dating from 1672, with open fires and serving real ale. Good food (V) *L and E daily,* with *Sun* roast. Children are welcome, and there is a garden. Quiz every other *Sun.*

⚓ ✕ **The Millhouse Hotel** London Road, Braunston (01788 890450). Once the Rose & Castle, it is now a welcoming hotel and restaurant, serving real ale. Grills, a *Sun* roast, carvery meals (V) *L and E.* Children's room and fine canalside garden with swings. Overnight mooring for patrons. Occasional local traditional entertainment.

✕ **The Gongoozler's Rest** Narrowboat café moored outside the Stop House (07730 125849). Breakfasts, sandwiches, omlettes and a variety of good fare. *Open daily 09.00–18.00 (16.00 winter).*

Napton Junction

The canal now passes through open countryside with a backdrop of hills, seeming very quiet and empty following all of the waterway activity around Braunston. The land is agricultural, with just a few houses in sight. There are initially no locks, no villages and the bridges are well spaced, making this a very pleasant rural stretch of canal running south west towards Napton Junction, on a length once used by both the Grand Junction Company and the Oxford Canal Company. As the Oxford Canal actually *owned* this stretch, they charged excessive toll rates in an attempt to get even with their rival, whose more direct route between London and the Midlands had attracted most of the traffic. At Napton Junction the Oxford Canal heads off to the south while the Grand Union Canal strikes off north towards Birmingham. The empty landscape rolls on towards Stockton, broken only by Calcutt Locks. The windmill on top of Napton Hill can be seen from Napton Junction.

Boatyards

Ⓑ **Napton Narrowboats** Napton Marina, Stockton (01926 813644). 🚿 🛒 🔧 D Pump out, gas, narrowboat hire, overnight and long-term mooring, boat and engine repairs, toilets, chandlery, gifts.

Ⓑ **Calcutt Boats** Calcutt

Top Lock (01926 813757; www.calcuttboats. com). 🚿 🛒 🔧 D Pump out, gas, narrowboat hire, day-boat hire, overnight mooring, long-term mooring, slipway, crane, dry dock, boat and engine sales and repairs, boatbuilding, chandlery, toilets, solid fuel, breakdown service.

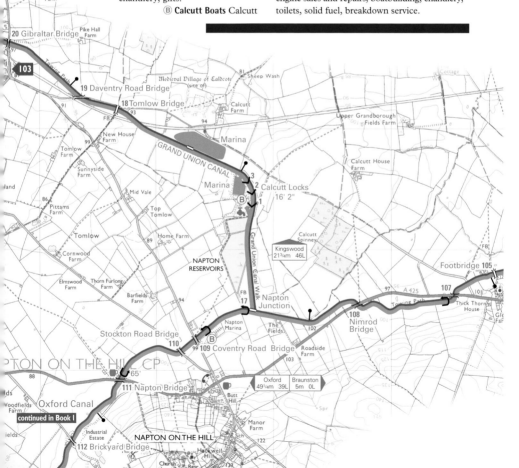

Pubs and Restaurants

⬤ ✕ **Napton Bridge Inn** (01926 812466). A haunted canalside pub at bridge 111 on the Oxford Canal. Real ale. Excellent bar and restaurant food (V) served *L and E, daily.* Range of choice from steaks to fish to spicy pasta. Separate smoking area. Children welcome. Pleasant garden with a children's playground, and often entertainment during *summer months.* Well-behaved dogs welcome.

⬤ **Old Olive Bush** Flecknoe (01788 891134). A cosy village pub serving home-cooked meals (booking preferred) (V) *E Tue–Sun,* and bar snacks *L Sat and Sun.* Children welcome, and there is a garden. *Closed L Mon–Fri in winter.*

⬤ **Lower Shuckburgh**
Warwicks. PO box. A tiny village along the main road. The church, built in 1864, is attractive in a Victorian way, with great use of contrasting brickwork inside.

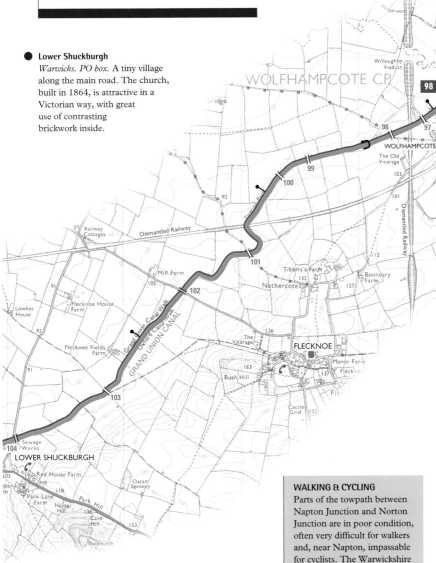

WALKING & CYCLING
Parts of the towpath between Napton Junction and Norton Junction are in poor condition, often very difficult for walkers and, near Napton, impassable for cyclists. The Warwickshire Feldon Cycleway crosses the canal at bridge 18.

Stockton

Continuing west, the canal passes to the north of Stockton and descends Stockton Locks, where you will notice the remains of the old narrow locks beside the newer wide ones. Around here there is a change in landscape, with the hills coming much closer to the canal, broken by old quarries and thick woods along the south bank. The quarries produced blue lias, a local stone, and cement which was used in the construction of the Thames Embankment. Huge fossils have been found in the blue lias clay, which is the lowest layer from the Jurassic period. This section contrasts greatly with the open landscape that precedes and follows it. The canal passes Long Itchington, a village with a large number of pubs, including two on the canal, all the while flanked by open arable land backed on both sides by hills. This pleasant emptiness is broken only by further locks continuing the fall to Warwick. Of particular interest are the top two locks at Bascote, just beyond the pretty toll house, which form a staircase. Then the canal is once again in quiet, wooded, countryside.

● **Stockton**
Warwicks PO, tel, stores, fish & chips, Indian take-away. Stockton is a largely Victorian village in an area which has been dominated by the cement works to the west. St Michael's church is built of blue lias, quarried near Stockton Locks, although the tower is of red sandstone.

● **Long Itchington**
Warwicks. PO, tel, stores, garage. A large housing estate flanks the busy A423; the village proper lies

a short walk to the north west, and is very attractive. Apart from several pubs there are houses of the 17th and 18th C, and impressive poplars around the village pond. St Wulfstan, who later became Bishop of Worcester, was born here in 1012.

Holy Trinity A largely 13th-C church whose tall spire was blown down in a gale in 1762, and replaced with a stump. Parts of the south aisle date from the 12th C, although the 13th-C windows are perhaps the building's best feature.

Boatyards

Ⓑ **Blue Lias Marina** Stockton (01926 815449; www.kateboats.co.uk). By bridge 20.
🚿 ⛽ D Pump out, gas, long-term mooring, slipway, toilets.
Ⓑ **Warwickshire Fly Boat Company** Stop Lock Cottage, Stockton (01926 812093). By the Kayes Arm. 🚿 🚿 ⛽ D Pump out, gas, long-term mooring, dry dock, boat sales and repairs, engine repairs, boatbuilding, chandlery, telephone, toilets, showers, solid fuel, laundrette, books and maps.

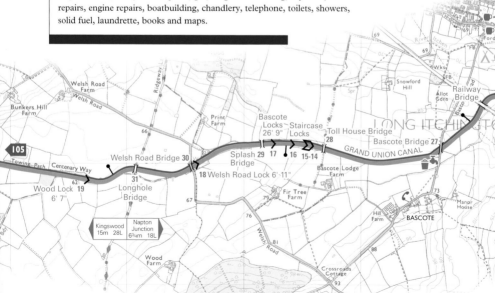

Pubs and Restaurants

🍺 **The Boat Inn** Birdingbury Wharf, Rugby Road (01926 812349). Canalside at bridge 21. A pleasant old pub with a fine map, painted by Dusty Miller, around the top of the bar. Real ale. Grills and bar meals (V) *L and E*. Children welcome, canalside garden with play area. Blues and jazz bands *Sat evening*. Annual beer and blues festival *June/July*.

🍺 **The Blue Lias Inn** Stockton Road, Stockton (01926 812249; www.bluelias.com). Canal-side at bridge 23. A well-kept and attractive pub, with a pleasant canalside garden. Be prepared for the uneven interior brickwork, which may look straighter when you have enjoyed one of the real ales they regularly keep. Bar meals (V) *L and E*. Live music outside *Sat evenings in summer*. Children are welcome, but they must remain seated.

🍺 ✕ **The Barley Mow** School Street, Stockton (01926 812713). A modernised pub where bar meals are served in large portions (V) *L and E*. Children welcome. Outside seating on the green, opposite the church.

🍺 **The Two Boats Inn** Southam Road, Long Itchington (01926 812640). Canalside at bridge 25. A good selection of real ale is available in this fine pub, built in 1743.

At one time there was a forge and stables here for the boat horses. Bar meals and grills (V) *L and E*. Children welcome. Garden. Live music *Sat*.

🍺 **The Green Man** Church Road, Long Itchington (01926 812208). Just past the church, this is a fine traditional community pub with a very low ceiling in the corridor. Real ale and bar snacks. Family room and garden.

🍺 ✕ **The Harvester** Church Road, Long Itchington (01926 812698). Opposite the village store, this is a small, family-run village local serving real ale. Bar and restaurant meals (V), including peppered steaks and lasagne, *L and E*. Children welcome. Outside seating. The Young Farmers meet here on *Wed evening*.

🍺 **The Duck on the Pond** The Green, Long Itchington (01926 815876). Specialising in food, this pub overlooks the village green and pond. Queen Elizabeth I once stayed in the black and white timbered building opposite. Real ale, and a wide range of meals (V) are served *L and E*. Non-smoking areas. Children welcome *L*, and there is sometimes jazz *during the summer*. Garden.

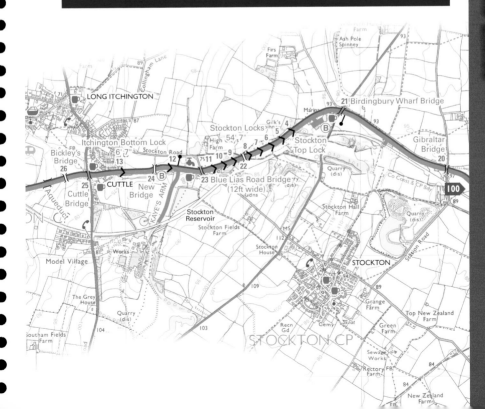

Royal Leamington Spa

The waterway makes its descent through the quiet Fosse Locks and continues west through attractive and isolated country to pass to the north of Radford Semele, where there is a fine wooded cutting. Emerging from the cutting, the canal joins a busy road for a short while, then carves a fairly discreet course through Leamington. Midway through the town the canal enters a deep cutting that hides it from the adjacent main road and railway. Leaving Leamington the canal swings north west under a main road and crosses the railway and the River Avon on aqueducts, to immediately enter the outskirts of Warwick. There are good *moorings*, *shops* and two *Indian takeaways* by bridge 40.

Pubs and Restaurants

● **The Stags Head** Welsh Road, Offchurch (01926 425801). A thatched 15th-C pub, serving real ale and food (V) *L and E (not Sun E or Mon)*. Children welcome *until 19.30*. Garden with swings.

● **The White Lion** Southam Road, Kingshurst, Radford Semele (01926 425770). Real ale, and meals (V) served *all day, every day*. Children welcome in the restaurant *until 21.00*.

● **The Fusilier** Sydenham Drive, Leamington Spa (01926 336048). Children welcome. Lawn at the back. Karaoke *Sat*, quiz and disco *Sun*. *Fish & chips* next door, and *shops* nearby.

✗ ♀ **The Grand Union** 66 Clemens Street (01926 421323; www.thegrandunion.co.uk). At bridge 40, overlooking the canal. Home-made English food (V) served as a six-course dinner *at 19.30, Mon–Sat*. Advisable to book. Children welcome, garden.

● **The Tiller Pin** Queensway, Leamington Spa (01926 435139). Real ale. Food (V) is available *L and E Mon–Fri, and all day until 21.00 at weekends*. Children welcome. Large garden. Quiz night *Mon*.

● ✗ **The Moorings** (01926 425043). By bridge 43. Real ale, and food available in the bar or restaurant *L and E, daily*. Children welcome *until 21.00*. Quiz night *Wed*. Barbecues in *summer*. Mooring.

● Offchurch
Warwicks. Tel. A scattered residential village reflecting the proximity of Leamington. It takes its name from Offa, the Saxon King of Mercia, reputedly buried near here. The church, with its tall grey stone tower, contains some Norman work. To the west lies Offchurch Bury, whose park runs almost to the canal. Originally this was a 17th-C house, but it

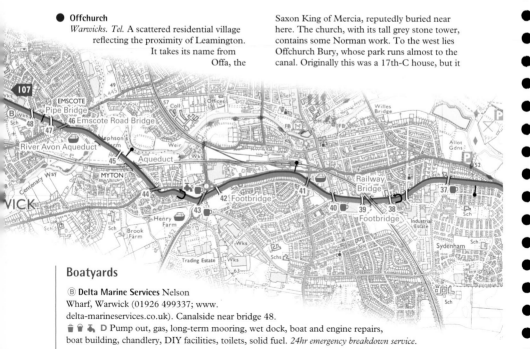

Boatyards

Ⓑ **Delta Marine Services** Nelson Wharf, Warwick (01926 499337; www. delta-marineservices.co.uk). Canalside near bridge 48.
🚽 ♀ ♿ D Pump out, gas, long-term mooring, wet dock, boat and engine repairs, boat building, chandlery, DIY facilities, toilets, solid fuel. *24hr emergency breakdown service.*

has since been entirely rebuilt. The façade is now early 19th-C Gothic.

- **Radford Semele**

  Warwicks. PO, tel, stores, garage. A main road suburb of Leamington, Radford Semele takes no notice of the canal that runs below the village, alongside the River Leam and what was once the railway line to Rugby. Among the bungalows are some fine large houses, including Radford Hall, a reconstructed Jacobean building. The Victorian church of St Nicholas is set curiously by itself, seeming to be in the middle of a field.

- **Royal Leamington Spa**

  Warwicks. PO, tel, stores (by bridge 40), garage, station, cinema. During the 19th C the population of Leamington increased rapidly, due to the late 18th- and 19th-C fashion for spas generally. As a result the town is largely mid-Victorian, and a number of Victorian churches and hotels dominate it, several designed by J. Cundall, a local architect of some note who also built the brick and stone town hall. The long rows of villas, elegant houses in their own grounds spreading out from the centre, all express the Victorian love of exotic styles – Gothic, Classical, Jacobean, Renaissance, French and Greek are all mixed here with bold abandon. Since the Victorian era, however, much industrialisation has taken place.

  Assembly Rooms, Art Gallery & Museum Royal Pump Rooms, The Parade, Royal Leamington Spa (01926 742700; tearooms@warwickdc. gov.uk). British, Dutch and Flemish paintings of the 16th and 17th C. Also a collection of modern art, pottery and porcelain through the ages and a specialist series of 18th-C English drinking glasses. Victorian costumes and

objects. *Open Tue, Wed, Fri and Sat 10.30– 17.00, Thur 13.30–20.00, Sun 11.00–16.00. Closed Mon.* Free.

All Saints' Church Bath Street. Begun in 1843 to the design of J. C. Jackson, who was greatly influenced by the then vicar, Dr John Craig. It is of Gothic style, apparently not always correct in detail. The north transept has a rose window patterned on Rouen Cathedral; the west window is by Kempe. The scale of the building is impressive, being fully 172ft long and 80ft high.

Jephson Gardens Alongside Newbold Terrace, north of bridge 40. Beautiful ornamental gardens named after Dr Jephson (1798– 1878), the local practitioner who was largely responsible for the spa's high medical reputation.

Tourist Information Centre Royal Pump Rooms, The Parade, Royal Leamington Spa (01926 742762).

BOAT TRIPS

Prince Regent II is a 50-seater wide-beam Edwardian luxury cruising restaurant, which departs from Offchurch Wharf *evenings and Sun lunchtimes*. Good food and wine, and entertainment can be arranged. Booking for a meal is essential. Telephone 01608 662216 for details. Their office address is: The Edwardian Dining Company, Wisteria House, 76 Hawthorn Way, Shipston-on-Stour, Warwicks CV36 4FD. The *Prince Regent II* is also available for private charter.

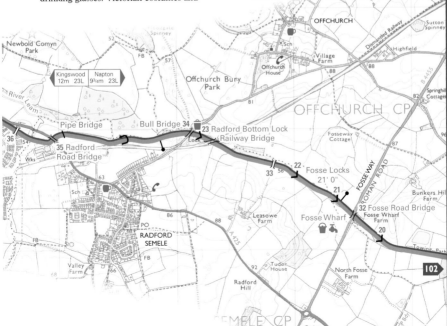

Warwick

The canal passes around the north side of central Warwick, so if you wish to visit the town centre, it is best to approach from bridge 49 (walking to the south for a little over half a mile), or from the Saltisford Canal Centre *(see below)*. After climbing the two Cape Locks, the canal swings south to Budbrooke Junction, where the old Warwick and Napton Canal joined the Warwick and Birmingham Canal. A short section of the arm to the east of the junction has been restored, and has a winding hole, moorings and other facilities. To the west of the junction, beyond a large road bridge, is the first of the 21 locks of the Hatton flight, with its distinctive paddle gear and gates stretching up the hill ahead, a daunting sight for even the most resilient boatman. Consolation is offered by the fine view of the spires of Warwick as you climb the flight. There is a small *shop* selling maps and canalia between locks 45 and 46. On reaching the top, the canal turns to the west, passing the wooded hills that conceal Hatton village and Hatton Park. The canal then enters the wooded cutting that leads to Shrewley Tunnel.

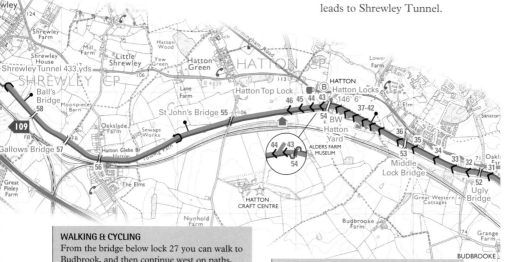

WALKING & CYCLING
From the bridge below lock 27 you can walk to Budbrook, and then continue west on paths, passing Grove Park Farm, to reach Hatton Country World. Returning to the canal at bridge 55, you then complete the circuit, enjoying fine views over Hatton Locks and passing The Waterman pub.

BOAT TRIPS
Saltie cruises *Jun–Aug on last Sun afternoon each month* from the Saltisford Canal Centre. It is also available for day hire. Telephone (01926) 490006 for details.

Boatyards

ⓑ **Saltisford Canal Centre** Budbrooke Road, Warwick (01926 490006). 🚿 🛒 🔧 Pump out, day-hire craft, overnight and long-term mooring, winter storage, telephone nearby, toilets, gifts. Gardens, picnic places, barbecue and snacks available. An excellent place in its own right, with good access to Warwick.
ⓑ **Kate Boats Warwick** The Boatyard, Nelson Lane, Warwick (01926 492968; www.kateboats.co.uk). 🚿 🛒 🔧 D Pump out, gas,

narrowboat hire, overnight and long-term mooring, boat and engine repairs, boatbuilding, chandlery, toilets, books and maps.
Get Knotted Lower Cape (01926 410588). Next door to the Cape of Good Hope pub. Rope fender-making specialist, plus general ropework and an expanding chandlery.
ⓑ **Stephen Goldsbrough Boats** Hatton (01564 778210). Dry dock on the Hatton flight, boat painting and repairs, DIY facilities.

● **Warwick**
Warwicks. All services. Virtually destroyed by fire in 1694 the town rose again, with Queen Anne styles now mixed with the medieval buildings which survived the blaze.

Warwick Castle Castle Hill (telephone 0870 442 2000 for information line). Built on the site of a motte and bailey constructed by William the Conqueror in 1068, the present exterior is a famous example of a 14th-C fortification, with the tall Caesar's Tower rising to a height of 147ft. The castle grounds were laid out by Capability Brown. *Open daily 10.00–18.00. Closed Xmas.* Charge. Programme of events *throughout the year.*

Collegiate Church of St Mary's Of Norman origin. The most striking feature of the rebuilt church is its pseudo-Gothic tower, built 1698–1704. Climb to the top to enjoy the view (*May–Sep, 10.00–16.00 weather permitting).* Church *open summer 10.00–18.00; winter 10.00–16.00.* Free (charge for tower).

Warwick County Museum Market Place (01926 412500). Housed in the Market Hall. Includes the Sheldon tapestry map of Warwickshire, which dates from 1588. *Open May–Sep, Tue–Sat and B Hols 10.00–17.00, Sun 11.30–17.00.* Free.

Lord Leycester Hospital High Street (01926 491422). A superbly preserved group of 14th-C timber-framed buildings. Chapel of St James, Great Hall and galleried courtyard. The Museum of the Queen's Own Hussars is also here. *Open Tue–Sun and B Hol Mon 10.00–17.00 (16.00 winter).* The restored gardens are *open during the summer.* Charge.

Oken's House & Doll Museum Castle Street (01926 495546). A superb collection of early dolls housed in one of the few timber buildings that survived the great fire. *Open Easter–Oct, Mon–Sat 10.00–17.00, Sun 11.00–17.00; Nov–Easter, Sat only 10.00–dusk.* Charge.

Tourist Information Centre The Court House, Jury Street, Warwick (01926 492212). Guided walks are arranged from here *during the summer.*

● **Hatton**
Warwicks. A heavily wooded village.

Hatton Country World George's Farm, Hatton (01926 843411). South of bridge 55. Rare breeds, craft workshops and a children's play area. *Open daily 10.00–17.00 (closed Xmas).* Entrance to the craft village is free, but a charge is made for the Farm Park.

● **Shrewley**
Warwicks. PO, tel, stores. Best approached from the north western end of the Shrewley Tunnel, through an exciting, but slippery, towpath tunnel.

Shrewley Tunnel 433yds long, the tunnel was opened in 1799 with the completion of the Warwick and Birmingham Canal. *This tunnel allows two 7ft boats to pass: keep to the right.*

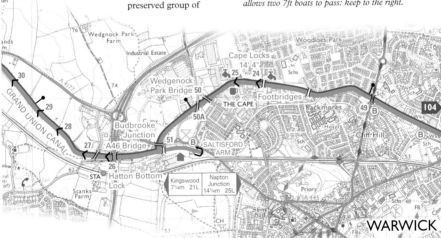

Pubs and Restaurants

There are many pubs and restaurants in Warwick which will repay exploration.

🍺 **The Cape of Good Hope** Cape Locks, 66 Lower Cape (01926 498138; www.capeof-goodhope.co.uk). A canalside pub where good food (V), especially fish, is served *L and E daily,* and there is a choice of real ales. Children welcome, lockside seating. Live music *Thur.*

🍺 ✕ **The Waterman** Birmingham Road (A4177), Hatton (01926 492427). Excellent and extensive bar menu (V) available *all day, every day* in this country pub, which has a comfortable beamed bar and fine views over the Hatton flight. It is also handy for Hatton Country World. Real ale. Children welcome. Large garden.

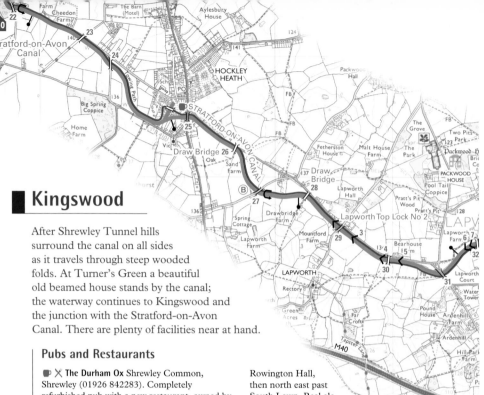

Stratford-on-Avon Canal

Kingswood

After Shrewley Tunnel hills surround the canal on all sides as it travels through steep wooded folds. At Turner's Green a beautiful old beamed house stands by the canal; the waterway continues to Kingswood and the junction with the Stratford-on-Avon Canal. There are plenty of facilities near at hand.

Pubs and Restaurants

🍺 ✕ **The Durham Ox** Shrewley Common, Shrewley (01926 842283). Completely refurbished pub with a new restaurant, owned by Olympic showjumper Nick Skelton. Real ale, and bar and restaurant meals (V), including an all-day *Sun* roast, served *L and E*. Children welcome, and there is a large garden.

🍺 ✕ **The Cock Horse** Old Warwick Road, Rowington (01926 841183). Country pub and à la carte restaurant (V) serving real ale and meals *L and E*. Children welcome, and there is a garden with a children's play area. Folk and jazz club, *mid-summer* charity ball, and beer and jazz festival.

🍺 **The Case is Altered** Case Lane, just off Five Ways, Haseley Knob (01926 484206). A brisk 45-minute walk from bridge 62, but worth it to find this quiet old-fashioned ale house. Pass

Rowington Hall, then north east past South Lawn. Real ale, but no children, food or dogs. Outside seating.

🍺 ✕ **Tom o' the Wood** Finwood Road, Rowington (01564 782252). Traditional country pub serving real ale, and bar and restaurant meals (V) *L and E*. Children welcome, and garden by the canal.

🍺 **The Navigation** Old Warwick Road, canalside at Kingswood (01564 783337). Real ale and real draught cider. Bar meals (V) *L and E*. Children welcome. Moorings.

WALKING & CYCLING
By walking west from the Tom o'the Wood pub and crossing Dick's Lane Bridge on the Stratford-on-Avon Canal, you can follow paths past Ardenhill Farm to bring you to bridge 31 on the Lapworth Flight. It is then an excellent and fascinating walk back, passing the locks and returning to the Grand Union via Kingswood Junction.

● **Rowington**
Warwicks. Tel. Near the canal the 13th-C church retains some furnishings and a fine peal of bells.

● **Kingswood**
Warwicks. Tel, garage, station. The village is scattered over a wide area from the Grand Union Canal to the Stratford-on-Avon Canal. The centre is a mile to the west, around the ambitious 15th-C church.

Packwood House *NT* (01564 782024). Hockley Heath, 2 miles west of bridge 66. Timber-framed Tudor house, dating from the late 16th C and enlarged in the 17th C, where Cromwell's general, Henry Ireton, slept before the Battle of Edgehill in 1642. *House open Mar–Oct, Wed–Sun 12.00–16.30.* Charge. Events are staged *during the summer.*

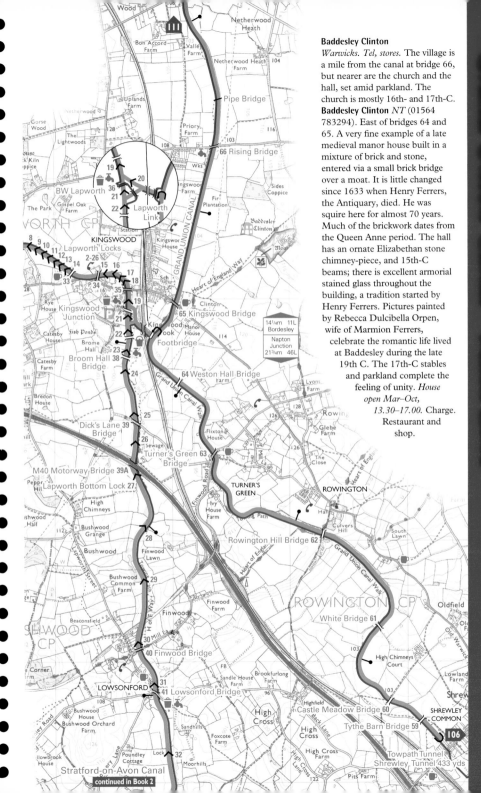

Baddesley Clinton

Warwicks. Tel, stores. The village is a mile from the canal at bridge 66, but nearer are the church and the hall, set amid parkland. The church is mostly 16th- and 17th-C. **Baddesley Clinton** *NT* (01564 783294). East of bridges 64 and 65. A very fine example of a late medieval manor house built in a mixture of brick and stone, entered via a small brick bridge over a moat. It is little changed since 1633 when Henry Ferrers, the Antiquary, died. He was squire here for almost 70 years. Much of the brickwork dates from the Queen Anne period. The hall has an ornate Elizabethan stone chimney-piece, and 15th-C beams; there is excellent armorial stained glass throughout the building, a tradition started by Henry Ferrers. Pictures painted by Rebecca Dulcibella Orpen, wife of Marmion Ferrers, celebrate the romantic life lived at Baddesley during the late 19th C. The 17th-C stables and parkland complete the feeling of unity. *House open Mar–Oct, 13.30–17.00.* Charge. Restaurant and shop.

Netherwood Heath

Bon Accord Farm

Uplands Farm

Pipe Bridge

Priory Farm

66 Rising Bridge

19
20
BW Lapworth 36
21
22 Lapworth Link

KINGSWOOD

8 9 10 11 12 13 14
Lapworth Locks
2-26
15 16
33 P 34 35 17
18
19
Rye House Kingswood Junction
21
65 Kingswood Bridge
22
Kings Wook Manor House Footbridge
23
Broom Hall 38 Bridge
24
64 Weston Hall Bridge

14¼m 11L Bordesley
Napton Junction 21¾m 46L

Dick's Lane 39 Bridge
25

26
Turner's Green 63 Bridge

M40 Motorway Bridge 39A
Lapworth Bottom Lock 27

TURNER'S GREEN

ROWINGTON

28

Rowington Hill Bridge 62

29

Finwood

30 Mill
40 Finwood Bridge

White Bridge 61

High Chimneys Court

LOWSONFORD
31
41 Lowsonford Bridge

Castle Meadow Bridge 60

SHREWLEY COMMON

Tythe Barn Bridge 59

106

Lock 32

Stratford-on-Avon Canal

Towpath Tunnel
Shrewley Tunnel 433 yds

continued in Book 2

Knowle

The canal now continues its northerly route, passing through countryside which is surprisingly peaceful. Knowle Locks introduce more hilly countryside again, and this green and pleasant land continues right through to Solihull, concealing the nearness of Birmingham. The flight of five wide locks at Knowle used to be six narrow ones, until the 1930 improvements; the remains of the old ones can still be seen alongside the new, together with the side ponds (originally built to save water). The locks are comparatively deep, and are well maintained and pleasantly situated. They are also the northernmost wide locks for many miles now, since all the Birmingham canals have narrow locks. Knowle is set back from the canal, but warrants a visit, especially to see the church. Continuing north west through wooded country, the canal passes under the M42 motorway and crosses the River Blyth on a small aqueduct.

● **Knowle**
W. Midlands. All services. Despite its proximity to Birmingham, Knowle still survives as a village, albeit rather self-consciously. A number of old buildings thankfully remain, some dating from the Middle Ages and including such gems as Chester House (now the library), which illustrate the advances in timber-frame construction from the 13th to the 15th C. Have a look at the splendid knot garden around the back. Half-a-mile north of the village is Grimshaw Hall, a gabled 16th-C house noted for its decorative brickwork. There are good views of it from the canal.
Church of St John the Baptist, St Lawrence and St Anne Knowle. This remarkable church was built as a result of the efforts of Walter Cook, a wealthy man who founded a chapel here in 1396, and completed the present church in 1402. Prior to its building the parishioners of Knowle had to make a 6-mile round trip each Sunday to the church at Hampton-in-Arden. This involved crossing the River Blythe, an innocuous brook today, but in medieval times 'a greate and daungerous water' which 'noyther man nor beaste can passe wt. owte daunger of peryshing'. The church is built in the Perpendicular style, with a great deal of intricate stonework. There is much of interest to be seen inside, including the roof timbers, the original font and a medieval dug-out chest. Behind the church is the 3-acre 'Children's Field', given to the National Trust by the Reverend T. Downing 'to be used for games'.

WE ARE THE OVALTINE-EES . . .

Dr George Wander founded the company which was to manufacture Ovaltine in Switzerland in 1864. Finding a ready market in England, the company established a factory at Kings Langley, beside what is now the Grand Union Canal. In 1925 they decided to build their own fleet of narrowboats to bring coal to this factory from Warwickshire. Their boats were always immaculately maintained, with the words 'Drink delicious Ovaltine for Health' emblazoned in orange and yellow on a very dark blue background. The last boat arrived at Kings Langley on 17 April 1959.

Pubs and Restaurants

● **The Black Boy** Warwick Road, at bridge 69 (01564 772655). Traditional family-owned pub, built in 1793, sporting a canalside garden with children's play area. Real ale and excellent bar meals with a wide choice of main courses (V) served *L and E.* Children welcome *until 20.00.* Large play area in the garden. Heated canalside patio for chilly evenings.
● ✕ **The Wilsons Arms** Warwick Road, Knowle (01564 772559). Toby Carvery pub which dates from the 16th C. The older part still retains much of its character. Real ale, and fresh food and carvery (V) served *L and E until 22.00.* Children welcome. Outside seating.
● **The Heron's Nest** (01564 771177). Canalside at bridge 70. Attractive country pub serving real ale, and traditional seasonal food (V) *L and E.* Children welcome. Garden with a heated terrace.

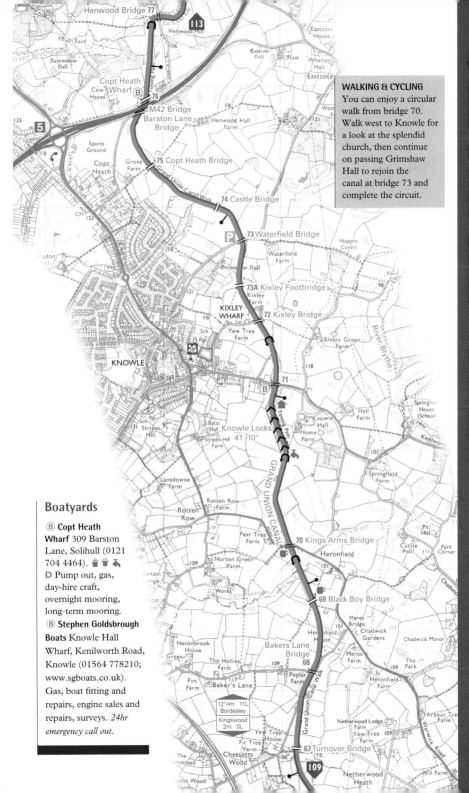

WALKING & CYCLING
You can enjoy a circular walk from bridge 70. Walk west to Knowle for a look at the splendid church, then continue on passing Grimshaw Hall to rejoin the canal at bridge 73 and complete the circuit.

Boatyards

Ⓑ **Copt Heath Wharf** 309 Barston Lane, Solihull (0121 704 4464). Ⓓ Pump out, gas, day-hire craft, overnight mooring, long-term mooring.
Ⓑ **Stephen Goldsbrough Boats** Knowle Hall Wharf, Kenilworth Road, Knowle (01564 778210; www.sgboats.co.uk). Gas, boat fitting and repairs, engine sales and repairs, surveys. *24hr emergency call out.*

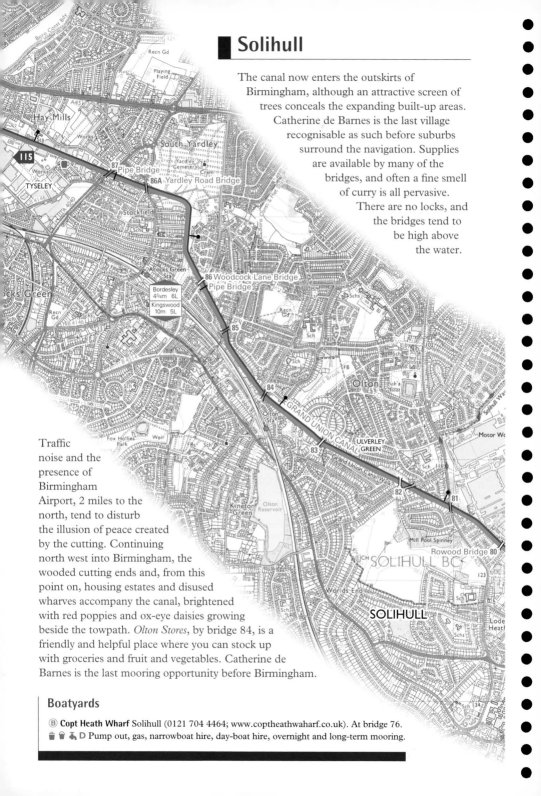

Solihull

The canal now enters the outskirts of Birmingham, although an attractive screen of trees conceals the expanding built-up areas. Catherine de Barnes is the last village recognisable as such before suburbs surround the navigation. Supplies are available by many of the bridges, and often a fine smell of curry is all pervasive. There are no locks, and the bridges tend to be high above the water.

Traffic noise and the presence of Birmingham Airport, 2 miles to the north, tend to disturb the illusion of peace created by the cutting. Continuing north west into Birmingham, the wooded cutting ends and, from this point on, housing estates and disused wharves accompany the canal, brightened with red poppies and ox-eye daisies growing beside the towpath. *Olton Stores*, by bridge 84, is a friendly and helpful place where you can stock up with groceries and fruit and vegetables. Catherine de Barnes is the last mooring opportunity before Birmingham.

Boatyards

Ⓑ **Copt Heath Wharf** Solihull (0121 704 4464; www.coptheathwaharf.co.uk). At bridge 76.
🛢 💧 ⚓ D Pump out, gas, narrowboat hire, day-boat hire, overnight and long-term mooring.

● **Catherine de Barnes**
W. Midlands. PO, tel, stores, garage. A higgledy-piggledy village far from the romanticism implied by the name. However, a convenient supply centre with easy access from the canal before the bulk of Birmingham begins to make its presence felt.

● **Elmdon Heath**
W. Midlands. PO, tel, stores, garage. A suburb of Solihull useful for supplies.

● **Solihull**
W. Midlands. PO, tel, stores, garage, cinema, *station.* A modern commuter development, with fine public buildings. What used to be the town centre, dominated by the tall spire of the parish church, is now a shopping area.

St Alphege Church Solihull. Built of red sandstone, it is almost all late 13th-C and early 14th-C. The lofty interior contains work of all periods, including a Jacobean pulpit, a 17th-C communion rail, 19th-C stained glass and a few notable monuments.

Tourist Information Centre Central Library, Homer Road, Solihull (0121 704 6130).

Pubs and Restaurants

🍺 **The Boat Inn** 222 Hampton Lane, Catherine de Barnes (0121 705 0474). A well-kept and friendly pub, offering real ale, together with bar meals (V) *all day, every day.* Children welcome, garden.

✕♀ **Longfellows English Restaurant** 255 Hampton Lane, Catherine de Barnes (0121 705 0547). Cosy and intimate family-run restaurant serving fresh food (V), including game and seafood, *L and E (not Sun or Mon)*. Bottled real ale. Gazebo.

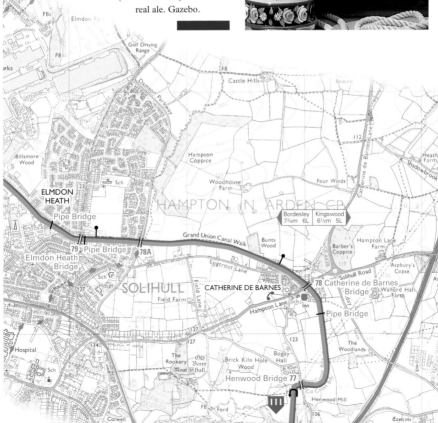

Birmingham

The canal curves past the large Energy from Waste plant and the Ackers Trust Basin before reaching Camp Hill Locks. These, and all the succeeding locks, are narrow. After passing through subterranean vaults formed by the criss-crossing of railway viaducts, Bordesley Junction is reached. Ahead, beyond the Junction, the canal continues towards the Birmingham Canal Main Line, joining the Birmingham & Fazeley Canal at Aston Junction, passing a very fine collection of old wharf buildings on the way. Heading north from Bordesley Junction, the Grand Union is accompanied by pleasantly transformed surroundings to join the Birmingham & Fazeley Canal at Salford Junction

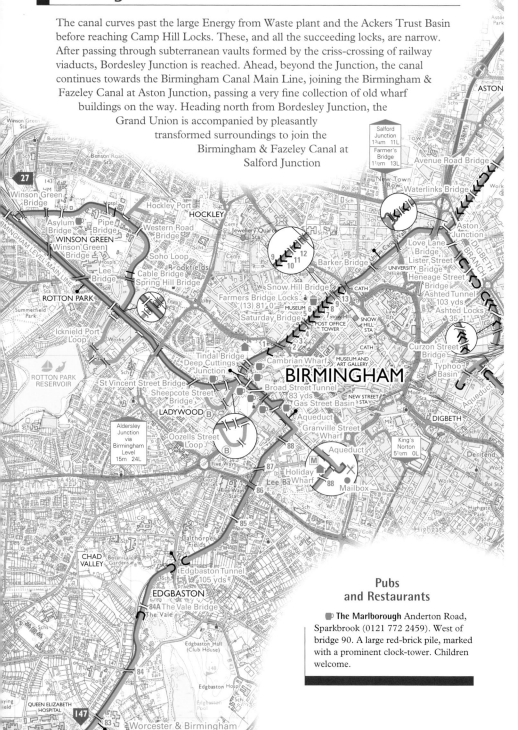

Pubs and Restaurants

🍺 **The Marlborough** Anderton Road, Sparkbrook (0121 772 2459). West of bridge 90. A large red-brick pile, marked with a prominent clock-tower. Children welcome.

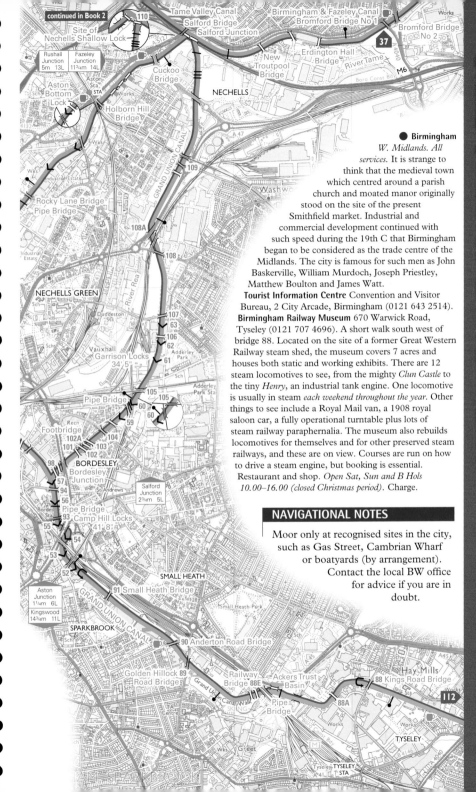

● **Birmingham**

W. Midlands. All services. It is strange to think that the medieval town which centred around a parish church and moated manor originally stood on the site of the present Smithfield market. Industrial and commercial development continued with such speed during the 19th C that Birmingham began to be considered as the trade centre of the Midlands. The city is famous for such men as John Baskerville, William Murdoch, Joseph Priestley, Matthew Boulton and James Watt.

Tourist Information Centre Convention and Visitor Bureau, 2 City Arcade, Birmingham (0121 643 2514).

Birmingham Railway Museum 670 Warwick Road, Tyseley (0121 707 4696). A short walk south west of bridge 88. Located on the site of a former Great Western Railway steam shed, the museum covers 7 acres and houses both static and working exhibits. There are 12 steam locomotives to see, from the mighty *Clun Castle* to the tiny *Henry*, an industrial tank engine. One locomotive is usually in steam *each weekend throughout the year*. Other things to see include a Royal Mail van, a 1908 royal saloon car, a fully operational turntable plus lots of steam railway paraphernalia. The museum also rebuilds locomotives for themselves and for other preserved steam railways, and these are on view. Courses are run on how to drive a steam engine, but booking is essential. Restaurant and shop. *Open Sat, Sun and B Hols 10.00–16.00 (closed Christmas period).* Charge.

NAVIGATIONAL NOTES

Moor only at recognised sites in the city, such as Gas Street, Cambrian Wharf or boatyards (by arrangement). Contact the local BW office for advice if you are in doubt.

Nettle Hill (see *page 122*)

OXFORD CANAL

MAXIMUM DIMENSIONS
Length: 70'
Beam: 7'
Headroom: 7'

MILEAGE
BRAUNSTON TURN to:
Hillmorton Bottom Lock: 7^1/$_2$
Rugby Wharf Arm: 10^1/$_4$
Stretton Stop: 15^3/$_4$

HAWKESBURY JUNCTION
(*Coventry Canal*): 22^3/$_4$ miles
Locks: 4

MANAGER
01788 890666
enquiries.braunston@britishwaterways.co.uk

The Oxford Canal was one of the earliest and, for many years, one of the most important canals in southern England. It was authorised in 1769, when the Coventry Canal was in the offing, and was intended to fetch coal southwards from the Warwickshire coalfield to Banbury and Oxford, at the same time giving access to the River Thames. James Brindley was appointed engineer: he built a winding contour canal 91 miles long which soon began to look thoroughly outdated and inefficient for the carriage of goods. Brindley died in 1772, and was replaced by Samuel Simcock: he completed the line from Longford, where a junction was made with the Coventry Canal, to Banbury, in 1778. After a long pause, the canal was finally brought into Oxford in 1790, and thereafter through-traffic flowed constantly along this important new trade route.

In 1780, however, the Grand Junction Canal opened (excepting the tunnel at Blisworth) from London to Braunston, and the Warwick & Napton and Warwick & Birmingham Canals completed the new short route from London to Birmingham. This had the natural – and intended – effect of drawing traffic off the Oxford Canal, especially south of Napton Junction, but the Oxford Company protected itself very effectively against this powerful opposition by charging outrageously high rates for their 5^1/$_2$-mile stretch between Braunston and Napton, which had become part of the new London–Birmingham through route. Thus the Oxford Canal maintained its revenue and very high dividends for many years to come.

By the late 1820s, however, the Oxford Canal had become conspicuously out of date with its extravagant winding course and, under the threat of various schemes for big new canals which, if built, would render the Oxford Canal almost redundant, the company decided to modernise the northern part of their navigation. Tremendous engineering works were executed which completely changed the face of the canal north of Braunston. Aqueducts, massive embankments and deep cuttings were built, carrying the canal in great sweeps through the countryside and cutting almost 14 miles off the original 36 miles between Braunston Junction and the Coventry Canal. Much of the old main line suddenly became a series of loops and branches leading nowhere, now crossed by elegant new towpath bridges inscribed Horseley Ironworks 1828.

This very expensive programme was well worthwhile. Although toll rates, and thus revenue, began to fall because of keen competition from the railways, dividends were kept at a high level for years – indeed a respectable profit was still shown right through to the 20th C.

Braunston and Willoughby

North of Braunston the Oxford Canal soon leaves behind the excitement and interest of the village to run through wide open country, backed by bare hills to the east. It is an ancient landscape, and by bridge 87 medieval ridge and furrow field patterns are in evidence. These were created as villagers cleared forested land, and each ploughed strips throwing soil towards the centre. Gradually a collection of strips, all running parallel to each other, made up a furlong or cultura. This was then enclosed by a low bank and an access track (usually difficult to identify today) was created. Fields, consisting of dozens of furlongs, were then sometimes fenced. Skirting round Barby Hill, the canal swings north east towards Hillmorton and Rugby. The M45 makes a noisy crossing after Barby Hill.

Boatyards

All the following are on the *Grand Union Canal* at Braunston.

The Boat Shop (01788 891310). Started on board a boat moored at Braunston Turn, this is now a shop by Braunston Bottom Lock selling basic chandlery, coal, groceries, fruit and vegetables and canal ware, brass ware and much more. *Open mid Mar–mid Oct 08.00–20.00; rest of the year 08.00–18.00.*

ⓑ **Braunston Boats** Bottom Lock, Braunston (01788 891079). Long-term mooring.

ⓑ **Union Canal Carriers** Canalside at Braunston Pump House, Dark Lane (01788 890784; www.unioncanalcarriers.co.uk). 🛠 D Pump out, gas, narrowboat hire, day-boat hire, dry dock, engine sales, boat and engine repairs.

ⓑ **Braunston Marina** The Wharf, Braunston (01788 891373; www.braunstonmarina.co.uk). Through the fine bridge dated 1834 and into an historic canal wharf. 🚮 🚽 🛠 D E Pump out, gas, overnight and long-term mooring, dry and wet dock, chandlery, boat building sales and repairs, engine repairs, limited chandlery, toilets, showers, public telephone, gift shop selling books and maps, laundrette, coal, DIY facilities. There are also boatbuilders, fitters, fender makers and furnishers at the marina.

ⓑ **Midland Chandlers** Canalside, Braunston Turn (01788 891401). A wide range of chandlery.

WALKING & CYCLING
The towpath is passable for walkers, but very bumpy in places for cyclists.

Pubs and Restaurants

🍺 ✕ **The Rose Inn** Main Street, Willoughby (01788 890567). Attractively maintained thatched village pub, offering real ale. Bar, restaurant and carvery meals (V) *L and E (not Sun or Mon E)*. Outside seating with children's play area. Regular entertainment with theme nights. Live singer *every Tue.*

🍺 ✕ **The Millhouse Hotel** London Road, Braunston (01788 890450). Once the Rose & Castle, it is now a welcoming hotel and restaurant, serving real ale. Grills, *Sun* roast, carvery meals (V) *L and E*. Children's room and fine canalside garden with swings. Overnight mooring for patrons. Occasional local traditional entertainment.

🍺 **The Wheatsheaf** The Green, Braunston. A locals' pub with a warm atmosphere. Real ale. Meals (V), including traditional *Sun* lunch, served *L Tue–Fri,* and *E Wed–Mon*. Children welcome *until 21.00*. Garden with a barbecue. Live music *Fri and Sat.*

🍺 ✕ **The Old Plough** 82 High Street, Braunston (01788 890000). Fine village pub dating from 1672, with open fires and serving real ale. Good food (V) *L and E daily*, with *Sunday* roast. Children are welcome, and there is a garden. Quiz every other *Sun.*

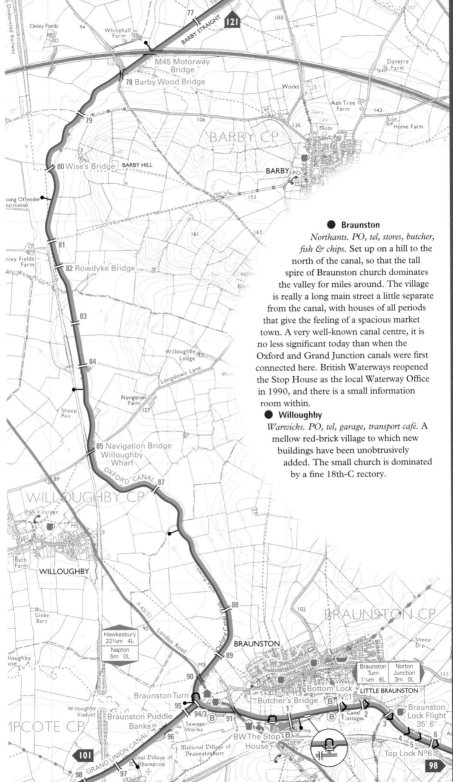

● **Braunston**
Northants. PO, tel, stores, butcher, fish & chips. Set up on a hill to the north of the canal, so that the tall spire of Braunston church dominates the valley for miles around. The village is really a long main street a little separate from the canal, with houses of all periods that give the feeling of a spacious market town. A very well-known canal centre, it is no less significant today than when the Oxford and Grand Junction canals were first connected here. British Waterways reopened the Stop House as the local Waterway Office in 1990, and there is a small information room within.

● **Willoughby**
Warwicks. PO, tel, garage, transport café. A mellow red-brick village to which new buildings have been unobtrusively added. The small church is dominated by a fine 18th-C rectory.

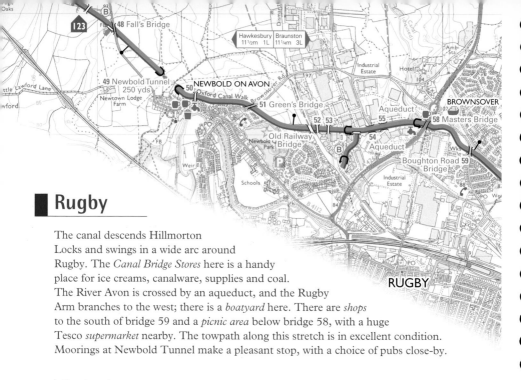

Rugby

The canal descends Hillmorton
Locks and swings in a wide arc around
Rugby. The *Canal Bridge Stores* here is a handy
place for ice creams, canalware, supplies and coal.
The River Avon is crossed by an aqueduct, and the Rugby
Arm branches to the west; there is a *boatyard* here. There are *shops*
to the south of bridge 59 and a *picnic area* below bridge 58, with a huge
Tesco *supermarket* nearby. The towpath along this stretch is in excellent condition.
Moorings at Newbold Tunnel make a pleasant stop, with a choice of pubs close-by.

Boatyards

Ⓑ **Hillmorton Boat Services** The Locks,
Hillmorton (01788 578661/mobile 07733
275336). 🚿 🚽 ⚓ Wet dock and dry dock, boat
sales, boat and engine repairs, chandlery, books
and maps, solid fuel. *24hr emergency breakdown
call out.*

Ⓑ **Clifton Cruisers** Clifton Wharf, Vicarage Hill,
Clifton on Dunsmore (01788 543570;
info@cliftoncruisers.com). 🚿 🚽 ⚓ D Pump out,
gas, narrowboat hire, overnight mooring, boat
and engine repairs, boatbuilding, toilets,
showers, gifts.

Ⓑ **Willow Wren Hire Cruisers** Rugby Wharf, off
Consul Road, Leicester Road, Rugby (01788
562183; www.willowwren.co.uk). 🚿 ⚓ D Pump
out, gas, narrowboat hire, overnight and long-
term mooring, boat sales and repairs, engine
repairs, toilets and showers, books and maps,
café, DIY facilities.

Ⓑ **T. F. Yates** Falls Bridge Works, Cathiron
Lane, Newbold-on-Avon (01788 569140).
East of bridge 44. 🚽 ⚓ D Pump out, gas,
crane, engine sales, boat and engine repairs,
boatbuilding, solid fuel.

● **Hillmorton**
*Warwicks. PO, tel, stores, garage, takeaways, but all
a fair distance from the canal.*

● **Rugby**
*Warwicks. PO, tel, stores, garage, station, theatre,
cinema, leisure centre.* There is a pedestrianised
shopping centre, a leisure centre and an open
market with a town crier. Look out for the tiny
shop in Chapel Street, which has stood for over
500 years and is reputedly the oldest building in
the town.
James Gilbert Rugby Football Museum 5 St
Matthews Street, Rugby (01788 333888).
Founded by the nephew of William Gilbert, who

made boots and shoes for Rugby School in his
original shop in the High Street. *Open Mon–Fri
09.00–17.00, Sat 09.00–14.00. Closed Sun.* Free.
Rugby School Museum 10 Little Church Street,
Rugby (01788 556109). Opposite the Temple
Speech Room, opened in 1909 by King Edward
VII and named after a headmaster of the school
who later became Archbishop of Canterbury.
Guided tours (ring and check availability). *Open
Mon–Sat 10.30–12.30 and 13.30–16.30, Sun
13.30–16.30.* Charge.
Tourist Information Centre 4 Lawrence Sherriff
Street, Rugby (01788 534970; visitor.centre@
rugby.gov.uk).

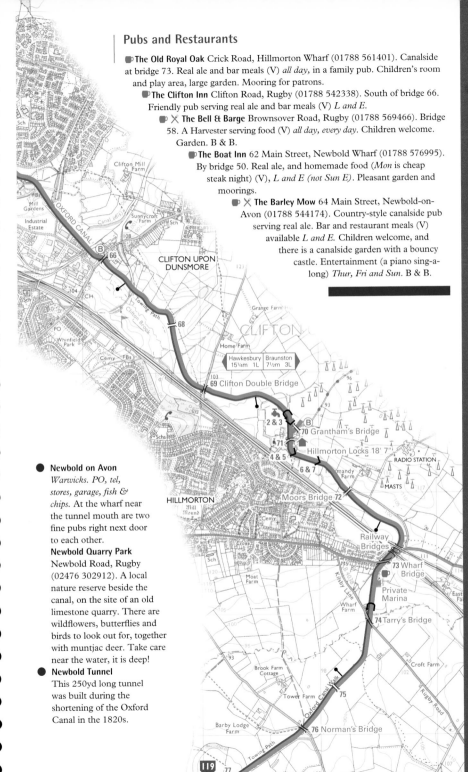

Pubs and Restaurants

🍺**The Old Royal Oak** Crick Road, Hillmorton Wharf (01788 561401). Canalside at bridge 73. Real ale and bar meals (V) *all day*, in a family pub. Children's room and play area, large garden. Mooring for patrons.

🍺**The Clifton Inn** Clifton Road, Rugby (01788 542338). South of bridge 66. Friendly pub serving real ale and bar meals (V) *L and E.*

🍺✕ **The Bell & Barge** Brownsover Road, Rugby (01788 569466). Bridge 58. A Harvester serving food (V) *all day, every day.* Children welcome. Garden. B & B.

🍺**The Boat Inn** 62 Main Street, Newbold Wharf (01788 576995). By bridge 50. Real ale, and homemade food (*Mon* is cheap steak night) (V), *L and E (not Sun E).* Pleasant garden and moorings.

🍺✕ **The Barley Mow** 64 Main Street, Newbold-on-Avon (01788 544174). Country-style canalside pub serving real ale. Bar and restaurant meals (V) available *L and E.* Children welcome, and there is a canalside garden with a bouncy castle. Entertainment (a piano sing-a-long) *Thur, Fri and Sun.* B & B.

● **Newbold on Avon**
Warwicks. PO, tel, stores, garage, fish & chips. At the wharf near the tunnel mouth are two fine pubs right next door to each other.

Newbold Quarry Park
Newbold Road, Rugby (02476 302912). A local nature reserve beside the canal, on the site of an old limestone quarry. There are wildflowers, butterflies and birds to look out for, together with muntjac deer. Take care near the water, it is deep!

● **Newbold Tunnel**
This 250yd long tunnel was built during the shortening of the Oxford Canal in the 1820s.

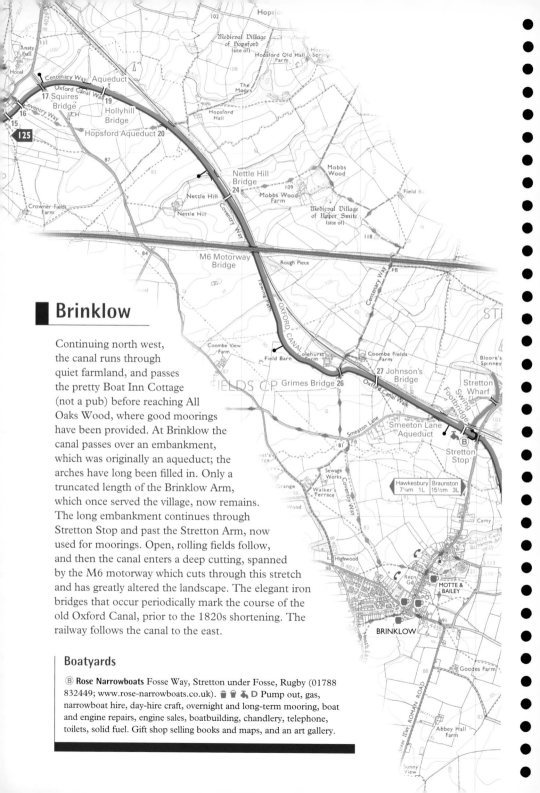

Brinklow

Continuing north west, the canal runs through quiet farmland, and passes the pretty Boat Inn Cottage (not a pub) before reaching All Oaks Wood, where good moorings have been provided. At Brinklow the canal passes over an embankment, which was originally an aqueduct; the arches have long been filled in. Only a truncated length of the Brinklow Arm, which once served the village, now remains. The long embankment continues through Stretton Stop and past the Stretton Arm, now used for moorings. Open, rolling fields follow, and then the canal enters a deep cutting, spanned by the M6 motorway which cuts through this stretch and has greatly altered the landscape. The elegant iron bridges that occur periodically mark the course of the old Oxford Canal, prior to the 1820s shortening. The railway follows the canal to the east.

Boatyards

Ⓑ **Rose Narrowboats** Fosse Way, Stretton under Fosse, Rugby (01788 832449; www.rose-narrowboats.co.uk). 🚻 🚿 ♨ **D** Pump out, gas, narrowboat hire, day-hire craft, overnight and long-term mooring, boat and engine repairs, engine sales, boatbuilding, chandlery, telephone, toilets, solid fuel. Gift shop selling books and maps, and an art gallery.

● **Harborough Magna**

Warwicks. PO box, tel, stores. Quiet red-brick village one mile to the north of the canal from bridges 43 or 48. The 13th–14th-C church has a Victorian west tower and many Victorian additions, including an interesting stained-glass window depicting Christ rising, with two angels, against a dark blue background.

● **Brinklow**

Warwicks. PO, tel, stores, garage, fish & chips. A spacious pre-industrial village built along a wide main street. The church of St John Baptist is of late Perpendicular style, and has some interesting 15th-C stained glass depicting birds, including a peacock. Its sloping floor climbs 12ft from west to east. Alongside is the substantial mound of a motte and bailey castle, built to defend the Fosse Way.

Pubs and Restaurants

🍺 **The White Lion** Broad Street, Brinklow (01788 832579; brinklowlion@aol.com). Traditional coaching inn with an old-fashioned bar, serving real ale and food (V) *L Mon–Sat.* Delightful garden with a play area. Folk music *Thur,* live music *weekends.* B & B.

🍺 **The Bulls Head** Broad Street, Brinklow (01788 832355; mrgriff@supanet.com). A smartly furnished family pub. Good food (V) served *L and E.*

Children welcome, indoor and outdoor play areas. Garden. B & B.

🍺 **The Raven** Broad Street, Brinklow (01788 832655). Friendly family pub at the top of the village, where real ale is served. Bar snacks *L (not Sun)* Children welcome, garden.

🍺 ✕ **The Dun Cow** Coventry Road, Brinklow (01788 810305). A locals' pub serving real ale, with food (V) *L and E.* Children welcome in the lounge. Courtyard. B & B.

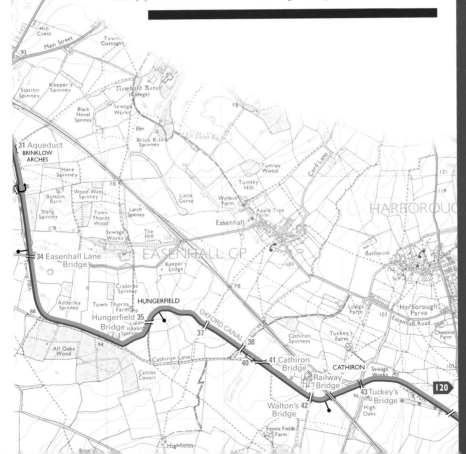

Hawkesbury Junction

The open landscape continues beyond Ansty, although the motorway is never far away. Soon the first signs of Coventry appear, with views of pylons and housing estates. The new Wyken Colliery Arm leaves to the west: it was built to replace the old one eaten up by the motorway which comes alongside the canal at this point: it is now used by the Coventry Cruising Club. Sharp bends then lead to the stop lock before Hawkesbury Junction, the end of the Oxford Canal where it joins the Coventry Canal. This last stretch of the Oxford Canal is characterised by the 1820s shortenings: straight cuttings and embankments date from this period, while the cast iron bridges mark the old route.

Pubs and Restaurants

🍺 **The Rose and Castle** Main Road, Ansty (02476 612822). Friendly and welcoming canalside pub serving real ale and an extensive range of good food (V) available *L and E*. Children welcome, play area and canalside garden. Moorings and 🚿.

🍺 **The Elephant & Castle** 445 Aldermans Green Road (02476 364606). Canalside, by Tusses Bridge (4). There is a good choice of real ale in this extended friendly local community pub. Bar snack are served *L*. Huge garden with a children's play area.

🍺 **The Old Crown** Aldermans Green Road (02476 365894). South of Tusses Bridge (4). Welcoming and cosy pub with carved woodwork, beams, brasses and snug settees, serving real ale. Children welcome, garden with play area. Karaoke *Tue*, disco *Fri*, live music *Sat*, quiz *Sun*.

🍺 ✕ **The Greyhound** Hawkesbury Junction (02476 363046). A fascinating pub beside the junction, decorated with canal and rugby memorabilia, together with an immense collection of Toby jugs, warmed by log fires in winter. An imaginative selection of food (V), especially pies and salads, served in the bar or restaurant *L and E*, and a choice of real ale is available. Canalside garden.

🍺 **The Boat Inn** Black Horse Road, Longford (02476 361438). A fine friendly pub with unspoilt rooms and a cosy lounge, all decorated with antiques, just a 3-minute walk north west of the junction. Real ale. Children welcome. Garden for the *summer* and a real fire for the *winter*.

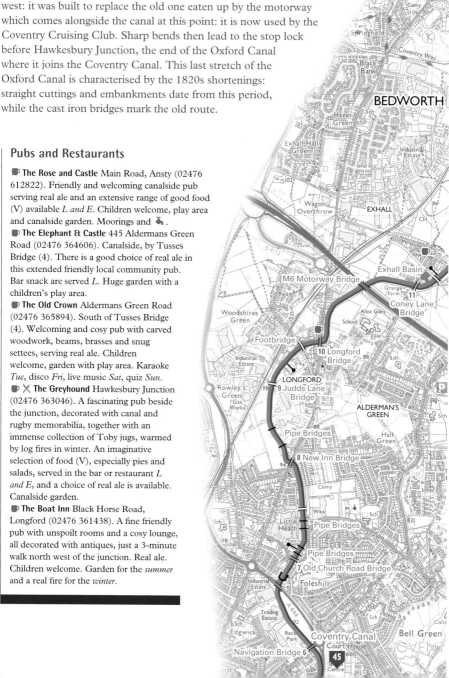

BEDWORTH

EXHALL

M6 Motorway Bridge

Exhall Basin

Coney Lane Bridge

11

ALDERMAN'S GREEN

10 Longford Bridge

LONGFORD

9 Judds Lane Bridge

Pipe Bridges

8 New Inn Bridge

Pipe Bridges

Pipe Bridges

7 Old Church Road Bridge

Foleshill

Navigation Bridge 6

Coventry Canal Court House

Bell Green

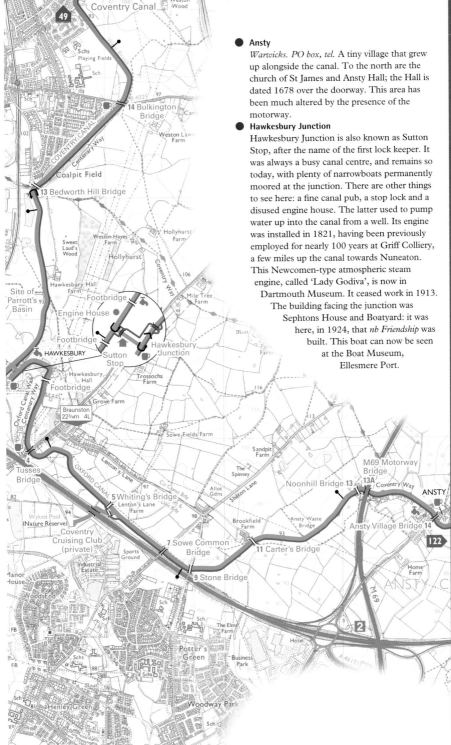

● **Ansty**

Warwicks. PO box, tel. A tiny village that grew up alongside the canal. To the north are the church of St James and Ansty Hall; the Hall is dated 1678 over the doorway. This area has been much altered by the presence of the motorway.

● **Hawkesbury Junction**

Hawkesbury Junction is also known as Sutton Stop, after the name of the first lock keeper. It was always a busy canal centre, and remains so today, with plenty of narrowboats permanently moored at the junction. There are other things to see here: a fine canal pub, a stop lock and a disused engine house. The latter used to pump water up into the canal from a well. Its engine was installed in 1821, having been previously employed for nearly 100 years at Griff Colliery, a few miles up the canal towards Nuneaton. This Newcomen-type atmospheric steam engine, called 'Lady Godiva', is now in Dartmouth Museum. It ceased work in 1913. The building facing the junction was Sephtons House and Boatyard: it was here, in 1924, that *nb Friendship* was built. This boat can now be seen at the Boat Museum, Ellesmere Port.

Brindley's Sow Aqueduct (see *page 135*)

STAFFORDSHIRE &
WORCESTERSHIRE CANAL: NORTH

MAXIMUM DIMENSIONS	MANAGER
Length: 70'	01785 284253
Beam: 7'	enquiries.norbury@britishwaterways.co.uk
Headroom: 6' 6"	

MILEAGE
AUTHERLEY JUNCTION to:
GREAT HAYWOOD JUNCTION: 20^1/$_2$ miles

Locks: 12

Construction of this navigation was begun immediately after that of the Trent &
Mersey, to effect the joining of the rivers Trent, Mersey and Severn. Engineered by
James Brindley, the Staffordshire & Worcestershire was opened throughout in 1772,
at a cost of rather over £100,000. It stretched 46 miles from Great Haywood on the
Trent & Mersey to the River Severn, which it joined at Stourport. The canal was an
immediate success. It was well placed to bring goods from the Potteries down to
Gloucester, Bristol and the West Country; while the Birmingham Canal, which
joined it half-way along at Aldersley Junction, fed manufactured goods northwards
from the Black Country to the Potteries via Great Haywood. In 1815 the Worcester
& Birmingham Canal opened, offering a more direct but heavily locked canal link
between Birmingham and the Severn. The Staffordshire & Worcestershire answered
this threat by gradually extending the opening times of the locks until, by 1830, they
were open 24 hours a day. When the Birmingham & Liverpool Junction Canal was
opened from Autherley to Nantwich in 1835, traffic bound for Merseyside from
Birmingham naturally began to use this more direct, modern canal. The
Staffordshire & Worcestershire lost a great deal of traffic over its length as most of
the boats now passed along only the ^{1}/$_2$-mile stretch of the Staffordshire &
Worcestershire Canal between Autherley and Aldersley Junctions. The company
levied absurdly high tolls for this tiny length. The B. & L. J. Company therefore
co-operated with the Birmingham Canal Company in 1836 to promote in
Parliament a Bill for the Tettenhall & Autherley Canal and Aqueduct. This project
was to be a canal flyover, going from the Birmingham Canal right over the
profiteering Staffordshire & Worcestershire and locking down into the Birmingham
& Liverpool Junction Canal. The Staffordshire & Worcestershire company had to
give way, and reduced its tolls to an acceptable level.
In spite of this set back, the Staffordshire & Worcestershire maintained a good
profit, and high dividends were paid throughout the rest of the 19th C. From the
1860s onwards, railway competition began to bite, and the company's profits began
to slip. Several modernisation schemes came to nothing, and the canal's trade
declined. Now the canal is used almost exclusively by pleasure craft. It is covered in
full *in Book 2* of this series.

Autherley Junction

Autherley Junction is marked by a big white bridge on the towpath side. The stop lock just beyond marks the entrance to the Shropshire Union: there is a useful boatyard just to the north of it. Leaving Autherley, the Staffordshire & Worcestershire runs through a very narrow cutting in rock, once known as 'Pendeford Rockin', after a local farm: there is only room for boats to pass in the designated places, so a good look out should be kept for oncoming craft. After passing the motorway and a rather conspicuous sewage works at Coven Heath, the navigation leaves behind the suburbs of Wolverhampton and enters pleasant farmland. The bridges need care: although the bridgeholes are reasonably wide, the actual arches are rather low.

● **Autherley Junction**
A busy canal junction with a full range of boating facilities close by.
● **Coven**
Staffs. PO, tel, stores, garage, fish & chips. The only true village on this section, Coven lies beyond a dual carriageway north west of Cross Green Bridge. There is a large number of shops, including a laundrette.

Near Gailey (see page 130)

Boatyards

Ⓑ **Water Travel** Autherley Junction, Oxley Moor Road, Wolverhampton (01902 782371). 🛉 🔧 D Pump out, gas, narrowboat hire, slipway, boat and engine repairs, chandlery, toilets.
Ⓑ **Oxley Marine** The Wharf, Oxley Moor Road, Wolverhampton (01902 789522). 🛉 D Pump out, gas, overnight and long-term mooring, slipway, crane, boat and engine sales and repairs. Licensed bar *each evening*, snacks.

WALKING & CYCLING
The towpath is generally in good condition for both walkers and cyclists.

BOAT TRIPS
Nb Stafford Carrying up to 42 passengers, with a bar and food. Public trips on the *first Sun each month*, plus private charter. For details telephone (01902) 789522.

Pubs and Restaurants

🍺 ✕ **Fox & Anchor Inn** Brewood Road, Cross Green (01902 790786). Canalside by Cross Green Bridge. Large and friendly pub with roof-top terrace. Real ale, and meals (V) available *all day*. Menu is traditional English, along with steaks and *Sun* roast. Children's menu, garden and good moorings.

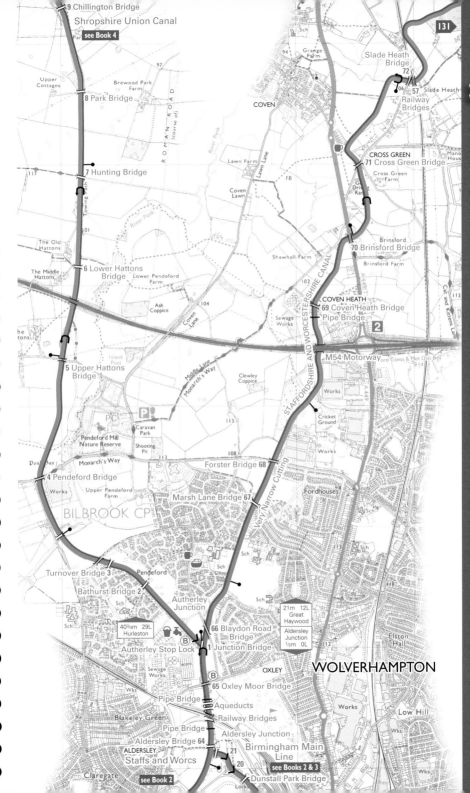

9 Chillington Bridge
Shropshire Union Canal
see Book 4

131

Slade Heath
Bridge

72

8 Park Bridge

57 Slade Heath
Railway
Bridges

Upper
Cottages

Brewood Park
Farm

COVEN

7 Hunting Bridge

CROSS GREEN
71 Cross Green Bridge

Cross Green
Farm

The Old
Hattons

70 Brinsford Bridge

The Middle
Hattons

6 Lower Hattons
Bridge

Lower Pendeford
Farm

Brinsford Farm

Ash
Coppice

COVEN HEATH
69 Coven Heath Bridge
Pipe Bridge

2

Sewage
Works

5 Upper Hattons
Bridge

Island
Pool

M54 Motorway

Clewley
Coppice

Cricket
Ground

Caravan
Park

Works

Pendeford Mill
Nature Reserve

Shooting
Pit

Forster Bridge 68

4 Pendeford Bridge

Fordhouses

Upper Pendeford
Farm

Marsh Lane Bridge 67

BILBROOK CP

Turnover Bridge 3

Pendeford

Bathurst Bridge 2

Autherley
Junction

21m 12L
Great
Haywood

40¾m 29L
Hurleston

66 Blaydon Road
Bridge
Junction Bridge

Aldersley
Junction
½m 0L

Autherley Stop Lock

OXLEY

WOLVERHAMPTON

Elston
Hall

65 Oxley Moor Bridge

Pipe Bridge

Works

Low Hill

Aqueducts
Railway Bridges

Aldersley Junction

Pipe Bridge

Aldersley Bridge 64

ALDERSLEY

Birmingham Main
Line
see Books 2 & 3

Staffs and Worcs

21
20

Claregate

see Book 2

Dunstall Park Bridge

Gailey Wharf

The considerable age of this canal is shown by its extremely twisting course, revealed after passing the railway bridge. There are few real centres of population along this stretch, which comprises largely former heathland. The canal widens just before bridge 74, where Brindley incorporated part of a medieval moat into the canal. Hatherton Junction marks the entrance of the former Hatherton Branch of the Staffordshire & Worcestershire Canal into the main line. This branch used to connect with the Birmingham Canal Navigations. It is closed above the derelict second lock, although the channel remains as a feeder for the Staffordshire & Worcestershire Canal. There is a campaign for its restoration. There is a *marina* at the junction. A little further along, a chemical works is encountered, astride the canal in what used to be woodlands. This was once called the 'Black Works', as lamp black was produced here. Gailey Wharf is about a mile further north: it is a small canal settlement that includes a boatyard and a large, round, toll keeper's watch-tower, containing a useful canal *shop*. The picturesque Wharf Cottage opposite has been restored as a bijou residence. The canal itself disappears under Watling Street and then falls rapidly through five locks towards Penkridge. These locks are very attractive, and some are accompanied by little brick bridges. The M6 motorway comes alongside for 1/2 mile, screening the reservoirs which feed the canal.

Pillaton Old Hall South east of bridge 85. Only the gate house and stone-built chapel remain of this late 15th-C brick mansion built by the Littleton family, although there are still traces of the hall and courtyard. The chapel contains a 13th-C wooden carving of a saint. Visiting is by appointment only: telephone (01785) 712200. The modest charge is donated to charity.
Gailey and Calf Heath reservoirs 1/2 mile east of Gailey Wharf, either side of the M6. These are feeder reservoirs for the canal, though rarely drawn on. The public has access to them as nature reserves to study the wide variety of natural life, especially the long-established heronry which is thriving on an island in Gailey Lower Reservoir. In Gailey Upper, fishing is available to the public from the riparian owner. In Gailey Lower a limited number of angling tickets are available on a season ticket basis each year from BW. There is club sailing on two of the reservoirs.

Boatyards

Ⓑ **Otherton Boat Haven** Otherton Hall Farm, Offerton (01785 712515; mobile 07966 184182; pdorrington@bun.com). 🚽 🚽 🛶 D Pump out, gas, overnight and long-term mooring, boat and engine sales and repairs, toilets.
Ⓑ **J D Boat Services** The Wharf, Watling Street, Standeford (01902 790811, www.jdboats.co.uk). Pump out, gas, boat and engine repairs, engine sales, boat building. Gifts and provisions opposite in the Roundhouse.
Ⓑ **Viking Afloat** At J B Boat Services (01905 610660, www.viking-afloat.com). Narrowboat hire.
Ⓑ **Calf Heath Marina** King's Road, Calf Heath (01902 790570, info@calf-heath-marina.co.uk). 🛶 D Pump out, gas, overnight and long-term moorings, telephone, toilet.

Pubs and Restaurants

✕ ♀ **Misty's Bar & Restaurant** Calf Heath Marina, King's Road, Calf Heath (01902 790570). Restaurant serving excellent and reasonably priced home-cooked food (V) *L and E.* Children welcome, garden.
🍺 **Spread Eagle** Watling Street, Gailey (01902 790212). About 1/2 mile west of Gailey Wharf. Large road house serving real ale and food (V) *all day.* Children welcome, and there is a spacious garden.
🍺 **Cross Keys** Filance Lane (01785 712826). Canalside, at Filance Bridge (84). Once a lonely canal pub, now it is modernised and surrounded by housing estates. Family orientated, it serves real ale and food (V) *L and E.* Garden, with *summer* barbecues. 🛶 There is a useful Spar *shop* 100yds north, on the estate.

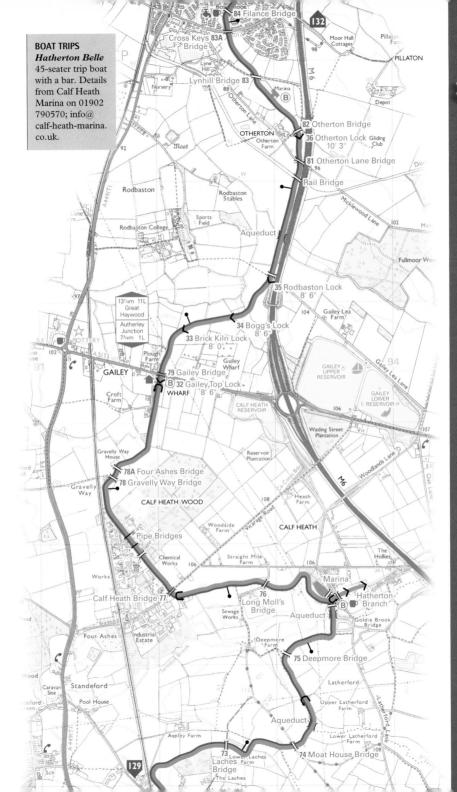

BOAT TRIPS
Hatherton Belle
45-seater trip boat with a bar. Details from Calf Heath Marina on 01902 790570; info@ calf-heath-marina. co.uk.

84 Filance Bridge

132

Cross Keys 83A Bridge

Moor Hall Cottages

Pillaton Farm

PILLATON

Depot

Lynhill Bridge 83

Lyne Hill

Nursery

Marina B

M6

OTHERTON

Otherton Lane

82 Otherton Bridge

36 Otherton Lock 10' 3"

Gliding Club

Moat

Otherton Farm

81 Otherton Lane Bridge

Rodbaston

Rodbaston Stables

Micklewood Lane

Rail Bridge

102

Micl

Sports Field

Aqueduct

Fullmoor Wood

Rodbaston College

35 Rodbaston Lock 8' 6"

104

Gailey Lea Farm

Gailey Lea Lane

94

13¼m 11L Great Haywood

Autherley Junction 7¾m 1L

34 Bogg's Lock 8' 6"

33 Brick Kiln Lock 8' 0"

Plough Farm

Gailey Wharf

GAILEY UPPER RESERVOIR

79 Gailey Bridge

GAILEY

B 32 Gailey Top Lock 8' 6"

WHARF

Croft Farm

CALF HEATH RESERVOIR

GAILEY LOWER L. RESERVOIR

106

107

Watling Street Plantation

Vic

Gravelly Way House

Reservoir Plantation

78A Four Ashes Bridge

78 Gravelly Way Bridge

Woodlands Lane

M6

Oak Lane

Gravelly Way

CALF HEATH WOOD

108

Heath Farm

Woodside Farm

Vicarage Road

CALF HEATH

Pipe Bridges

Chemical Works

106

Straight Mile Farm

106

The Hollies

Works

Marina

Calf Heath Bridge 77

Long Moll's Bridge

Hatherton Branch

B

Sewage Works

Aqueduct

Goldie Brook Bridge

Four Ashes

Industrial Estate

Deepmore Farm

75 Deepmore Bridge

Caravan Site

Standeford

Pool House

Latherford

Upper Latherford Farm

Aqueduct

Lower Latherford Farm

108

Aspley Farm

129

73 Lower Laches Laches Farm Bridge

74 Moat House Bridge

The Laches

Penkridge

The navigation now passes through Penkridge and is soon approached by the little River Penk: the two water courses share the valley for the next few miles. Apart from the noise of the motorway this is a pleasant valley: there are plenty of trees, a handful of locks and the large Teddesley Park alongside the canal. At Acton Trussell the M6 roars off to the north west and once again peace returns to the waterway. Teddesley Park Bridge was at one time quite ornamental, and became known as 'Fancy Bridge'. It is less so now. At Shutt Hill an iron post at the bottom of the lock is the only reminder of a small wharf which once existed here. The post was used to turn the boats into the dock.

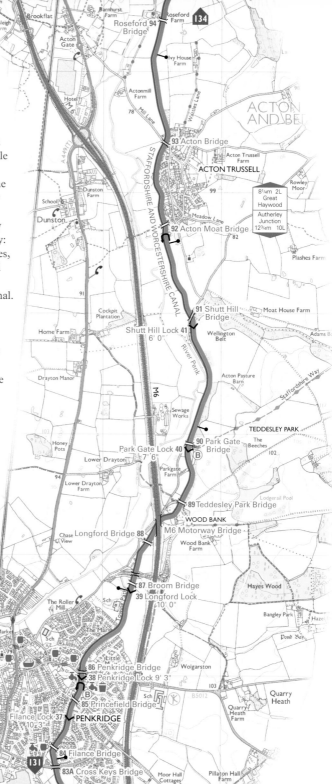

8¼m 2L
Great
Haywood
Autherley
Junction
12¾m 10L

● **Penkridge**
Staffs. PO, tel, stores, garage, bank, station.
Above Penkridge Lock is a good place to tie up
in this relatively old village. It is bisected by a
trunk road, but luckily most of the village lies
to the east of it. The church of St Michael is tall
and sombre, and is well-kept. A harmonious
mixture of styles, the earliest part dates from
the 11th C, but the whole was restored in
1881. There is a fine Dutch 18th-C wrought
iron screen brought from Cape Town, and the
tower is believed to date from about 1500.
There are fine monuments of the Littletons of

Pillaton Hall (see the previous section), dating
from 1558 and later.
Teddesley Park On the east bank of the canal.
The Hall, once the family seat of the Littletons,
was used during the last war as a prisoner-of-
war camp, but has since been demolished. Its
extensive wooded estate still remains.
● **Acton Trussell**
Staffs. Tel, stores. A village overwhelmed by
modern housing: much the best way to see it
is from the canal. The church stands to the
south, overlooking the navigation. The west
tower dates from the 13th C, topped by a
spire built in 1562.

Boatyards

Ⓑ **Teddesley Boat Company** Park Gate Lock,
Teddesley Road, Penkridge (01785 714692,
www.narrowboats.co.uk). **D** Pump out, gas,
narrowboat hire, overnight and long-term
mooring, winter storage, crane, boat and
engine sales and repairs, boat building,

telephone, books and maps, café. *Closed Sun.*
For chandlery telephone (01785) 712437.
Ⓑ **Tom's Moorings** Cannock Road, Penkridge
(01543 414808). Above Penkridge Lock.
⚓ Pump out, gas, overnight and long-term
mooring.

*Tixall Lock (*see *page 135)*

Pubs and Restaurants

🍺 **The Boat** Cannock Road (01785 714178).
Canalside, by Penkridge Lock. Mellow and
friendly red-brick pub dating from 1779, with
plenty of brass and other bits and pieces in
the homely bars. Real ale is served, and food
(V) is available *L and E (not Sun E)*. Children
welcome, garden.
🍺 **Star** Market Place, Penkridge (01785
712513). Fine old pub, tastefully renovated
and serving real ale and bar meals (V) *12.00–
17.00 in summer, reduced hours in winter.*
Children welcome. Outside seating.

🍺 **White Hart** Stone Cross, Penkridge (01785
712242). This historic former coaching inn,
visited by Mary, Queen of Scots, and
Elizabeth I, has an impressive frontage, timber
framed with three gables. It serves real ale,
and meals (V) *L and E.* Outside seating.
🍺 **Railway** Wolverhampton Road, Penkridge
(01785 712685). Real ale is available in this
listed and historic main road pub, along with
meals (V) *L and E.* Children welcome.
Garden.

WALKING & CYCLING
The Staffordshire Way crosses the canal between bridges 89 and 90. This 90-mile path strtetches
from Mow Cop in the north (near the Macclesfield Canal) to Kinver Edge in the south, using the
Caldon Canal towpath on the way. It connects with the Gritstone Trail, the Hereford & Worcester
Way and the Heart of England Way. A guide book is available from local Tourist Information Centres.

Tixall

Continuing north along the shallow Penk valley, the canal soon reaches Radford Bridge, the nearest point to Stafford. It is about 1½ miles to the centre of town: there is a frequent bus service. A mile further north the canal bends around to the south east and follows the pretty valley of the River Sow. At Milford the navigation crosses the Sow via an aqueduct – an early structure by James Brindley, carried heavily on low brick arches; there is a good *farm shop* south of bridge 105, through the railway bridge. Dredging around here revealed the presence of great numbers of freshwater mussels. Tixall Lock offers some interesting views in all directions: the castellated entrance to Shugborough Railway Tunnel at the foot of the thick woods of Cannock Chase and the distant outline of Tixall Gatehouse. The canal now completes its journey to the Trent & Mersey Canal at Great Haywood. It is a length of waterway quite unlike any other. Proceeding along this very charming valley, the navigation enters Tixall Wide – an amazing and delightful stretch of water more resembling a lake than a canal, and navigable to the edges. The Wide is noted for its kingfisher population. On the low hill to the north is the equally remarkable Tixall Gatehouse, while woods across the valley conceal Shugborough Hall. The River Trent is met, on its way south from Stoke-on-Trent, and crossed on an aqueduct. There is a wharf, and fresh produce can be purchased at the *farm* near here; gifts are sold in the old canal toll booth. The Trent & Mersey Canal is entered through an elegantly arched bridge, the subject of a very famous photograph taken by the canal historian Eric de Maré.

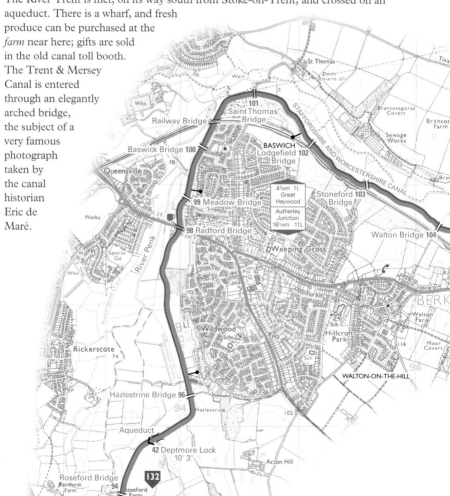

BOAT TRIPS
Milford Star (01785 663728).
Regular *hourly trips* from
Great Haywood, *departing
Apr–Sep on Wed, Thur, Sat
and Sun from midday.* Up to
40 people can be carried on
this comfortable boat which
has a ship's bar. *Book for
weekends and B Hols.* Also
available for private charter,
when food and music can be
arranged.

WALKING & CYCLING
There is a Nature Trail at
Milford Common, and visitors
to Shugborough Hall can enjoy
excellent walks in the park.

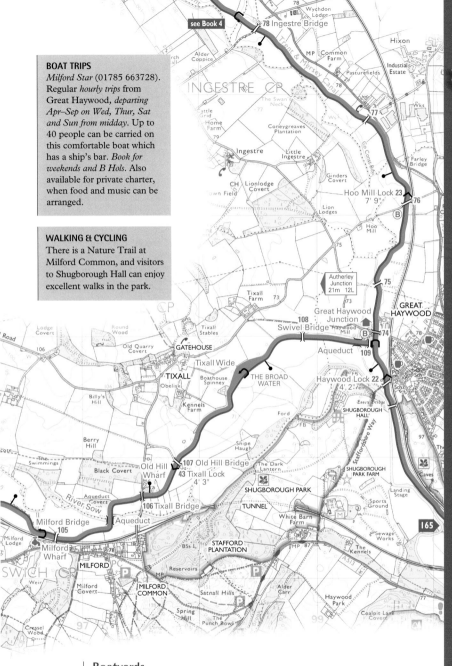

Boatyards

Ⓑ **Anglo Welsh** The Canal Wharf, Mill Lane, Great Haywood (01889 881711,
www.anglowelsh.co.uk). 🚽 🏮 ♨ D Pump out, gas, narrowboat hire, day-hire
craft, overnight and long-term mooring, boat sales, engine repairs, chandlery,
toilets, books, maps and gifts.

Stafford

Staffs. All services. This town is well worth visiting, since there is a remarkable wealth of fine old buildings. These include a handsome City Hall complex of ornamental Italianate buildings, c.1880. The robust-looking gaol is nearby; and the church of St Mary stands in very pleasing and spacious grounds. There are some pretty back alleys: Church Lane contains a splendid-looking eating house, and at the bottom of the lane a fruiterer's shop is in a thatched cottage built in 1610.

The Shire Hall Gallery Market Square, Stafford (01785 278345). A stimulating variety of work by local artists, craftsmen, printmakers, jewellers, photographers and others. *Open Mon–Sat 09.30–17.00.*

Tourist Information Centre Market Street, Stafford (01785 619619, tic@staffordbc.gov.uk).

The Stafford Branch

Just west of bridge 101 there was once a lock taking a branch off the Staffordshire & Worcestershire to Stafford. One mile long, it was unusual in that it was not a canal but the canalised course of the River Sow.

Milford

Staffs. PO, tel, stores, garage. Best reached from Tixall Bridge (106). Milford Hall is hidden by trees.

Tixall

Staffs. Tel, stores. Just to the east are the stables and the gatehouse of the long-vanished Tixall Hall. This massive square Elizabethan building dates from 1598 and is fully four storeys high. It stands alone in a field and is considered to be one of the most ambitious gatehouses in the country. The gatehouse is now available for holiday lets: telephone the Landmark Trust (01628 825925) for details.

Great Haywood

Staffs. PO, tel, stores. Centre of the Great Haywood and Shugborough Conservation Area, the village is not particularly beautiful, but it is closely connected in many ways to Shugborough Park, to which it is physically linked by the very old Essex Bridge, where the crystal clear waters of the River Sow join the Trent on its way down from Stoke.

Shugborough Hall *NT.* Walk south along the road from bridge 106 to the A513 at Milford Common. The main entrance is on your left. The present house dates from 1693, but was substantially altered by James Stuart around 1760 and by Samuel Wyatt around the turn of the 18th C. The Trust has leased the whole to Staffordshire County Council who now manage it. The house has been restored at great expense. There are some magnificent rooms and treasures inside.

Museum of Staffordshire Life This excellent establishment, Staffordshire's County Museum, is housed in the old stables adjacent to Shugborough Hall. Open since 1966, it is superbly laid out and contains all sorts of exhibits concerned with old country life in Staffordshire.

Shugborough Park There are some remarkable sights in the large park that encircles the Hall. Thomas Anson, who inherited the estate in 1720, enlisted in 1744 the help of his famous brother, Admiral George Anson, to beautify and improve the house and the park. In 1762 he commissioned James Stuart, a neo-Grecian architect, to embellish the grounds. 'Athenian' Stuart set to with a will, and the spectacular results of his work can be seen scattered round the park.

The Park Farm Designed by Samuel Wyatt, it contains an agricultural museum, a working mill and a rare breeds centre. Traditional country skills such as bread-making, butter-churning and cheese-making are demonstrated.

Shugborough Hall, Grounds, Museum and Farm (01889 881388; www.nationaltrust.org.uk). *Open Apr–Sep Tue–Sun 11.00–17.00 (also first 3 Suns Oct).* Charge. Parties must book. Tea rooms, shop.

Pubs and Restaurants

The Radford Bank Inn Canalside at bridge 98. (01785 2428250). Food (V) is served *all day, every day until 21.00,* along with real ale. Children are welcome *until 21.00,* and there is a garden.

The Clifford Arms Main Road, Great Haywood (01889 881321). There has apparently been a pub on this site for almost 1000 years. At one time it was a coaching inn. Now it is a friendly village local with an open fire, serving real ale and bar and restaurant meals (V) *L and E.* Small garden with yews.

Lockhouse Restaurant Trent Lane, Great Haywood (01889 881294). Personally run, very friendly and handy for Anglo-Welsh visitors, they offer morning and afternoon tea, coffee and cakes, hot and cold carvery *L daily* and home-cooked English food (V – but book for special dishes) *E Fri–Sat only (booking advisable).* Real ale is available for the thirsty. Canalside garden, and just a couple of minutes' walk from the village.

The Fox & Hounds Main Road, Great Haywood (01889 881252). Plush village pub with an open fire, serving a good selection of real ale. Home-made food (V) *L Thur–Sun and E Mon–Sat.* Children welcome, and there is a garden.

STRATFORD-ON-AVON CANAL

MAXIMUM DIMENSIONS
King's Norton to Kingswood
Length: 70'
Beam: 7'
Headroom: 7' 3"

MILEAGE
KING'S NORTON JUNCTION to:
Hockley Heath: 9³/4 miles

KINGSWOOD Junction with Grand Union Canal: 12¹/2
Locks: 14

MANAGER
01564 784634
enquiries.lapworth@britishwaterways.co.uk

The opening of the Oxford Canal in 1790 and of the Coventry Canal throughout shortly afterwards opened up a continuous waterway from London to the rapidly developing industrial area based on Birmingham. It also gave access, via the Trent & Mersey Canal, to the expanding pottery industry based around Stoke-on-Trent, to the Mersey, and to the East Midlands coalfield. When the Warwick & Birmingham and Warwick & Napton Canals were projected to pass within 8 miles of Stratford-on-Avon, the business interests of that town realised that the prosperity being generated by these new trade arteries would pass them by unless Stratford acquired direct access to the network. And so on 28 March 1793 an Act of Parliament was passed for the construction of the Stratford-on-Avon Canal, to start at King's Norton on the Worcester & Birmingham Canal.

Progress was rapid at first, but almost the total estimated cost of the complete canal was spent on cutting the 9³/4 lock-free miles to Hockley Heath within the first three years. It then took another four years, more negotiations, a revision of the route and another Act of Parliament to get things going again. By 1803 the canal was open from King's Norton Junction to its junction with the Warwick & Birmingham Canal (now part of the Grand Union main line) near Lapworth. Cutting recommenced in 1812, the route being revised yet again in 1815 to include the present junction with the River Avon at Stratford.

In its most prosperous period, the canal's annual traffic exceeded 180,000 tons, including 50,000 tons of coal through the complete canal, down to Stratford. By 1835 the canal was suffering from railway competition. This grew so rapidly that in 1845 the Canal Company decided to sell out to the Great Western Railway. In 1890 the tonnage carried was still a quarter of what it had been 50 years before, but the fall in ton-miles was much greater. This pattern of decline continued in the 20th C, and by the 1950s only an occasional working boat used the northern section; the southern section (Lapworth to Stratford) was badly silted, some locks were unusable and some of the short pounds below Wilmcote were dry.

After World War II interest began to grow in boating as a recreation. In 1955 a Board of Survey had recommended sweeping canal closures, including the southern section of the Stratford Canal, but public protest was such that a Committee of Enquiry was set up in 1958, and this prompted the start of a massive campaign to save the canal. The campaign was successful: the decision not to abandon it was announced by the Ministry on 22 May 1959. On 16 October of the same year the National Trust announced that it had agreed a lease from the British Transport Commission under which the Trust would assume responsibility for restoring and maintaining the southern section.

The reopening ceremony was performed by Queen Elizabeth the Queen Mother on 11 July 1964, after more than four years of hard work by prison labourers, canal enthusiasts, Army units and a handful of National Trust staff. On 1 April 1988 control of the southern section of the Stratford-on-Avon Canal was passed to the British Waterways Board (now British Waterways).

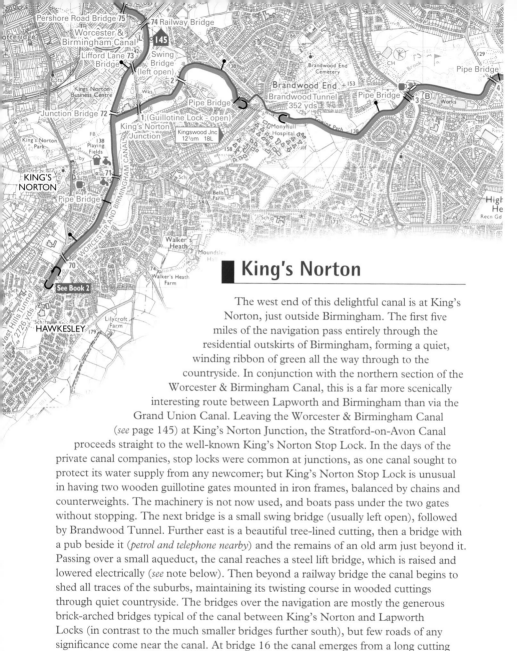

King's Norton

The west end of this delightful canal is at King's Norton, just outside Birmingham. The first five miles of the navigation pass entirely through the residential outskirts of Birmingham, forming a quiet, winding ribbon of green all the way through to the countryside. In conjunction with the northern section of the Worcester & Birmingham Canal, this is a far more scenically interesting route between Lapworth and Birmingham than via the Grand Union Canal. Leaving the Worcester & Birmingham Canal (*see* page 145) at King's Norton Junction, the Stratford-on-Avon Canal proceeds straight to the well-known King's Norton Stop Lock. In the days of the private canal companies, stop locks were common at junctions, as one canal sought to protect its water supply from any newcomer; but King's Norton Stop Lock is unusual in having two wooden guillotine gates mounted in iron frames, balanced by chains and counterweights. The machinery is not now used, and boats pass under the two gates without stopping. The next bridge is a small swing bridge (usually left open), followed by Brandwood Tunnel. Further east is a beautiful tree-lined cutting, then a bridge with a pub beside it (*petrol and telephone nearby*) and the remains of an old arm just beyond it. Passing over a small aqueduct, the canal reaches a steel lift bridge, which is raised and lowered electrically (*see* note below). Then beyond a railway bridge the canal begins to shed all traces of the suburbs, maintaining its twisting course in wooded cuttings through quiet countryside. The bridges over the navigation are mostly the generous brick-arched bridges typical of the canal between King's Norton and Lapworth Locks (in contrast to the much smaller bridges further south), but few roads of any significance come near the canal. At bridge 16 the canal emerges from a long cutting and is joined by a feeder from the nearby Earlswood Reservoir. Boats are moored along this, since it is the base of the Earlswood Motor Yacht Club. There are no villages along this rural stretch of canal, but at Salter Street there is a modern school and a strange Victorian church.

NAVIGATIONAL NOTES

You will need a BW key to operate bridge 8.

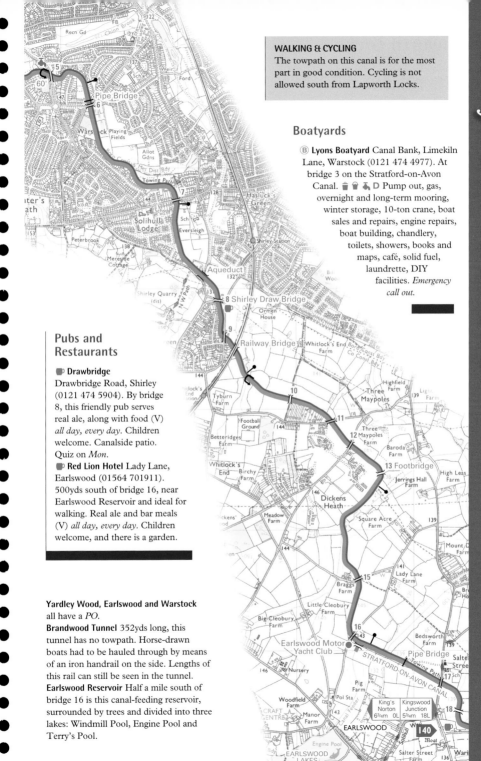

WALKING & CYCLING
The towpath on this canal is for the most part in good condition. Cycling is not allowed south from Lapworth Locks.

Boatyards

Ⓑ **Lyons Boatyard** Canal Bank, Limekiln Lane, Warstock (0121 474 4977). At bridge 3 on the Stratford-on-Avon Canal. 🚿 🛢 🔧 D Pump out, gas, overnight and long-term mooring, winter storage, 10-ton crane, boat sales and repairs, engine repairs, boat building, chandlery, toilets, showers, books and maps, café, solid fuel, laundrette, DIY facilities. *Emergency call out.*

Pubs and Restaurants

🍺 **Drawbridge** Drawbridge Road, Shirley (0121 474 5904). By bridge 8, this friendly pub serves real ale, along with food (V) *all day, every day.* Children welcome. Canalside patio. Quiz on *Mon.*

🍺 **Red Lion Hotel** Lady Lane, Earlswood (01564 701911). 500yds south of bridge 16, near Earlswood Reservoir and ideal for walking. Real ale and bar meals (V) *all day, every day.* Children welcome, and there is a garden.

Yardley Wood, Earlswood and Warstock all have a *PO*.

Brandwood Tunnel 352yds long, this tunnel has no towpath. Horse-drawn boats had to be hauled through by means of an iron handrail on the side. Lengths of this rail can still be seen in the tunnel.

Earlswood Reservoir Half a mile south of bridge 16 is this canal-feeding reservoir, surrounded by trees and divided into three lakes: Windmill Pool, Engine Pool and Terry's Pool.

Lapworth Locks

The canal continues on its south easterly course, passing through quiet countryside interrupted only by the incessant roar of the M42 motorway, crossing overhead. There is a good *bakery* north of bridge 20. There are no locks, and the bridges – especially those in the cuttings – are still the big brick arches worthy of a broader canal. At Hockley Heath (bridge 25) there is a tiny arm that once served a coal wharf. Nearby the Wharf Inn overlooks the canal, and there is a useful *petrol station* here. East of here things change dramatically, for the first of the locks down to Kingswood Junction is reached. The top lock is numbered 2, as the old stop lock at King's Norton is number 1. The surroundings of the top lock are indeed pleasant: a white house enclosed by walls and hemmed in by trees stands beside the lock, while a cottage with a delightful garden faces the towpath just below.

To the south west can be seen the spire of Lapworth church. After the first four locks, there is a ¹/₂-mile breathing space: then the Lapworth flight begins in earnest, with each of the next nine locks

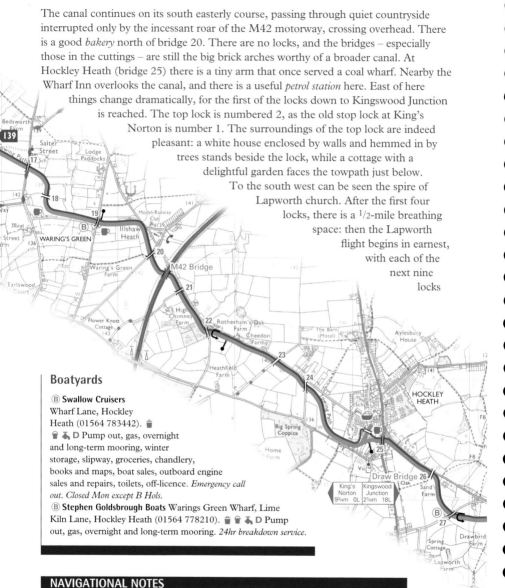

Boatyards

(B) **Swallow Cruisers**
Wharf Lane, Hockley
Heath (01564 783442). 🚿
🚻 ♨ **D** Pump out, gas, overnight and long-term mooring, winter storage, slipway, groceries, chandlery, books and maps, boat sales, outboard engine sales and repairs, toilets, off-licence. *Emergency call out. Closed Mon except B Hols.*
(B) **Stephen Goldsbrough Boats** Warings Green Wharf, Lime Kiln Lane, Hockley Heath (01564 778210). 🚿 🚻 ♨ **D** Pump out, gas, overnight and long-term mooring. *24hr breakdown service.*

NAVIGATIONAL NOTES

1 Bank erosion is a serious problem on all canals, and especially so on this one. *Please go slowly* to minimise your wash.
2 Bridges 26 and 28 operate hydraulically, using a lock windlass.
3 Due to rebuilding, the chamber of lock 15 on the Lapworth flight is now over 2ft shorter than the other locks. Those in full-length boats should take extra care when descending.

spaced only a few yards from its neighbour. There is a useful *canal shop* by lock 14 selling groceries, home-made bread and cakes, brassware and gifts. The short intervening pounds have been enlarged to provide a bigger working reservoir of water, so that one side of each lock is virtually an isthmus. The locks have double bottom gates and are not heavy going. They are interspersed with the old cast iron split bridges that are such a charming feature of the Stratford-on-Avon Canal. These bridges are built in two halves, separated by a one inch gap so that the towing line between a horse and a boat could be dropped through the gap without having to disconnect the horse. Below lock 19 is Kingswood Junction: boats heading for Stratford should keep right here. A short branch to the left leads under the railway line to the Grand Union Canal, or you can use the Lapworth Link after lock 22 if you are heading north to the GU, avoiding unnecessary lockage.

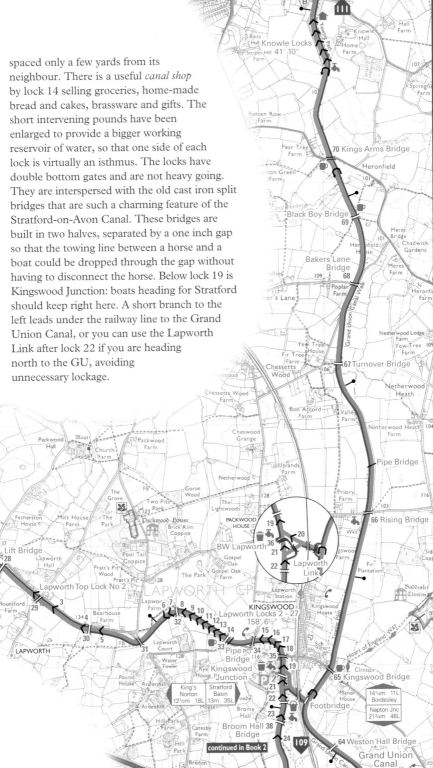

● **Hockley Heath**
Warwicks. PO, tel, stores, garage. A featureless place, but the several shops are conveniently close to the canal bridge, and the pub is pleasant.

● **Lapworth**
Warwicks. PO, tel, stores, garage, station. Indivisible from Kingswood, this is more a residential area than a village. Two canals pass through Lapworth: the heavily locked Stratford-on-Avon Canal and, to the east, the main line of the Grand Union Canal. These two waterways, and the short spur that connects them, are easily the most interesting aspect of Lapworth. The canalside buildings are attractive and there are two small reservoirs at the junction. The mostly 15th-C church is quite separate from the village and is 1¹/2 miles west of the junction; it contains an interesting monument by Eric Gill, 1928.

Packwood House *NT* (01564 782024). Hockley Heath, 2 miles west of bridge 66. Timber-framed Tudor house, dating from the late 16th C and enlarged in the 17th C, where Cromwell's general, Henry Ireton, slept before the Battle of Edgehill in 1642. Owned by the Featherstones until 1869, it was eventually purchased by Alfred Ash, who repaired the house and reinstated the gardens. Collection of tapestry, needlework and furniture. Park with formal grounds and 17th-C yew garden possibly laid out to represent the Sermon on the Mount, the trees taking the place of Jesus and his followers. *House open Mar–Oct, Wed–Sun 12.00–16.30.* Charge. Events are staged *during the summer.*

Pubs and Restaurants

🍺 **The Bull's Head** Lime Kiln Lane, Salter Street (01564 702335). ¹/4 mile south of bridge 17. Pleasant, low-ceilinged country pub in converted cottages, serving traditional and continental food (V) *L and E Mon–Sat, and Sun 12.00–18.00.* Real ale. Garden with a water pump, and there is a resident ghost – a 17th-C limekiln worker who appears during July and August. Games in the cupboard, and dominoes are played *Thur and Sun.* Live music *middle Sat of month.*

🍺 **The Blue Bell Cider House** Warings Green Road, Hockley Heath (01564 702328). Canalside, at bridge 19. A pretty, traditional cider house serving real draught cider and a couple of guest real ales. It is a drinkers pub, but bar meals and snacks (V) are available *L and E (not Sun and Mon E)* with a children's menu. Garden with playground. *Wed* is quiz night. Good mooring jetty for patrons.

✗ ♀ **Kam-Shun** 2362 Stratford Road, Hockley Heath (01564 782782). Highly recommended Cantonese food *E Tue–Sun.* Children welcome.

🍺 ✗ **The Wharf Tavern** Stratford Road, Hockley Heath (01564 782075). Canalside, at bridge 25. A smart pub with a pleasant canalside garden and adventure playground, offering real ale and bar meals (V) (carvery) *L and E daily.* Children very welcome. *Thur* is quiz night. Moorings.

🍺 **The Boot Inn** Old Warwick Road, Lapworth (01564 782464). Near lock 14. Quaint cosmopolitan country pub serving real ale. Fashionable bar meals (V) from chargrill to oysters *L and E.* Garden with gas heaters for cooler nights!

🍺 **The Navigation** Old Warwick Road, canalside at Kingswood (01564 783337). By bridge 65 on the Grand Union. Real ale and real draught cider. Bar meals (V) *L and E.* Children welcome. Moorings.

Lapworth Locks (see page 141)

WORCESTER & BIRMINGHAM CANAL

MAXIMUM DIMENSIONS
Length: 71' 6"
Beam: 7'
Headroom: 8'

MANAGER
01564 784634
enquiries.lapworth@britishwaterways.co.uk

MILEAGE
KING'S NORTON JUNCTION to:
BIRMINGHAM Gas Street Basin: 5¹/2 miles
No locks

The Bill for the Worcester & Birmingham Canal was passed in 1791 in spite of fierce opposition from the Staffordshire & Worcestershire Canal proprietors, who saw trade on their route to the Severn threatened. The supporters of the Bill claimed that the route from Birmingham and the Black Country towns would be much shorter, enabling traffic to avoid the then notorious shallows in the Severn below Stourport. The Birmingham Canal Company also opposed the Bill and succeeded in obtaining a clause preventing the new navigation from approaching within 7ft of their water. This resulted in the famous Worcester Bar separating the two canals in the centre of Birmingham.

Construction of the canal began at the Birmingham end following the line originally surveyed by John Snape and Josiah Clowes. Even at this early stage difficulties with water supply were encountered. The company was obliged by the Act authorising the canal to safeguard water supplies to the mills on the streams south of Birmingham. To do this, and to supply water for the summit level, ten reservoirs were planned or constructed. The high cost of these engineering works led to a change of policy: instead of building a broad canal, the company decided to build it with narrow locks, in order to save money in construction and water in operation.

The canal was completed in 1815. In the same year an agreement with the Birmingham Canal proprietors permitted the cutting of a stop lock through Worcester Bar. The canal had cost £610,000, exceeding its original estimate by many thousands of pounds. Industrial goods and coal were carried down to Worcester, often for onward shipping to Bristol, while grain, timber and agricultural produce were returned to the growing towns of the Midlands. However the opening of railways in the 1840s and 1850s reduced traffic considerably and had a profound effect on the fortunes of the canal.

By the early 1900s the commercial future of the canal was uncertain, although the works were in much better condition than on many other canals. Schemes to enlarge the navigation as part of a Bristol–Birmingham route came to nothing. Commercial carrying continued until about 1964, the traffic being mostly between the two Cadbury factories of Bournville and Blackpole, and to Frampton on the Gloucester & Sharpness Canal. After nationalisation, several proposals were made to abandon the canal, but the 1960s brought a dramatic increase in the number of pleasure boats using the waterway thus securing its future use. The whole of the canal is covered *in Book 2*.

King's Norton

To the north of King's Norton Junction, where the Stratford-on-Avon Canal (*see* page 138) joins the Worcester & Birmingham Canal, the canal passes through an industrial area, but thankfully seems to hold the factories at bay on one side, while a railway line, the main line from Worcester and the south west to Birmingham, draws alongside on its west flank. Canal and railway together drive through the middle of Cadbury's Bournville works, which is interesting rather than oppressive. Beyond it is Bournville station, followed by a cutting.

Bournville Garden Factory The creation of the Cadbury family, who moved their cocoa and chocolate manufacturing business south from the centre of Birmingham. The Bournville estate was begun in the late 1800s and is an interesting example of controlled suburban development. There were once old canal wharves here, which became disused when most of the ingredients travelled by rail – but the sidings closed in the late 1960s and now regrettably everything comes by road.

Cadbury World Linden Road (Information line 0121 451 4180). It is by the factory and signposted from the canal, where there are moorings. An exhibition dedicated to the history and the love of chocolate. Audio-visual displays, a jungle to explore, and Victorian Birmingham. *Open daily*

Mar–Nov (restricted in winter), telephone 0121 451 4159 for details. Charge.

Selly Manor and Minworth Greaves Sycamore Road, Bournville (0121 472 0199). Two half-timbered Birmingham houses of the 13th and early 14th C re-erected in the 1920s and 1930s in Bournville. They contain a collection of old furniture and domestic equipment. *Open all year Tue–Fri 10.00–17.00; also Apr–Oct, Sat and Sun 14.00–17.00.* Charge. The nearest point of access from the canal is at Bournville station: walk west to the Cadbury's entrance. There is a public right of way (Birdcage Walk) through the works: bear right at the fork, then turn right at the village green. The two houses are close by, on the left. Selly Oak and Bournville both have a *PO*.

King's Norton

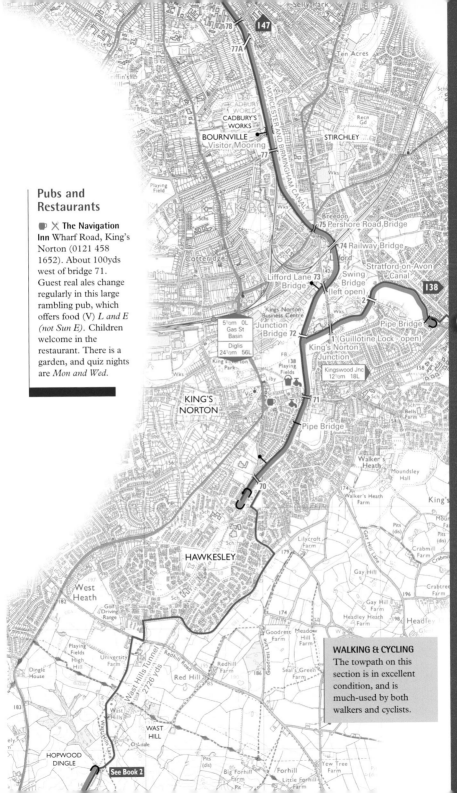

Pubs and Restaurants

🍺 ✕ **The Navigation Inn** Wharf Road, King's Norton (0121 458 1652). About 100yds west of bridge 71. Guest real ales change regularly in this large rambling pub, which offers food (V) *L and E (not Sun E)*. Children welcome in the restaurant. There is a garden, and quiz nights are *Mon and Wed*.

WALKING & CYCLING
The towpath on this section is in excellent condition, and is much-used by both walkers and cyclists.

Birmingham

Soon the railway vanishes briefly behind the buildings of Selly Oak. Between bridge 80 and the next, skewed, railway bridge is the site of the junction with the Dudley Canal, but no trace remains now of either the junction or the canal itself. North of here the canal and railway together shrug off industry and town, and head north on an embankment towards Birmingham in splendid isolation and attractive surroundings. Below on either side is the green spaciousness of residential Edgbaston, its botanical gardens and woods. A hospital is on the west side. The University of Birmingham is on the east side; among its many large buildings the most conspicuous is the Chamberlain Campanile Tower, which was erected in 1900. At one of the bridges near the University, two Roman forts used to stand; but most evidence of them was obliterated by the building of the canal and railway. Only a reconstructed part of the larger fort now exists. There is a useful *Sainsbury's* just south of bridge 80. Past the University's moorings, canal and railway enter a cutting, in which their enjoyable seclusion from the neighbourhood is complete; the charming old bridges are high, while the cutting is steep and always lined by overhanging foliage. It is a remarkable approach to Birmingham. The railway is the canal's almost constant companion, dipping away here and there to reappear a short distance further on; but trains are not too frequent, and in a way their occasional appearance heightens the remoteness that attaches to this length of canal. At one stage the two routes pass through short tunnels side by side: the canal's tunnel, Edgbaston, is the northernmost of the five on this canal and the only one with a towpath through it. It is a mere 105yds long. The Worcester & Birmingham Canal now completes its delightful approach to Birmingham. The railway disappears underneath in a tunnel to New Street station, while the canal passes Holiday Wharf and makes a sharp left turn to the basin. The terminus of the Worcester & Birmingham Canal is the former stop lock at Gas Street Basin; this is known as Worcester Bar, for originally there was a physical barrier here between the Worcester & Birmingham Canal and the much older Birmingham Canal. The latter refused to allow a junction, and for several years goods had to be transhipped at this point from one canal to the other. This absurd situation was remedied by an Act of Parliament in 1815, by which a stop lock was allowed to be inserted to connect the two canals. Nowadays the stop gates are kept open and one can pass straight through, on to the Birmingham Canal (*see* page 36). Don't leave your boat unattended in this area, although Gas Street Basin should be OK.

The Dudley Canal This canal used to join the Worcester & Birmingham Canal at Selly Oak, thus providing a southern bypass round Birmingham. The eastern end of the canal has been closed for many years, and will certainly remain so. The tremendously long (3795yd) Lappal Tunnel, now collapsed, emerged 2 miles from Selly Oak. This bore was more like a drainpipe than a navigable tunnel – it was only 7ft 9in wide, a few inches wider than the boats that used it, and headroom was limited to a scant 6ft. Boats were assisted through by a pumping engine flushing water along the tunnel, but it must still have been a nightmarishly claustrophobic trip for the boatmen.

● **Edgbaston**
West Midlands. A desirable residential suburb of Birmingham, Edgbaston is bisected by the canal.
Botanical Gardens Edgbaston. Founded over 100

years ago. Alpine Garden, lily pond and a collection of tropical birds. *Open daily.*
Perrott's Folly Waterworks Road, off Monument Road, Edgbaston. About ¾ mile west of bridge 86, not far from the Plough & Harrow Hotel. This seven-storey tower was built in 1758 by John Perrott and claims to be Birmingham's most eccentric building. One theory as to its origin is that Mr Perrott could, from its height, gaze upon his late wife's grave 10 miles away. One of the Two Towers of Gondor, featured in J.R.R. Tolkien's *Lord of the Rings*, is thought to have been based upon this building. Tolkien's last address in Birmingham was at 4 Highfield Road, opposite the Plough & Harrow. From 1884–1984 the folly was used as a weather station and was subsequently renovated. *Open Easter–Sep, Sun and B Hols 14.00–17.00.* Modest charge. Tearoom.

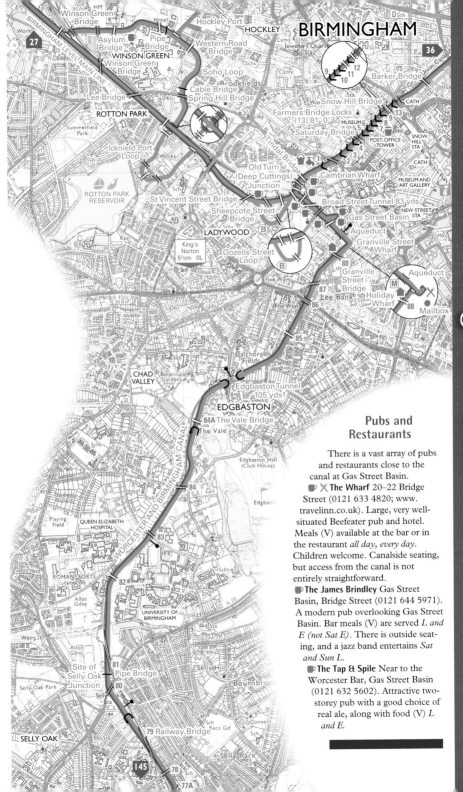

Worcester & Birmingham Canal

Birmingham

Pubs and Restaurants

There is a vast array of pubs and restaurants close to the canal at Gas Street Basin.

The Wharf 20–22 Bridge Street (0121 633 4820; www. travelinn.co.uk). Large, very well-situated Beefeater pub and hotel. Meals (V) available at the bar or in the restaurant *all day, every day*. Children welcome. Canalside seating, but access from the canal is not entirely straightforward.

The James Brindley Gas Street Basin, Bridge Street (0121 644 5971). A modern pub overlooking Gas Street Basin. Bar meals (V) are served *L and E (not Sat E)*. There is outside seating, and a jazz band entertains *Sat and Sun L*.

The Tap & Spile Near to the Worcester Bar, Gas Street Basin (0121 632 5602). Attractive two-storey pub with a good choice of real ale, along with food (V) *L and E*.

Shardlow (see page 150)

■ TRENT & MERSEY CANAL

MAXIMUM DIMENSIONS

Derwent Mouth to Burton upon Trent
Length: 72'
Beam: 10'
Headroom: 7'

Burton upon Trent to south end of Harecastle Tunnel
Length: 72'
Beam: 7'
Headroom: 6' 3"

MILEAGE

DERWENT MOUTH to:
Swarkestone Lock: 7 miles

Willington: $12^{1}/4$ miles
Horninglow Wharf: $16^{1}/2$ miles
Barton Turn: $21^{1}/4$ miles
Fradley, junction with Coventry Canal: $26^{1}/4$ miles
GREAT HAYWOOD, junction with Staffs & Worcs Canal: 39 miles

Locks: 76

MANAGER

Derwent Mouth to Colwich: 01283 790236
enquiries.sawley@britishwaterways.co.uk
Colwich to Trentham: 01785 284253
enquiries.fradley@britishwaterways.co.uk

This early canal was originally conceived partly as a roundabout link between the ports of Liverpool and Hull, while passing through the busy area of the Potteries and mid-Cheshire, and terminating either in the River Weaver or in the Mersey. Its construction was promoted by Josiah Wedgwood (1730–95), the famous potter, aided by his friends Thomas Bentley and Erasmus Darwin. In 1766 the Trent & Mersey Canal Act was passed by Parliament, authorising the building of a navigation from the River Trent at Shardlow to Runcorn Gap, where it would join the proposed extension of the Bridgewater Canal from Manchester.

The ageing James Brindley was appointed engineer for the canal. Construction began at once and in 1777 the Trent & Mersey Canal was opened. In the total 93 miles between Derwent Mouth and Preston Brook, the Trent & Mersey gained connection with no fewer than nine other canals or significant branches.

By the 1820s the slowly sinking tunnel at Harecastle had become a serious bottleneck. Thomas Telford recommended building a second tunnel beside the old one. His recommendation was eventually accepted by the company and the whole tunnel was completed in under three years, in 1827.

Although the Trent & Mersey was taken over in 1845 by the new North Staffordshire Railway Company, the canal flourished until World War I. Today it is assured (by statute) of its future as a pleasure cruising waterway. Look out for the handsome cast iron mileposts, which actually measure the mileage from Shardlow, not Derwent Mouth. There are 59 originals, from the Rougeley and Dixon foundry in Stone, and 34 replacements, bearing the mark T. & M. C. S. 1977 of the Trent & Mersey Canal Society.

Shardlow

The Trent & Mersey Canal begins at Derwent Mouth, some 2¹/₂ miles upstream of the point where the Soar Navigation enters

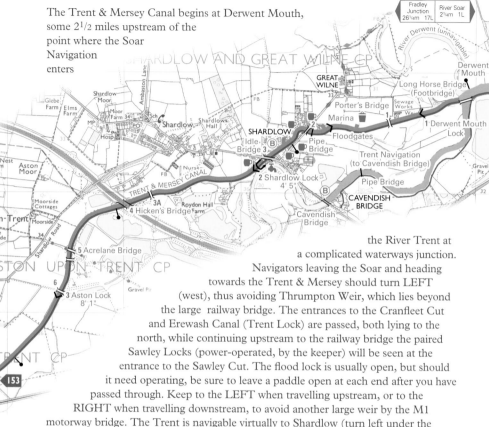

the River Trent at a complicated waterways junction. Navigators leaving the Soar and heading towards the Trent & Mersey should turn LEFT (west), thus avoiding Thrumpton Weir, which lies beyond the large railway bridge. The entrances to the Cranfleet Cut and Erewash Canal (Trent Lock) are passed, both lying to the north, while continuing upstream to the railway bridge the paired Sawley Locks (power-operated, by the keeper) will be seen at the entrance to the Sawley Cut. The flood lock is usually open, but should it need operating, be sure to leave a paddle open at each end after you have passed through. Keep to the LEFT when travelling upstream, or to the RIGHT when travelling downstream, to avoid another large weir by the M1 motorway bridge. The Trent is navigable virtually to Shardlow (turn left under the concrete footbridge if you wish to explore as far as Cavendish Bridge). The 1758 tolls are engraved on a plaque on the bridge – it was washed away in the floods in 1947, and was re-erected in 1960. The first lock on the Trent & Mersey is Derwent Mouth Lock, beyond which is Shardlow, one of the most interesting inland canal ports on the whole inland waterway network. Note, for example, the old salt warehouse by Shardlow Lock.

Boatyards

ⓑ ✗ **British Waterways Sawley Marina** Long Eaton, Nottingham (01159 734278). 🚿 🚽 ⚓ P D Pump out, gas, overnight and long-term mooring, winter storage, slipway, crane, boat and engine sales, engine repairs, telephone, chandlery, toilets, showers, restaurant, laundrette. Day-boat hire from Thompsons (0115 972 5373).
ⓑ **BB Marine** Sawley Marina, Long Eaton, Nottingham (0115 973 5000). Boat and engine repairs. *24hr emergency call out.*
ⓑ **Dobsons Boatyard** The Wharf, Shardlow

(01332 792271) 🚿 🚽 ⚓ D Pump out, gas, overnight and long-term mooring, winter storage, slipway, chandlery, boat building, boat and engine sales, engine repairs, wet dock, books and maps.
ⓑ ✗ **Shardlow Marina** London Road, Shardlow (01332 792832). On the River Trent. 🚿 🚽 ⚓ D Pump out, gas, overnight and long-term mooring, winter storage, slipway, boat sales, chandlery, toilets and showers. 🍴 ✗ **The Old Marina Bar & Restaurant** Meals (V) *L and E.* Outside seating.

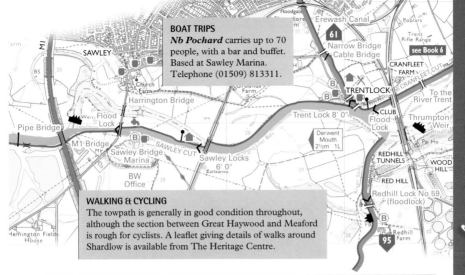

BOAT TRIPS
Nb Pochard carries up to 70 people, with a bar and buffet. Based at Sawley Marina. Telephone (01509) 813311.

WALKING & CYCLING
The towpath is generally in good condition throughout, although the section between Great Haywood and Meaford is rough for cyclists. A leaflet giving details of walks around Shardlow is available from The Heritage Centre.

NAVIGATIONAL NOTES

1 Those leaving the canal and heading towards the River Trent should not pass Shardlow floodgates if the warning light shows red.
2 The Derwent is not navigable north of Derwent Mouth.

● **Sawley Cut**
In addition to a large marina and a well-patronised BW mooring site, the Derby Motor Boat Club has a base on the Sawley Cut where well over 100 boats are kept. There are windlasses for sale at Sawley Lock, as well as the more conventional facilities, and BW showers. It is beautifully tended, with lots of flowers and some jokey sculptures. Have a look at the flood level markers – they are astonishing!

● **Shardlow**
Derbs. PO, tel, stores, garage. Few canal travellers will want to pass through Shardlow without stopping. Everywhere there are living examples of large-scale canal architecture, as well as long-established necessities such as canal pubs. By the lock is the biggest and best of these buildings – the 18th-C Trent Mill, now the Clock Warehouse, which has a large central arch where boats once entered to unload. Restored in 1979, it still retains all its original proud elegance.

Shardlow Heritage Centre Adjacent to the Clock Warehouse (01332 792489; www.homepages.which.net/~shardlow.heritage). Exhibitions of local canal history, replica of a narrowboat back cabin, Edwardian boaters' clothing for visiting children to try on, plus a calendar of canal-centred events. *Open Easter–Oct, Sat, Sun and B Hols 12.00–17.00.* Very modest entry charge.

Pubs and Restaurants

🛥 **The Clock Warehouse** London Road, Shardlow (01332 792844). Real ale, and food (V) *L and E.* Children welcome, and there is a garden and adventure playground.

🛥 **The Navigation Inn** 143 London Road, Shardlow (01332 792918). By bridge 3. Haunted pub, serving real ale, and home-made food (V) *L and E*, including *Sun* carvery. Garden with a play area. Regular quiz nights. Jazz on *Tue*, quiz on *Thur*, karaoke on *Fri* and live group on *Sat*.

🛥 **The Malt Shovel** 49 The Wharf, Shardlow (01332 799763). By bridge 2. Friendly canalside pub, built in 1779 and serving real ale. Excellent and inventive food (V) with home-made specials *L only (not Sun)*.

Children welcome. Outside seating by the canal.

🛥 **The New Inn** The Wharf, Shardlow, next to the Malt Shovel (01332 793330). Real ale, and bar meals *L and E (not Sun E)*. Children welcome. Garden and outside seating.

✕ 🍷 **The Thai Kitchen** Shardlow (01332 792331). Authentic Thai food (V) *L and E* in a restaurant haunted by the 'lady in grey'. Children welcome.

🛥 **The Old Crown** Cavendish Bridge, Shardlow (01332 792392; oldcrown@yahoo.com). Friendly riverside pub, decorated with old advertising ephemera. Real ale. Bar meals (V) *L only.* Children welcome. Garden with play area. B & B.

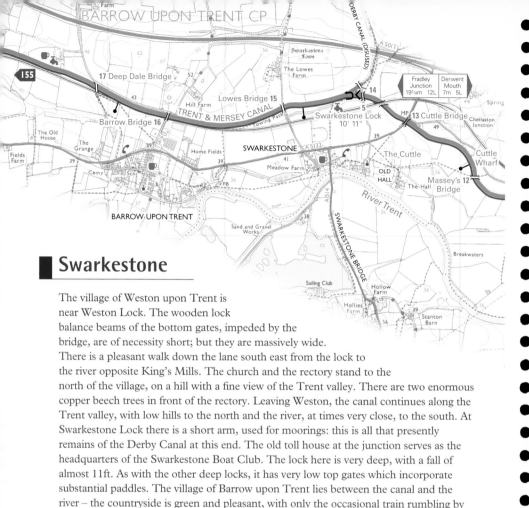

Swarkestone

The village of Weston upon Trent is near Weston Lock. The wooden lock balance beams of the bottom gates, impeded by the bridge, are of necessity short; but they are massively wide. There is a pleasant walk down the lane south east from the lock to the river opposite King's Mills. The church and the rectory stand to the north of the village, on a hill with a fine view of the Trent valley. There are two enormous copper beech trees in front of the rectory. Leaving Weston, the canal continues along the Trent valley, with low hills to the north and the river, at times very close, to the south. At Swarkestone Lock there is a short arm, used for moorings: this is all that presently remains of the Derby Canal at this end. The old toll house at the junction serves as the headquarters of the Swarkestone Boat Club. The lock here is very deep, with a fall of almost 11ft. As with the other deep locks, it has very low top gates which incorporate substantial paddles. The village of Barrow upon Trent lies between the canal and the river – the countryside is green and pleasant, with only the occasional train rumbling by to disturb the peace.

● **Weston upon Trent**
Derbs. Tel, stores. A scattered village that is in fact not very close to the Trent. The isolated church is splendidly situated beside woods on top of a hill, its sturdy tower crowned by a short 14th-C spire. Inside are fine aisle windows of the same period. The lock gardens make the approach from the canal particularly attractive.

● **Swarkestone**
Derbs. Tel, stores. The main feature of Swarkestone is the 18th-C five-arch stone bridge over the main channel of the River Trent. An elevated causeway then carries the road on stone arches all the way across the Trent's flood plain to the village of Stanton by Bridge. It was at Swarkestone that Bonnie Prince Charlie, in the rising of 1745, gave up his attempt for the throne

of England and returned to his defeat at Culloden. In a field nearby are the few remains of Sir Richard Harpur's Tudor mansion, which was demolished before 1750. The Summer House, a handsome, lonely building, overlooks a square enclosure called the Cuttle. Jacobean in origin, it is thought that it may have been the scene of bull-baiting, although it seems more likely it was just a 'bowle alley'. Restored by the Landmark Trust, two people may now have holidays here – telephone (01628) 825925 for details. The Harpurs moved to Calke following the demolition of their mansion after the Civil War. The pub in the village, and monuments in the church, which is tucked away in the back lanes, are a reminder of the family.

● **Barrow upon Trent**

Derbs. Tel, stores. A small, quiet village set back from the canal. A lane from the church leads down to the River Trent. Opposite there is a 'pinfold', once an enclosure for stray animals. The surviving lodge house stands opposite a mellow terrace of old workmen's cottages.

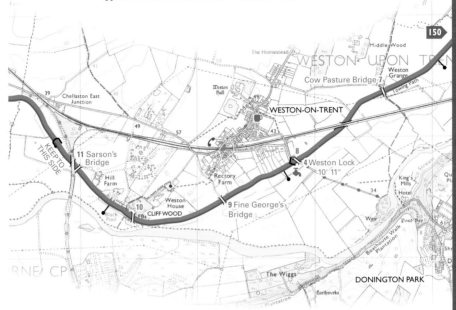

Pubs and Restaurants

🍺 **The Old Plough Inn** 1 Main Street, Weston upon Trent (01332 700331). Serving real ale. Exciting range of food (V), with good choice for children, available *all day.* Children welcome. Outside seating.

🍺 **The Crew & Harpur Arms** Woodshop Lane, Swarkestone (01332 700641). By the river bridge. Real ale, and bar meals (V) served *all day* in this handsome pub. Riverside seating and garden.

🍺 **The Ragley Boat Stop** Deepdale Lane, off Sinfin Lane, Barrow-on-Trent (01332 703919). Large pub 300yds west of bridge 17, serving real ale. Food (V) is available *L and E, and all day Sun.* Extensive vegetarian and children's menus. Children welcome. Outside seating in a 3-acre garden. Good moorings with 🚰

A HOP, A SKIP, AND A JUMP TO DERBY

The Derby Canal, which left the Trent & Mersey at Swarkestone and joined the Erewash at Sandiacre, has long been disused. One condition of its building, and a constant drain on its profits, was the free carriage of 5000 tons of coal to Derby each year, for the use of the poor.

But one of the most unusual loads was transported on 19 April 1826, when 'a fine lama, a kangaroo, a ram with four horns, and a female goat with two young kids, remarkably handsome animals' arrived in Derby by canal 'as a present from Lord Byron to a Gentleman whose residence is in the neighbourhood, all of which had been picked up in the course of the voyage of the *Blonde* to the Sandwich Islands in the autumn of 1824'.

Willington

Just by bridge 18 is Arleston House, an attractive old building with ground-floor walls of stone and the upper tiers of brick. This is followed by Stenson Lock, the last of the wide locks until Middlewich – it has a massive fall of 12ft 4in. Stenson is a small farming centre and a popular mooring spot with a large marina. After passing through a railway bridge, the canal changes course and heads off in a south easterly

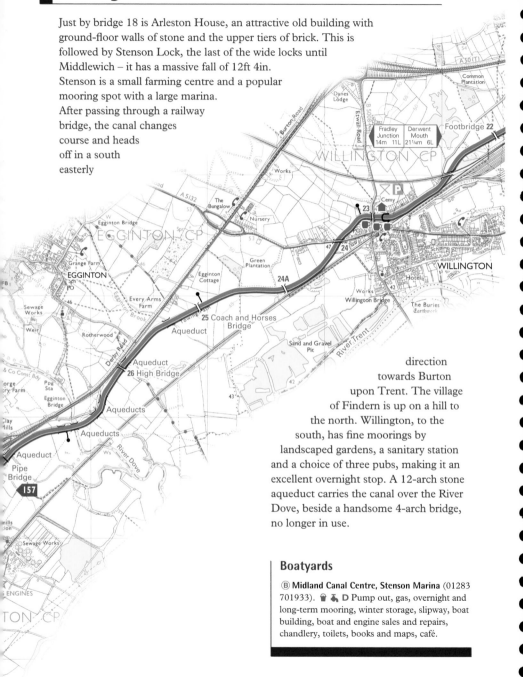

direction towards Burton upon Trent. The village of Findern is up on a hill to the north. Willington, to the south, has fine moorings by landscaped gardens, a sanitary station and a choice of three pubs, making it an excellent overnight stop. A 12-arch stone aqueduct carries the canal over the River Dove, beside a handsome 4-arch bridge, no longer in use.

Boatyards

Ⓑ **Midland Canal Centre, Stenson Marina** (01283 701933). D Pump out, gas, overnight and long-term mooring, winter storage, slipway, boat building, boat and engine sales and repairs, chandlery, toilets, books and maps, café.

● **Repton**
Derbs. PO. 1¹/₂ miles south east of Willington
(over the River Trent) is Repton, one of the
oldest towns in England, which was once the
capital of Mercia. The crypt below St
Wystan's Church was built in the 10th C.
One of the finest examples of Saxon
architecture in the country, this crypt was
completely forgotten until the end of the
18th C when a man fell into it while digging
a grave. Repton public school dates from
1551, and there is much of historical interest
in the school and the town.

● **Willington**
Derbs. PO, tel, stores. The railway bisects this
busy little village on an embankment. There
are three pubs, all close together.

● **Findern**
Derbs. PO, tel, stores. A small, quiet village
where Jedekiah Strutt, the inventor of the
ribbed stocking frame, served a 7-year
apprenticeship with the local wheelwright. At
one time the village green was no more than a
waste patch used by cars as a short cut, and a
parking place. When suggestions were made to
turn it into a formal cross roads, the indignant
Women's Institute galvanised the villagers into
actually uprooting all traces of tarmac from
the green and turfing the whole area properly.

● **Egginton**
Derbs. PO, tel, stores. A quiet village lying
off the A38. The church, set apart from the
village, is pleasingly irregular from the outside,
with a large chancel and a squat tower.

Pubs and Restaurants

🍺 **The Bubble Inn** Stenson (01283 703113;
www.stensonbubble.com). Alongside Stenson
Lock and Marina, this modern pub in a
converted barn serves real ale and bar meals
(V) *L and E (not E Sun)*. Children welcome.
Garden. DJ on *Sun eves.*
🍺 **The Greyhound** Heath Lane, Findern.
Completely refurbished. Garden.
🍺 **The Rising Sun** The Green, Willington
(01283 702116). Friendly village pub serving

real ale. Reasonably priced bar food (V),
including home-made pies, available *L and E*.
Children welcome. Outside seating.
🍺 **The Green Dragon** 11 The Green,
Willington (01283 702327). Popular and
welcoming pub, with plenty of low beams.
Real ale. Wide range of food (V) available *L
and E*. Garden. Children welcome away from
the bar. Karaoke every other week on *Sun
evening*.

Burton upon Trent

Logs, coal and *diesel* are available between bridges 28 and 29. *Fish & chips* can be obtained 100yds north of Horninglow Basin. The canal then passes along one side of Burton upon Trent, without entering the town. Many of the old canalside buildings have been demolished, but the waterside has been nicely tidied up, making the passage very pleasant. The lovely aroma of brewing – malt and hops – often pervades the town, often strongest to the west. Dallow Lock is the first of the narrow locks, an altogether easier job of work than the wider ones to the east. Shobnall Basin is now used by a boatyard, and visitor moorings nearby are available from which to explore the town. The A38 then joins the canal, depriving the navigator of any peace. Up on the hills to the north west is the well-wooded Sinai Park – the moated 15th-C house here, now a farm, used to be the summer home of the monks from Burton Abbey. There is a fine canalside pub at bridge 34, and a *shop* selling provisions, home-made cakes and crafts. It is *open Easter–Oct, daily 09.00–18.00.* The canal enters the new National Forest at bridge 30 – indeed an intricately carved seat reminds us of this – and will leave it just beyond Alrewas. The Bass Millennium Woodland, to the west of Branston Lock, is part of this major project.

● **Burton upon Trent**
Staffs. All services. Known widely for its brewing industry, which originated here in the 13th C, when the monks at Burton Abbey discovered that an excellent beer could be brewed from the town's waters, because of their high gypsum content. At one time there were 31 breweries producing 3 million barrels of ale annually: alas, now only a few remain. The advent of the railways had an enormous effect on the street geography of Burton, for gradually a great network of railways took shape, connecting with each other and with the main line. These branches were mostly constructed at street level, and until recent years it was common for road traffic to be held up by endless goods trains chugging all over the town. Only the last vestiges of this system now remain. The east side of the town is bounded by the River Trent, on the other side of which are pleasant hills. The main shopping centre lies to the east of the railway station.
The Bass Museum Horninglow Street (01283 511000; www.bass-museum.com). ¾ mile from Horninglow Basin. All aspects of brewing during the late 19th C. Also a preserved steam engine, café and shop. Conducted tours around the brewery. *Open daily 10.00–17.00 (last admission 16.00). Closed Xmas.* Admission charge.

Marston's Brewery Visitor Centre Shobnall Road, Burton upon Trent (01283 507391). Tours of the brewery, including the unique and world-famous Burton Union system are available *Mon–Fri.* At the end of the tour you can enjoy a drink of real ale in the Visitor Centre. *Please telephone in advance to check availability and to book.*
Brewhouse Arts Centre Union Street car park (01283 516030; www.brewhouse.co.uk). Live entertainment in a 230-seat theatre, plus a gallery and bistro bar.
Tourist Information Centre 183 High Street, Burton upon Trent (01283 516609; www. burtonwindow.com).
● **Shobnall Basin**
This is all that remains of the Bond End Canal, which gave the breweries the benefit of what was modern transport, before the coming of the railways.
● **Branston**
Staffs. PO, tel, stores, garage, butcher, Chinese takeaway, fish & chips. This is apparently the place where the famous pickle originated.

Boatyards

Ⓑ **Tom's Moorings** Horninglow (01543 414808). 🔧 Pump out, overnight and long-term mooring.
Ⓑ **Jannel Cruisers** Shobnall Marina, Shobnall Road, Burton upon Trent (01283 542718). In Shobnall Basin. 🛒 🏪 🔧 **D** Pump out, gas, narrowboat hire, overnight mooring, long-term mooring, winter storage, slipway, dry dock, chandlery, books and maps, boat-fitting, boat sales, engine sales and repairs, toilets.

NAVIGATIONAL NOTES

A BW key is needed for Dallow Lock.

Pubs and Restaurants

The Mill House Milford Drive, Stretton Park (01283 535133). Family friendly pub nicely situated by the canal. Real ale. Food (V) available *all day*, with a children's menu. *24hr* mooring.

The Bass Museum Horninglow Street (01283 511000; www.bass-museum.com). Pay to visit the museum and enjoy their own real ales and food (*L*). Children welcome. *See* page 128 for opening times.

WALKING & CYCLING

Cycle Route 54 uses the towpath north of Burton upon Trent. It links Lichfield with Derby. Three walking trails around Burton upon Trent are available from the TIC. There are pleasant walks through Branston Water Park – telephone (01283) 508573 for more information.

✕ ♀ **The Brewhouse** Union Street car park (01283 540041; www. brewhouse.co.uk). At the Arts Centre. Coffee and meals, *L and E (up to 1 hour before a performance)*.

The New Inn 273 Horninglow Road North (01283 540812). Real ale and food *L and E*. Garden.

The Navigation Inn 120 Horninglow Road (01283 568977). Friendly pub. Real ale. Bar snacks (V) *L*. Children welcome. Garden.

The Star & Garter 69 Grange Street (01283 509014). Real ale and food *L* in a pub with one of the largest cellars in Burton. Children welcome. Patio.

The Loaf & Cheese 114 Waterloo Street (01283 534101). Friendly local. Bar meals (V) *12.00–18.00 (and Sun L if you book in advance)*. Children's room. Garden with climbing frame and slide. Barbecues on B Hols.

Coopers Tavern 43 Cross Street (01283 532551). Once the brewery tap. Real ale. Bar meals (V) *L Mon–Fri*. Children welcome.

Bill Brewer Centrum 100, Wellington Road (01283 542321) North east of the A38 bridge. Friendly pub decorated with brewery memorabilia, serving food (V) *all day*. Large beer garden with children's play area (bouncy castle during *summer*). Entertainment on *Wed, Sat and Sun*.

The Blacksmith's Arms Main Street, Branston (01283 564332). Comfortable pub serving real ale and home-made gourmet sandwiches (V) *L Tue–Sat*. Children welcome. Garden and patio. Occasional karaoke and food theme nights.

The Bridge Tatenhill Lane, Branston (01283 564177). At Branston Bridge (34). Real ale served straight from the cask, and good food *L and E (not Sun E)*. Children welcome. Canalside garden.

Barton Turn

Beside Tatenhill Lock there is an attractive cottage; at the tail of the lock is yet another of the tiny narrow brick bridges that are such an engaging feature of this navigation. Note the very fine National Forest seat just north of the lock – there is another at Bagnall Lock, along with a 'living willow' sculpture. After passing flooded gravel pits and negotiating another tiny brick arch at bridge 36, the canal and the A38, the old Roman road, come very close together – thankfully the settlement of Barton Turn has been bypassed, leaving the main street (the old Roman road of Ryknild Street) wide and empty. It is with great relief that Wychnor Lock, with its diminutive crane and warehouse, is reached – here the A38 finally parts company with the canal, and some peace returns. To the west is the little 14th-C Wychnor church. Before Alrewas Lock the canal actually joins the River Trent – there is a large well-marked weir which should be given a wide berth. The canal then winds through the pretty village of Alrewas, passing the old church, several thatched cottages and a charming brick bridge.

● **Barton-under-Needwood**
Staffs. PO, tel, stores, bank, garage. Many years ago, when there were few roads and no canals in the Midlands, the only reasonable access to this village was by turning off the old Roman road, Ryknild Street: hence, probably, the name Barton Turn. The village is indeed worth turning off for, although unfortunately it is nearly a mile from the canal. A pleasant footpath from Barton Turn Lock leads quietly to the village, which is set on a slight hill. Its long main street has many attractive pubs. The church is battlemented and surrounded by a very tidy churchyard. Pleasantly uniform in style, it was built in the 16th C by John Taylor, Henry VIII's private secretary, on the site of his cottage birthplace. The former Royal Forest of Needwood is to the north of the village.
● **Wychnor**
Staffs. A tiny farming settlement around the church of St Leonards.
● **Alrewas**
Staffs. PO, tel, stores, garage, butcher, chemist, tea-room, fish & chips. Just far enough away from the A513, this is an attractive village whose rambling back lanes harbour some excellent timbered cottages. The canal's unruffled passage through the village gives the place a restful air, and the presence of the church and its pleasant churchyard adds to this impression. The River Trent touches the village, and once fed the old Cotton Mill (now converted into dwellings), and provides it with a fine background which is much appreciated by fishermen. The somewhat unusual name Alrewas, pronounced 'olrewus', is a corruption of the words Alder Wash – a reference to

the many alder trees which once grew in the often-flooded Trent valley and gave rise to the basket weaving for which the village was once famous.
Alrewas Church A spacious building of mainly 13th-C and 14th-C construction, notable for the old leper window, which is now filled by modern stained glass.

Boatyards

ⓑ **Barton Turns Marina** Barton Turn, Barton-under-Needwood (01283 711666). 🚽 🚿 ⚓ D Pump out, gas, narrowboat hire, overnight and long-term mooring, winter storage, boat sales and repairs, engine repairs, chandlery, toilets, showers, books, maps and gifts, laundrette.
Boat Doctor (01332 771622). Emergency marine engineer with *24 hour emergency breakdown call out.*
ⓑ **Wychnor Moorings** Wychnor, Burton upon Trent (07778 668388). 🚽 🚿 ⚓ Pump out, gas, long-term mooring, coal.

NAVIGATIONAL NOTES

In times of flood *great caution* should be exercised along the stretch immediately north of Alrewas Lock – keep well over to the towpath side at all times.

Pubs and Restaurants

🍺 **The Three Horseshoes** Station Road, Barton-under-Needwood (01283 716268). Quiet pub, with no juke box or pool table, but with extremely friendly staff serving a changing range of real ales and excellent bar meals (V) *L and E*. Children are welcome. Garden.

✕ 🍴 **Little Chef** Canalside at Barton, and very handy (01283 716135). *Open 07.00–22.00 daily.* Vegetarian options.

🍺 **The Shoulder of Mutton** Main Street, Barton-under-Needwood (01283 712568). A 17th-C pub serving real ale and bar meals (V) *L and E*. Children welcome. Garden with a play area.

🍺 **Barton Turns** Barton Turn (01283 712142). Opposite Barton Lock, this is a basic but friendly pub serving real ale and bar meals (V) *L and E*. Small garden.

🍺 **The Crown Inn** Post Office Road, Alrewas, near bridge 46 (01283 790328). Friendly village pub serving real ale, and home-cooked food (V) *L and E*, with a fish night each *Thur*. Children welcome. Garden, with a bouncy castle during the summer.

🍺 **The Old Boat** Canalside at Alrewas, Kings Bromley Road (01283 791468). With a boat-themed and quirky interior, and a traction engine in the car park, this relaxed and popular pub offers excellent meals (V) *L and E*, along with real ale. Children (and also dogs) welcome. Pleasant garden with play area. Regular entertainment. Moorings. Fishing facilities.

🍺 **The George & Dragon** Main Street, Alrewas (01283 791476). Real ale and bar meals (V) *L and E (not Sun)*, in an old village local. Children welcome. Garden.

🍺 **William IV** William IV Road, Alrewas (01283 790206). Village local with friendly staff. Real ale. Wide range of unusual and inspiring food (V) *L and E, and all day Sat and Sun*. Children welcome *until 21.00*. Patio. Quiz nights *first Sun of month*, live music *second Fri of month*.

✕ 🍴 **Rafters Restaurant** Claymar Hotel, Alrewas (01283 790202). Welcoming and informal restaurant with fine collection of Royal commemorative mugs. Real ale, bar meals and an à la carte menu (V) served *E and Sun L*. Children welcome. Garden.

WALKING & CYCLING
There is an excellent circular walk from Alrewas along the east side of the Trent, then along the A38 for a short while before turning back beside the canal at Wychnor Lock.

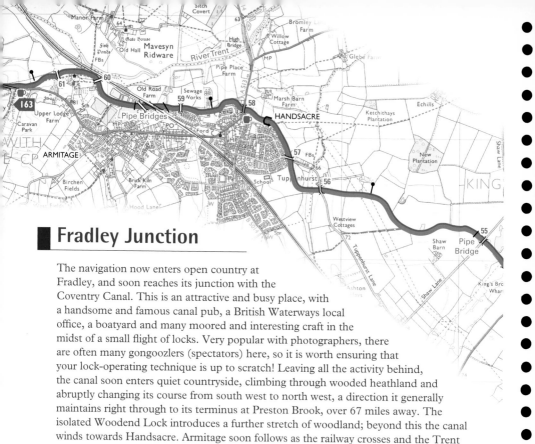

Fradley Junction

The navigation now enters open country at Fradley, and soon reaches its junction with the Coventry Canal. This is an attractive and busy place, with a handsome and famous canal pub, a British Waterways local office, a boatyard and many moored and interesting craft in the midst of a small flight of locks. Very popular with photographers, there are often many gongoozlers (spectators) here, so it is worth ensuring that your lock-operating technique is up to scratch! Leaving all the activity behind, the canal soon enters quiet countryside, climbing through wooded heathland and abruptly changing its course from south west to north west, a direction it generally maintains right through to its terminus at Preston Brook, over 67 miles away. The isolated Woodend Lock introduces a further stretch of woodland; beyond this the canal winds towards Handsacre. Armitage soon follows as the railway crosses and the Trent comes very close. There is a useful general *store* 500yds south of bridge 59, and *fish & chips* and a *café* near bridge 58.

NAVIGATIONAL NOTES

West of bridge 61 the canal is very narrow, due to the removal of Armitage Tunnel, and wide enough for one boat only. Check that the canal is clear before proceeding.

Boatyards

ⓑ **BW Waterways Office** Fradley Junction (01283 790236). 🚻 🛈 ♨ Overnight mooring, long-term mooring, toilets.

ⓑ **Swan Line Cruisers** Fradley Junction (01283 790332). ♨ D Pump out (*not Sat*), gas, narrowboat hire, overnight mooring, boat and engine sales and repairs, chandlery,

books and maps, gifts, groceries, laundry service.

ⓑ **King's Bromley Wharf Marina** Bromley Hayes, Lichfield (01543 417209). 🚻 🛈 ♨ D Pump out, gas, overnight and long-term mooring, toilets, showers, laundrette. A new marina still developing as we go to press.

● **Fradley Junction**
A long-established canal centre where the Coventry Canal joins the Trent & Mersey. Like all the best focal points on the waterways, it is concerned solely with the life of the canals, and has no relationship with local roads or even with

the village of Fradley. The junction bristles with boats for, apart from it being an inevitable meeting place for canal craft, there is a boatyard, a British Waterways maintenance yard, BW moorings, a boat club and a popular pub – all in the middle of a 5-lock flight.

● **Kings Bromley**
Staffs. PO, tel, stores. A village 1¹/₂ miles north
of bridge 54, along the A515. There are some
pleasant houses and an old mill to be seen
here, as well as what is reputed to have been
Lady Godiva's early home. The Trent flows
just beyond the church, which contains some
old glass. A large cross in the southern part of
the churchyard is known locally as
Godiva's cross.

● **Armitage**
Staffs. PO, tel, stores, garage. A main road
village, whose church is interesting: it was
rebuilt in the 19th C in a Saxon/Norman style,
which makes it rather dark. The organ is 200
years old and it is enormous: it came from
Lichfield Cathedral and practically deafens the
organist at Armitage.

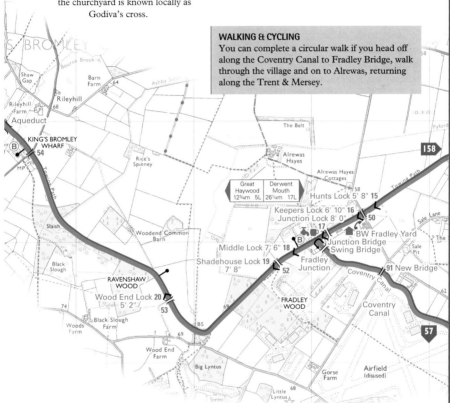

WALKING & CYCLING
You can complete a circular walk if you head off
along the Coventry Canal to Fradley Bridge, walk
through the village and on to Alrewas, returning
along the Trent & Mersey.

Pubs and Restaurants

🍺 **The Swan** Fradley Junction (01283
790330). Known as 'The Mucky Duck'.
Canalside, it is the focus of the junction
and justly famous, this is reputedly one of
the most photographed pubs in the
country! It is in a 200-year-old listed
building, with a fine public bar warmed by
a coal fire, a comfortable lounge, and a
vaulted cellar room. Real ale, and bar
meals are served *L and E*, with a carvery
Sun L. There is a flowered patio at the
rear.

🍺 **The Crown** The Green, Handsacre (01543
490239). At bridge 58. Welcoming 300-year-

old pub serving real ale. Family room, and a
garden. Good moorings.

✕ 🍷 🍺 **Tom Cobleigh's Spode Cottage**
Armitage (01543 490353). A very popular
restaurant (V) in a timbered 17th-C farmhouse, sensitively converted. Imaginative
menu, and a real ale. *Open Mon–Sat
11.00–23.00 and Sun 12.00–22.30.* Children
welcome *until 21.00.* Large garden.

🍺 **The Plum Pudding** Rugeley Road, Armitage
(01543 490330; www.plumpudding.co.uk).
Well-kept canalside pub serving real ale, with
bar meals (V) *L and E*. Children welcome for
meals only. Outside seating and garden.

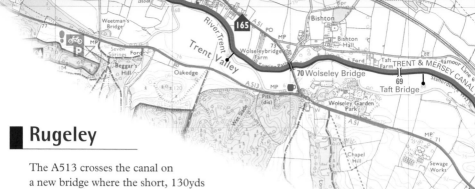

Rugeley

The A513 crosses the canal on
a new bridge where the short, 130yds
long, Armitage Tunnel used to run before its
roof was removed in 1971 to combat the subsidence
effects of coal being mined nearby. There is a *restaurant* just
across the road here, very much a rarity on canals in general and
this area in particular. To the west stands Spode House, a former home
of the pottery family. The huge power station at Rugeley, tidied up now,
comes into view – and takes a long time to recede. There are pleasant
moorings at Rugeley, by bridge 66, with the town centre and *shops* only a short
walk away. North of the town, the canal crosses the River Trent via a substantial
aqueduct. The canal then enters an immensely attractive area full of interest.
Accompanied by the River Trent, the canal moves up a narrowing valley bordered by
green slopes on either side, Cannock Chase being clearly visible to the south. Wolseley
Hall has gone, but Bishton Hall (now a school) still stands: its very elegant front faces
the canal near Wolseley Bridge. There is a *pub*, an *Indian restaurant* and an *antique*, *craft*
and *garden centre* just a short way to the south.

● **Spode House** Spode House and Hawkesyard
Priory stand side by side. The priory was founded
in 1897 by Josiah Spode's grandson and his niece
Helen Gulson when they lived at Spode House.
The Priory now provides office accommodation.
● **Rugeley**
Staffs. PO, tel, stores, garage, banks, station, cinema.
An unexciting place with a modern town centre
and a dominating power station. There are two
churches by bridge 67; one is a 14th-C ruin, the
other is the parish church built in 1822 as a
replacement.
● **Cannock Chase**
Covering an area of 26 square miles, and designated as an Area of Outstanding Natural Beauty
in 1949, the Chase is all that remains of what was
once a Norman hunting ground known as the
King's Forest of Cannock. Large parts are
recognised as Sites of Special Scientific Interest,
and exceptional flora and fauna are abundant.
This includes a herd of fallow deer whose
ancestors have grazed in this region for centuries.

An area of 4½ square miles forms a Country Park,
one of the largest in Britain. Near the Sherlock
Valley an area was chosen in 1964 as the site of
the Deutscher Soldatenfriedhof, and was built by
the German War Graves Commission. It contains
the graves of 2143 German servicemen from
World War I, and 2786 from World War II. It is
an intentionally sombre place. A small area is
devoted to the crews of German airships, shot
down over the UK in 1916 and 1917. There
were two huge army camps on the Chase during
World War I, but today little remains, apart
from some anonymous and overgrown concrete
foundations.
Museum of Cannock Chase Valley Road, Hednes-
ford (01543 877666; www.museumofcannockchase.
co.uk). This site was at one time The Valley
Colliery. Exhibits illustrate the life of the Chase,
from a medieval Royal hunting ground to a
19th-C colliery. *Open daily Easter–Sep 11.00–
17.00; Oct–Easter Mon–Fri 11.00–16.00.* Free.
Coffee shop and visitor information.

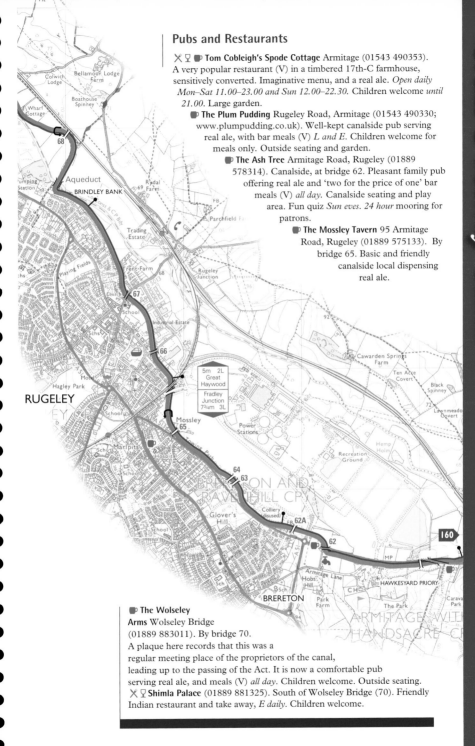

Pubs and Restaurants

✗ ♀ 🍺 **Tom Cobleigh's Spode Cottage** Armitage (01543 490353). A very popular restaurant (V) in a timbered 17th-C farmhouse, sensitively converted. Imaginative menu, and a real ale. *Open daily Mon–Sat 11.00–23.00 and Sun 12.00–22.30.* Children welcome *until 21.00.* Large garden.

🍺 **The Plum Pudding** Rugeley Road, Armitage (01543 490330; www.plumpudding.co.uk). Well-kept canalside pub serving real ale, with bar meals (V) *L and E.* Children welcome for meals only. Outside seating and garden.

🍺 **The Ash Tree** Armitage Road, Rugeley (01889 578314). Canalside, at bridge 62. Pleasant family pub offering real ale and 'two for the price of one' bar meals (V) *all day.* Canalside seating and play area. Fun quiz *Sun eves.* *24 hour* mooring for patrons.

🍺 **The Mossley Tavern** 95 Armitage Road, Rugeley (01889 575133). By bridge 65. Basic and friendly canalside local dispensing real ale.

🍺 **The Wolseley Arms** Wolseley Bridge (01889 883011). By bridge 70. A plaque here records that this was a regular meeting place of the proprietors of the canal, leading up to the passing of the Act. It is now a comfortable pub serving real ale, and meals (V) *all day.* Children welcome. Outside seating.

✗ ♀ **Shimla Palace** (01889 881325). South of Wolseley Bridge (70). Friendly Indian restaurant and take away, *E daily.* Children welcome.

Great Haywood

The pleasant surroundings continue as the canal passes Colwich. As the perimeter of Shugborough Park is reached the impressive façade of the Hall can be seen across the parkland. Haywood Lock and a line of moored craft announce the presence of Great Haywood and the junction with the Staffordshire & Worcestershire Canal (*see* page 135), which joins the Trent & Mersey under a graceful and much photographed towpath bridge: just the other side there is a useful boatyard. Beyond the junction the Trent valley becomes much broader and more open. There is another boatyard by Hoo Mill Lock.

● **Great Haywood**
Staffs. PO, tel, stores. Centre of the Great Haywood and Shugborough Conservation Area, the village is not particularly beautiful, but it is closely connected in many ways to Shugborough Park, to which it is physically linked by the very old Essex Bridge, where the crystal clear waters of the River Sow join the Trent on its way down from Stoke. Haywood Lock is beautifully situated between this packhorse bridge (which is an Ancient Monument) and the unusually decorative railway bridge that leads into Trent Lane. The lane consists of completely symmetrical and very handsome terraced cottages: they were built by the Ansons to house the people evicted from the former Shugborough village, the site of which is now occupied by the Arch of Hadrian within the park, built to celebrate Anson's circumnavigation of the globe in 1740–44. About 100yds south of Haywood Lock is an iron bridge over the canal. This bridge, which now leads nowhere, used to carry a private road from Shugborough Hall which crossed both the river and the canal on its way to the church just east of the railway. This was important to the Ansons, since the packhorse bridge just upstream is not wide enough for a horse and carriage, and so until the iron bridge was built the family had to *walk* the 300yds to church on Sunday mornings!
Shugborough Hall *NT*. Milford, nr Stafford. Walk west from Haywood Lock and through the park. The present house dates from 1693, but was substantially altered by James Stuart around 1760 and by Samuel Wyatt around the turn of the 18th C. It was at this time that the old village of Shugborough was bought up and demolished by the Anson family so that they should enjoy more privacy and space in their park. Family fortunes fluctuated greatly for the Ansons, the Earl of Lichfield's family; and crippling death duties in the 1960s brought about the transfer of the estate to the National Trust. The Trust has leased the property to Staffordshire County Council who now manage the whole estate. The house has been restored at great expense, and there are some magnificent rooms and many treasures inside.
Museum of Staffordshire Life This excellent establishment, Staffordshire's County Museum, is housed in the old stables adjacent to Shugborough Hall. Open since 1966, it is superbly laid out and contains all sorts of exhibits concerned with old country life in Staffordshire. Amongst many things it contains an old-fashioned laundry, the old gun-room and the old estate brew-house, all completely equipped. Part of the stables contains harness, carts, coaches and motor cars. There is an industrial annexe up the road, containing a collection of preserved steam locomotives and some industrial machinery.
Shugborough Park There are some remarkable sights in the large park which encircles the hall. Thomas Anson, who inherited the estate in 1720, enlisted in 1744 the help of his famous brother, Admiral George Anson, to beautify and improve the house and the park. In 1762 he commissioned James Stuart, a neo-Grecian architect, to embellish the park. 'Athenian' Stuart set to with a will, and the spectacular results of his work can be seen scattered round the grounds. The stone monuments that he built have deservedly extravagant names such as the Tower of the Winds, the Lanthorn of Demosthenes and so on.
The Park Farm Designed by Samuel Wyatt, it contains an agricultural museum, a working mill and a rare breeds centre. Traditional country skills such as bread-making, butter-churning and cheese-making are demonstrated.
Shugborough Hall, Grounds, Museum and Farm (01889 881388; www.nationaltrust.org.uk). *Open Apr–Sep Tue–Sun 11.00–17.00 (also first 3 Suns Oct)*. Charge. Parties must book. Tea rooms, shop.

Boatyards

Ⓑ **Anglo Welsh** The Canal Wharf, Mill Lane, Great Haywood (01889 881711, www. anglowelsh.co.uk). 🛶 🚽 🔧 D Pump out, gas, narrowboat hire, day-hire craft, overnight and long-term mooring, boat sales, engine repairs, chandlery, toilets, books, maps and gifts.
Ⓑ **Engineering & Canal Services** Hoo Mill Boatyard, Hoo Mill Lane, Great Haywood (01889 882611, mobile 07721 487561, engcanal@globalnet.co.uk) 🚽 🔧 (modest charge) D Pump out, gas, overnight and long-term mooring, winter storage, boat and engine sales and repairs, toilets, showers, laundrette.

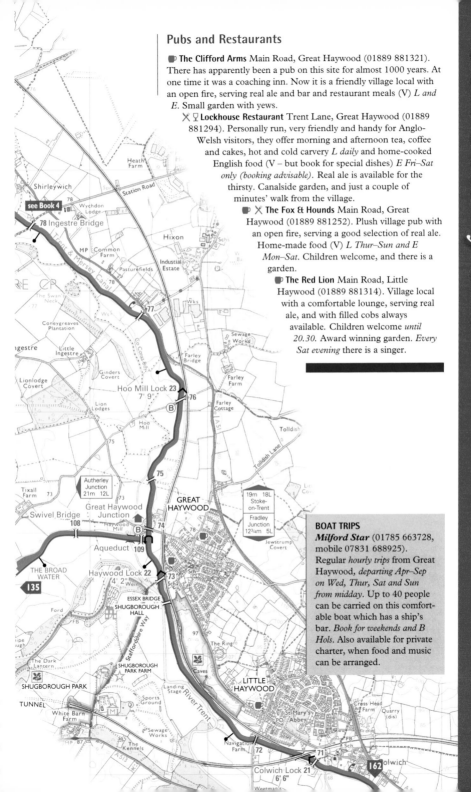

Pubs and Restaurants

🍺 **The Clifford Arms** Main Road, Great Haywood (01889 881321). There has apparently been a pub on this site for almost 1000 years. At one time it was a coaching inn. Now it is a friendly village local with an open fire, serving real ale and bar and restaurant meals (V) *L and E*. Small garden with yews.

✗ 🍷 **Lockhouse Restaurant** Trent Lane, Great Haywood (01889 881294). Personally run, very friendly and handy for Anglo-Welsh visitors, they offer morning and afternoon tea, coffee and cakes, hot and cold carvery *L daily* and home-cooked English food (V – but book for special dishes) *E Fri–Sat only (booking advisable)*. Real ale is available for the thirsty. Canalside garden, and just a couple of minutes' walk from the village.

🍺 ✗ **The Fox & Hounds** Main Road, Great Haywood (01889 881252). Plush village pub with an open fire, serving a good selection of real ale. Home-made food (V) *L Thur–Sun and E Mon–Sat*. Children welcome, and there is a garden.

🍺 **The Red Lion** Main Road, Little Haywood (01889 881314). Village local with a comfortable lounge, serving real ale, and with filled cobs always available. Children welcome *until 20.30*. Award winning garden. *Every Sat evening* there is a singer.

BOAT TRIPS

Milford Star (01785 663728, mobile 07831 688925). Regular *hourly trips* from Great Haywood, *departing Apr–Sep on Wed, Thur, Sat and Sun from midday*. Up to 40 people can be carried on this comfortable boat which has a ship's bar. *Book for weekends and B Hols*. Also available for private charter, when food and music can be arranged.

INDEX